Principles of Faith

Principles of Faith

Charles G. Finney

BETHANY HOUSE PUBLISHERS
MINNEAPOLIS, MINNESOTA 55438
A Division of Bethany Fellowship, Inc.

Copyright © 1988
Louis Gifford Parkhurst, Jr.
All Rights Reserved

Published by Bethany House Publishers
A Division of Bethany Fellowship, Inc.
6820 Auto Club Road, Minneapolis, Minnesota 55438

Printed in the United States of America

Library of Congress Cataloging-in-Publication Data

Finney, Charles Grandison, 1792–1875.
    Principles of faith / Charles G. Finney ; Louis Gifford Parkhurst, Jr.,
compiler and editor.
        p.   cm.
    Contains twenty-one of Finney's major sermons on faith and salvation.

    1. Evangelistic sermons. 2. Faith (Theology)—Sermons.
3. Salvation—Sermons. 4. Sermons, American.
I. Parkhurst, Louis Gifford, 1946–   . II. Title.
BV3797.F525P75 1988
252'.3—dc19   88–18711
ISBN 0-87123-993-0   CIP

CHARLES G. FINNEY was one of America's foremost evangelists. Over half a million people were converted under his ministry in an age that offered neither amplifiers nor mass communication as tools. Harvard Professor Perry Miller affirmed that "Finney led America out of the eighteenth century." As a theologian, he is best known for his *Revival Lectures* and his *Systematic Theology*.

LOUIS GIFFORD PARKHURST, JR., is pastor of Christ Community Church in Oklahoma City, Oklahoma. He garnered a B.A. and an M.A. from the University of Oklahoma and an M.Div. degree from Princeton Theological Seminary. He is married and the father of two children. This is his twelfth volume of the works of Charles G. Finney for Bethany House Publishers.

BOOKS IN THIS SERIES

Answers to Prayer
Principles of Devotion
Principles of Discipleship
Principles of Faith
Principles of Holiness
Principles of Liberty
Principles of Love
Principles of Prayer
Principles of Revival
Principles of Sanctification
Principles of Union with Christ
Principles of Victory

OTHER BOOKS BY FINNEY

Finney's Systematic Theology
Heart of Truth, Finney's Outline of Theology
Reflections on Revival
Finney on Revival
Promise of the Spirit
Autobiography of Charles G. Finney
The Believer's Secret of Spiritual Power (with Andrew Murray)

Life and Ministry of Charles Finney / Lewis Drummond

CONTENTS

INTRODUCTION

Principles of Faith is a book I have wanted to compile and edit for a long time. Along with its companion volume *Principles of Salvation,* I have collected Finney's major sermons on faith and salvation. None of the more than forty sermons in these two books are in any of the other books published by Bethany House Publishers. My purpose is to provide a collection of sermons dealing with why a person should be a Christian, and how to become a Christian. Most of the readers of these two books will be Christians already, but I believe many of us are looking for better ways to present the Christian faith to non-Christians. And many of us are seeking a better comprehension of major biblical doctrines.

These two books will also be valuable for the *thinking* non-Christian, because they answer many of the questions non-Christians ask. These sermons will remove many of the stumbling blocks false theologies have put in the pathway to Christian faith. I, for one, would never have become a Bible-believing Christian if Finney's works had not helped me deal with questions of human ability and moral responsibility. These sermons also show the difficulties non-Christians face in coming to God, why they need Christ, and the necessity for the work of the Holy Spirit in conversion.

Finney closely joined justification by faith and sanctification by faith in his presentation of salvation by faith. These sermons demonstrate more clearly than many others already published just how justification and sanctification relate to each other, and how indispensable faith is to both. These sermons also exhibit how Finney used "Moral Government Theology" to explain the work of

9

Christ as Advocate and Mediator, and the necessity of His atoning work. Finney carefully showed how the atonement relates to God's government of the world, and why God required the atonement of Christ in order to extend pardon to repentant sinners. Furthermore, many have misunderstood Finney's views on human ability, and these sermons define what people must do and what God must do in salvation.

Everyone has generic faith. Generic faith is confidence in someone or something. Christian faith is confidence in the Son of God. Faith in Jesus Christ brings forth love. Only through faith in Jesus Christ can we obey the first and second commandments to love God and our neighbors. Saving faith is truly saving, in the sense that through our relationship with Christ we are saved from eternal death and we are saved from sin. Through faith in Jesus Christ, we are justified and sanctified. We can and should know whether or not we have saving faith, and these sermons help us know by teaching what saving faith is and by helping us to evaluate whether or not we are living by Christian faith.

Other books in the *Principles Series* have dealt with the Christian's relationship with Christ, holiness, prayer, revival, sanctification, and themes from Romans. *Principles of Faith* and *Principles of Salvation* are primarily foundational to all of the other books in this series. Finney brought revival to spiritually dead or dying churches. The Holy Spirit so anointed his preaching that church members became vibrant, effective Christians. As vibrant Christians, they began to live holy lives and seek a more intimate relationship with Christ—an area of Christianity that is covered in the other books in this series.

But these vibrant Christians also looked beyond their own personal piety and demonstrated love and concern for their lost family members and neighbors by sharing with them the gospel of Christ. When we truly become Christians, we take seriously Christ's call to share the gospel with every person. Sometimes we are not as effective witnesses for Christ as we want to be, and I for one had much false theology to unlearn after I became a Christian. The sermons in *Principles of Faith* and *Principles of Salvation* give us truths that we can understand and share with every person, in the sure and certain hope that some will respond to Christ and be saved. As you learn the truths in these books, truths found in Scripture and logically deduced from Scripture, you will be a stronger Christian and you will be able to solve many problems that are currently keeping many from embracing Christ and His gospel.

In conclusion, I wish to thank those at Bethany House Publishers for their commitment to the publication of Finney's works. I also wish to thank my wife, Pat Parkhurst, for typing many of these sermons and speeding up my work considerably. What a joy to work with a Christian wife!

I am also deeply grateful for the life and ministry of Charles G. Finney. I am grateful that God blessed his labors over one hundred years ago. I am grateful that God is still blessing the words he left behind in numerous books and sermons. I look forward to the day when Finney and I will be able to visit about the fruits of his labors. I know that in the years to come people will enter paradise and greet Finney with thanksgiving for his faithful ministry, one that has reached into this new generation. I am grateful and humbled to think that I have had a small part in making his thoughts more accessible to people today.

> In the Risen and Reigning
> Lamb of God,
> L. G. Parkhurst, Jr.

1

LIVING BY FAITH*

"The just shall live by his faith" (Habakkuk 2:4).

These words that occur first in Habakkuk are quoted in Galatians 3:11 and in Hebrews 10:38. They express a great truth that has an especially rich and important development in the gospel. I will explain the sense in which *all people* live by faith, and then show the sense in which *the just* live by faith.

Faith is not merely an intellectual state. It is more than a mere conviction or state of being convinced that something is true or right. We do not reach the root idea of faith until we get to the heart. Faith is "the heart's confidence," a trusting in which the heart rests on the word or character of one deemed worthy of confidence. Faith is a phenomenon of the will, of necessity a thing of free choice. Whenever a person puts his trust in someone or something, it is supposed that he has good reason for such confidence.

Faith in the generic sense may be applied to anything in which we place our confidence. Faith is any exercise of the mind in which we yield it up to confide and trust in someone or something. All intelligent beings live by faith in something. Little children live by faith, and it is striking to observe how much this is true of them. Indeed, unreflecting people do not by any means conceive how universal this principle is and must be, and how necessary to the existence of social and reasonable beings. Even little children must learn to have faith in the use of their muscles, or else they will not venture to trust themselves upon their feet at all. Nor would any

---

The Oberlin Evangelist, June 7, 1854.

sane person eat his daily food except by faith. He has faith in his cook, that she has not poisoned it. He must have faith that his food will do him good and not kill him. Without faith people would not dare to lie down to sleep. They must have some confidence in their fellow beings, that they will be permitted to sleep without being murdered. In fact, people would not dare to do anything that implies peaceful rest and relaxation unless they lived by faith. Without faith, there could be no repose of mind—nothing but sleepless and intense solitude. In this state no person could live. His very solitudes would wear out his nerves and crush his physical system.

All families must live by faith, or rather they could not live without it. Even a pirate ship could not be managed without faith. An old adage says, "There is honor among thieves"; obviously, if there were not, then there could be no such thing as organized crime or cooperation in mischief of any sort. Those who need the help or sympathies of others in their enterprise must of necessity live by faith.

It is astonishing to see how much faith there is in everything. Look at people anywhere in any area of life and you will see them living by faith. If young people did not have faith, they would not try to get an education. Society could not get along in any form without faith. Farmers would not plant or reap. No one would bestow labor for the sake of future good results. Without faith, nothing would be done. If faith should utterly cease, the human race would perish. You would be surprised if you were to reflect to see how soon the entire race would perish if *all* faith were to cease. Faith is the great secret of our being—the underlying condition of our continued existence.

Without faith, we would overcome no obstacles; for we would make no efforts. And who does not know that we never accomplish anything useful without effort? If it were not for faith, all useful things would go undone. God has so constituted the universe that faith must be in exercise or its necessary processes must cease and ruin come down on all created beings.

On the other hand, in proportion as faith is present, society moves along admirably. An army, held together in strong and perfect discipline, owes its bond of strength to faith. A well-ordered school, in diligence pursuing its noble work, lives by faith. A family, living by promoting each others' interests, moving along with helpful labors and cares, has its central power in faith.

Of course, I am speaking here only of *faith* in the generic sense and not in the Christian sense. If confidence really exists, in all these multiform relations, then all goes right, all moves along smoothly. But if faith is lacking, everything is wrong, necessarily and eternally so.

Commonly, skeptics will sneer at Christianity, because it makes so much of faith.They seem to assume *they* have no need of faith in anything. It would be easy to show that of all people religious skeptics must be most credulous and have the most faith. The chief peculiarity in their case is that having rejected the light and the evidence of truth through their radical enmity of heart against it, they are locked into believing things without evidence, and against evidence, even being forced to believe that to "leap into the dark" at death is the best ending of human life.

It is important for us to see how all people live by faith in the generic sense so we can understand *Christian faith*. Christian faith differs from other faith in its objects, but not essentially in its nature. Naturally, Christians have faith in the generic sense like other men and women. They have the same faith in a general sense that is common to society and human nature everywhere. But they have more than this. They have a Christian faith by which they live a Christian life. *The secret of the Christian life is the faith Christians have in the Son of God.* This faith "works by love." Their confidence in Christ, in all He says and does, joins their souls to Him and brings forth unceasing love.

The Christian's confidence in Christ's benevolence makes love a present reality to his soul, and hence the influence of such a *presence of love* cannot fail to inspire a corresponding love in his heart toward Christ and His people, and indeed, toward all creatures. Thus Christians become conscious of both affectional and emotional love. Without confidence in God and in Christ, they could not live such a life of faith. The motive would be lacking. How could they have peace with God without faith in Christ's atonement as the ground of reconciliation? How could they walk in the strength of the Lord without faith in His exceedingly great and precious promises? How can they bring their hearts under the influence of all the great truths of the gospel unless they have faith in all those truths?

Many Christians complain of a lack of emotion in their religious exercises, but overlook the great reason for their deficiency. They do not seem to see that the fountain out of which proceeds the strong, deep, flow of emotion is *faith*. For example, look at a daughter. She sits down to write to pour out her soul. See how her faith in her mother's love opens the great fountain of her emotions.

Her mother's character is before her mind as a present reality. She never can question the strength or the fullness of her mother's love. Hence, when her attention turns to her mother, a thousand thoughts rush upon her mind and tears flow unbidden. Is it any wonder that a Christian's faith should likewise inspire his affections and quicken his emotions?

By faith, the just live a life of obedience. Faith works by love, and love inspires the heart to obey. Faith brings the soul into such union and harmony with God that love and obedience become second nature. Nothing can be more easy and natural than to obey where there is love and faith. If you confide in your Heavenly Father, you will naturally try to please Him.

By faith, you will live a life of submission to all God's providences. Adverse circumstances will cross your path in this earthly state, but if you confide in your Heavenly Father, you will pass smoothly along, submissive and satisfied that He who rules all does all things well. Only the other day a man said to me, "I believe that whatever occurs to me will work for my good. If any loss befalls me, I know it shall be in some way for my gain. I know it must be. If one of my horses dies, it is all best. God will make it up in some spiritual good." Another man said to me, "If I set my heart upon accomplishing any object, make efforts for it, and succeed, it is well. And if I do not succeed, it is well. I know the failure must be better than the success, or else God would have given me the success. I know that He will always give me the best thing. It does not follow that God was displeased with me for making the efforts that He saw it best to frustrate. He expects me to act according to my best light and judgment. Then, if He sees a still better way and frustrates my way, all is well." Now, I ask you, how could these men feel this rest and this submission to God's providence without faith?

A person learns to adjust himself to the providence of God as a ship at sea on the tops of the bounding waves. If anything comes dashing across his path and blasts his plans, gradually by his faith in God he adjusts himself to the blast and sings, "All is well, for it is my Father!" From his conversion he trains himself by faith to this self-adjustment, even as the infant on his new and untrained legs learns to balance himself on the center of gravity, gaining new skill with each day's practice, until soon he surprises you with the acrobatics he can make with apparently the utmost ease and safety. So in the Christian's life, the believer learns to adjust himself to the blasts that strike him under the vicissitudes of God's providence, keeping his mind upright and on its balance however sudden may be the changes that pass over him. He learns to always apply those great truths he has learned about God. He holds practically that all God does is best. Hence, he can pass through trials with calm and heavenly resignation. He expects to come out at last as Jacob did.

You recollect Jacob began by saying, "Joseph is not, and Simeon is not, and ye will take Benjamin away: *all these things are against me*" (Gen. 42:36). Did he ever make a greater mistake? Joseph was not dead, but was sent before him to the granary of the world to provide means of subsistence, not for Jacob's family only, but for whole nations. Simeon was not dead. All these things were not *against him*, but *for him* in the highest sense. And the good old man lived to see how sadly he had misinterpreted the ways of God toward himself and his house.

Likewise, the fierce blast smites many a person, and the poor person, weak in faith, staggers under the blow and trembles through great fear. But soon, he gathers up his confidence and lifting his head above the surging billows, cries out, "All is well!" Even though the lightnings flash and the thunders roar; even though darkness and storm combine their terrors; why should he tremble? Is not God on the throne, high above and over all?

So the Christian lives exempt from care, bearing his burdens without distraction because he rolls them over upon the Lord. In the midst of business, ever so complicated, his mind rests sweetly in the Lord—his faith causing his soul to have rest.

He has peace in God, because he is justified by faith. His own soul has internal peace, because through faith he is sanctified. How could he have peace in either of these respects if he did not embrace Jesus Christ and His revealed plan of atonement by His blood and the cleansing by His Spirit?

Similarly, by faith, people live a joyous and useful life. Faith lays the foundation for both the silent influence of a good example and for the active influence of direct efforts. You can look for neither without a living faith.

By faith people live a humble life. By faith, they learn to take a low place. Indeed, the very idea of faith involves humility, just as the idea of doing all yourself and trusting no one for help implies self-sufficiency and independence. The Christian is emptied of self-reliance before he can be filled with Christ. He sees he has nothing to be proud of, that humility becomes him, and that his spirit must accept this low position before he can receive all fullness of grace from His Lord.

By faith he lives a cheerful life. Generally, the tenor of the life of faith is cheerful. Satisfied with God and His providence, why should he not be cheerful? He has occasion to rejoice evermore. God will bring out such glorious results, and his faith so distinctly anticipates them, that he knows the church and all he loves on earth is safe.

By faith he lives a self-denying life. If he has faith, he will not make much of the petty comforts of this life. His soul is upon far greater and better things. Why should he care for these little things, when souls are to be saved or lost? He can afford to deny himself of almost every earthly comfort in order to save a soul or to please his Lord and Master. When he encounters labor and toil, glad to go to the very ends of the earth on the gospel mission, he knows he has nothing to fear and no reason to anticipate loss to himself. It is true he does not go for the sake of personal gain, but he goes deeply conscious that he is pursuing the most truly valuable objects, and pursuing them because they are most truly valuable. As for his own reward, he knows he finds it in large measure in his work itself, and as for the future, he cheerfully leaves it with God. Without faith, such a life would be hard indeed. But with faith, why should he fear poverty or persecution or shame? All is right—all is well enough. Who cannot afford to submit to all this, so long as his soul reposes in faith in his God?

By faith he lives a spiritual life, and not a merely natural life. His life is spiritual, not in the abused and perverted sense in which modern necromancers use the word, but in the sense of being in real communion with the Father, with the Son and with the Holy Spirit. The Spirit of God dwells in his heart by faith.

By faith he lives a prayerful life. He naturally prays. He loves prayer, and breathes it even as he breathes the atmosphere. He has confidence in God and expects blessings in answer to prayer. Such a person has reason enough for much prayer.

His life of faith is hopeful. He is not easily discouraged, for his confidence rests in the mighty God. He expects to succeed in doing all that God would have him do; and why should he wish to do more? He is a minister of the gospel, going forth to preach. He goes hopeful. Why should he not? He expects success in the name of the Lord, if he has faith.

By faith he will lead an active life. Faith will spur on his activities. Under an earnest faith in divine truth, how can he help being active and zealous? If he believes God's Word, he will believe in the fearful peril of sinners, and in the awful doom that awaits them. How can he abstain from labor for souls as long as he sees them stand on slippery places, with fiery billows rolling below? Will he not devote himself with untiring diligence to pluck whomever he can from the ruin of a lost sinner?

Faith secures sympathy with God. Confidence in anyone ensures your sympathy with him. So if you have confidence in God, you will give Him the warm and earnest sympathies of your heart. Unbelief locks up the heart against sympathy with God, but faith opens it wide. It is wonderful to see how true faith in God opens the gateways of the soul and lets in the waters of spiritual life and power.

Faith makes the Christian's life humane. Faith trains him to look on all as God's children and to love them and care for them as such. Seeing how much pity and forbearance God has toward His sinning creatures, he is drawn by his faith to exercise the same.

By faith he lives a life of gospel liberty. He is not in bondage to law or to fear. He does not pray because he is obliged to, but because he trusts and loves. All right mental exercises are spontaneous, God's Spirit writes His own law on his heart. It would be easy to show that a life of faith secures all these results.

The results of faith constitute real life. Hence, we see how eminently and how universally it must be true that the *just shall live by his faith*.

The Fruits of Faith

Natural faith, faith that unconverted people have in things and other people, is useful to society, to the purposes of business, and to the comfort and the subsistence of families. Natural faith is always useful as far as it goes; but it is not virtuous, since it does not have regard for God, for His character or His law. It may be good and useful, but not virtuous, because it co-exists with selfishness and hatred of God. Pirates may, yes *must*, have natural faith. But it does not follow that pirates are good citizens. It is not *saving faith*, for it does not save people from sin, nor fit them for heaven.

In its foundation and exercise, faith is perfect in heaven. Faith is perfect there; therefore, the state of the society and the happiness of reasonable beings must be perfect there. If faith were not perfect in heaven, then society even in heaven could not be perfect. All is right in heaven, because in heaven faith is perfect and universal.

All people who come to the knowledge of the gospel ought to live lives of faith. Curiously, some people do not see its value and its excellence. In my early life, I took this view of faith and of the Christian life. In studying the great truths that Christians claimed to believe, I thought I could account for the way Christians lived by the nature of what they believed. Believing that Christ died for them, how could they not love Him and live to please and serve Him? Believing thus, rationally, they should act thus. This belief must be of the utmost value to them, as long as they live in this world, whether the things they believed were true or false. This reasoning of mine did not assume the truth of the Bible, but merely brought out the relation of the Christian life to those statements, whether true or false.

But after a little more reflection on the matter, it occurred to me that the very fact of the universal utility of this faith proves its divine origin and the divine truth of the things believed. Christian faith does in fact fit people for heaven; this proves its doctrine to be divine. It cannot be a lie, for no lie could produce such results. It is impossible for a system to be false which, when believed, makes a person so pure and holy. The fruits of Christian faith prove the Bible is true; unless we accept the absurdity that to believe a lie will lift people above the world, will renovate their hearts and restore them to God's own image—but who can believe this?

True Christian faith is the essential condition for a perfect society either in this world or in the world to come. It must be the necessary condition of the mind's being in a perfect state. It must be ever present in that society which constitutes heaven.

The life of faith in Christ is too peculiar to be mistaken. Christians are a "peculiar people." They have a peculiar faith. They believe things that elevate the soul. They believe in purity of heart. And by faith, they raise their minds above the influence of sordid things and place them above the debasing influence of sensuality, and all things low and mean. Faith in Christ must produce a life that will be its own witness. Look over society anywhere, and your eye must recognize the person who lives by faith in Christ. Such faith as the true Christian has must create a life so peculiar as to be readily distinguished from every other life.

Saving faith is in its very nature *saving*. Many think of saving faith as only future, as only rescuing the soul at death from final perdition.This is a great and grievous mistake. Christian faith is that by which people live, not that by which they die. They are saved here first, and then saved hereafter, *because* they are first saved here. If faith ever saves the soul, it must be saved first here on this earth. Faith saves souls into happiness in heaven, because it has first saved them into holiness on earth.

All people who are not grossly ignorant can see the nature and value of gospel faith. A person must be exceedingly stupid who can live in a world where faith is exhibited before his eyes, talked about all around him, and yet not be interested in the questions, "What is this? How are these results produced?" If he looks into this matter, he cannot help but see that the truths taught in the gospel only need to be believed, and the results will be of the very greatest value to the soul. Let me ask the sinner, whose aims hitherto have never risen above the mere enjoyments of time, "Suppose you were now to believe the gospel for yourself. Understanding it in a good degree, you give it full credence, embracing it with all its precious provisions and promises. Do you think it would be strange for you to then say, 'I have enjoyed more in one hour than in all my life before'?"

You who are still in your sins can know but very little of the great things of the gospel. You have never yet believed things which could give you more than a feverish pleasure, transient and deceptive. You have never yet believed anything high, inspiring, ennobling. Now take your standpoint of vision above the great ocean of truth. Ascend the "Delectable Mountains" from whence you can take in a broad and clear view of the "Celestial City." Lo, there is a palace, built of God, for His saints from earth.

Did you ever see a royal palace? Have you ever scanned the lofty walls, the glittering towers, the artificial lakes, the gardens, lawns, trees and flowers? If so, you may have said, "How noble to be the owner of this! To be able to survey it all and say, 'This is mine!'" But when you become a true Christian and open your heart to a Christian's faith, you can say, "All this will not begin to compare with my Master's palace to which He will take me home after a few days. This earthly king's palace, compared with heaven, is only as the merest dunghill! 'In my Father's house are many mansions.'" Jesus said that He was going to get His Father's house ready for us, and then He would take us home. There we shall indeed be "at home in the presence of Jesus." He can tell us the thousand things that took place ages ago before we were born. If you believed that you were to be there, would it be strange if you were too happy to sleep at night?

Many times I have heard people say, "I have been too happy in God to sleep!" One of the most active businessmen, who had been skeptical, was brought to see his sins and to be greatly concerned for himself. After attending meetings many evenings, he finally said to his wife, "It does me no good to go to these meetings. I must stop. I am going out of town today." He went to meet the train, but it had already left! Upon his return his wife said, "Now please go with me to the meeting once more." He consented. The truth took hold of his soul with power. She had been praying for him for many years, and now he is converted. What is the result? She is too happy to sleep, and so is he! They have a thousand things to talk over, to recount the mercies of the Lord and to celebrate His love. There was no sleep in that house for at least one night. And here is another most beautiful result: their two children are also converted and they rejoice, believing in God with all their house.

The reason sinful people live as they do is they lack faith. They fail to trust in God. They do not realize the great things of God's promises and of His love.

Finally, without faith, no one can be happy even in heaven. Unless they can confide in God, it is vain to suppose they can be quiet and blessed even there. For, in that world, perhaps even more than in this, there will be things brought before their minds that they cannot understand. Under the government of an infinite God, there must always be things done or permitted by the Great Ruler of all that minds so small and shortsighted as ours can by no means fathom. There is no alternative then but either to trust or to rebel. Christian faith or sin—this is the only alternative. How wise, therefore, that God should train His children in faith before He ventures to take them up to heaven! And let them all take care that they do not even ask to go there until they have faith enough to trust God as revealed to them here! It must be a fearful thing to go to heaven unprepared to endure its discipline. God will take no one who cannot bear it.

2

THE RATIONALITY OF FAITH*

"He staggered not at the promise of God through unbelief; but was strong in faith, giving glory to God" (Romans 4:20).

These words were spoken of Abraham, as you will see by reading the context in which they are found. Faith is the heart's confidence in God. Specific faith relates to particular things: belief in the promises of God, in Christ, in the doctrines of the Bible, and in all the various assertions that God makes in His Word. This specific form of faith differs from faith in its simple form, which implies a general confidence in the existence, attributes, and character of God. The mind's resting in these things is the simple form of faith. Observe, faith in God is not a mere assent to these things, nor a mere intellectual conviction that they are true. Faith is the heart, the mind, and the will resting in this truth: that God is, that He possesses certain attributes and a certain character. Faith in its specific form is the belief of the heart in certain declarations of God, a belief in His wisdom and goodness, in His assertions respecting Christ, and in all those things He has said and promised. There are a great many specific forms in which faith develops itself, but the root of it is heart confidence in God.

Our Faith Is Meant to Be Tested

One fact calculated to challenge our faith is the existence of so much evil and misery in this world. God declares that He is ac-

---

The Penny Pulpit, preached on Sunday morning, January 12, 1851, at the Tabernacle, Moorfields.

quainted with everything. He affirms that He is omnipresent, omniscient, omnipotent; He is everywhere present, knows all things, and is all-powerful. He declares He is infinitely good and disposed to do good. Now, that under the government of such a Being as this there should be so much evil, so much sin, and so much misery is greatly calculated to try the faith of mankind. That these things should exist, and be everywhere observable in this world to an immense extent, is to many people so great a mystery, so difficult to reconcile with the existence and declared attributes of God, that they stumble and call into question the fact that there is a God at all.

Another thing that God asserts, and that reason also affirms, is the existence of a providence that guides and controls all events. God has a design in everything that He does. At the very beginning God had a design, and in what He does He is pursuing this design to its accomplishment. This design proceeds from a being who is infinitely good and infinitely wise. Now, the existence of evil in the world does not seem to harmonize with the things that God says of himself regarding His wisdom and goodness. Therefore, many find great difficulty in getting over these facts; and it is more than unbelief ever can accomplish. Please understand, at present I will not attempt to explain this, but simply to notice the facts at which unbelief stumbles, which are calculated to try the faith of God's creatures.

The manner in which the Bible reveals God is also a great stumbling block to many. For example, a great many stumble at the doctrine of the Trinity. They cannot understand the Trinity any better than they can understand a great many other things, but because they cannot understand it, they reject it and say that it cannot be. They will not receive it simply because they cannot explain it. Likewise, they will not receive the incarnation of the Son of God, because they cannot explain it. They cannot understand how humanity and deity could be united, so they reject the doctrine, and will not believe it. I admit at once that these doctrines are very mysterious; but they are announced facts, that God was in Christ and Christ was both God and man. I readily admit that this declaration is a great trial to the faith of finite creatures; but the announcement is made by God himself and ought to be believed.

The doctrine of the atonement is another stumbling block. The fact that God should actually suffer is a difficulty that can only be overcome by faith—unbelief will suggest a multitude of difficulties and reject it. The resurrection, the doctrine of justification by faith, the doctrine of sanctification by faith, and all the other doctrines of the Bible, are stumbling blocks to the human mind. Indeed, people who find no difficulties in them do not have faith, and they show that they have not well considered them. But however difficult they may be, there is ten thousand times greater absurdity in disbelieving than in exercising faith in them, since they are the testimony of God. But, nevertheless, unbelief finds great difficulty in admitting them. The mind that has no confidence in God refuses to believe, because it cannot explain how all these things are; of course, such a mind will stumble and stagger at every step.

The manner in which sin was introduced into the world is a great stumbling block to those who have no confidence in God. Unless God gives them His reasons for everything that He does, some will find great difficulty in getting along. Suppose a child should have no confidence in his father, and should therefore want the reasons for his father's conduct in everything that he did. What if he required his father to explain to him in a satisfactory manner how everything was done before he could believe it? Who cannot see that a family of such unbelievers, stumbling and staggering at every step, would have no confidence in their father at all? If he was a man conducting a very extensive business on a vast scale, they could not understand as children what even perhaps many men could not comprehend if it were explained to them. How absurd then for the children not to put confidence in their father because they could not understand the reasons for all his conduct.

The very greatness of God's promises is often a severe trial to faith. He promises things so great to people so undeserving, indeed so ill-deserving, that unbelief finds it difficult to believe Him, because He says so much, and promises so much.

And again: the providence of God is often a great trial to faith. How remarkable was the conduct of God toward Abraham, and how greatly calculated to try his faith. He called him out of his father's house, and Abraham obeyed not knowing where he went. God had reasons in His own mind for His conduct in this matter. He intended to make of Abraham a great nation, and through him to communicate His will to men. From Abraham's family, the Savior would come, but He gave Abraham no such intimation of what He was going to do. God called him and told him to go to a certain place that He would show him. After Abraham had obeyed the command, God promised to give him a certain land for a possession, and to his seed after him. And although he had no family, God called him and said, "Look now toward heaven, and tell the stars, if thou be able to number them: and he said unto him, So shall thy seed be" (Gen. 15:5).

This promise was long and remarkably delayed. He lived with much hardship in the land that was promised to him for a possession, and when his wife died, he was obliged to purchase a burial place in that very land that God had promised should be his own— yet we see no signs of any stumbling in his faith. After a long period of time, God promised Abraham that he would have a son by his wife Sarah. Now both Abraham and Sarah were very old, she was long past the age when it was common for women to have children; nevertheless, Abraham believed that God would do what He had promised. Those who will read and ponder well all the circumstances connected with the trial of Abraham's faith will see that he must have been very severely tried indeed.

Now after a long time, this promised son was born. The lad grew—when all at once God took Abraham by surprise—He seems always to have taken Abraham by surprise—and He said, "Take now thy son, thine only son Isaac, whom thou lovest, and get thee into the land of Moriah; and offer him there for a burnt offering" (Gen. 22:2). He not only said to Abraham, "take now thy son," but He reminded him that it was his only son, whom he loved. This son, this son of promise, this beloved son, he was to offer upon the altar. Now, how infinitely strange is all this. Yet Abraham staggered not. He believed that God was able to raise him from the dead. He had such strength of faith that he appears not to have been in much trouble of mind about it. He does not seem even to have revealed to Sarah that he had received any such communication from God. He was so calm that Sarah did not perceive anything was the matter with him.

The next morning he started out with his servants to offer Isaac at the place that God was to point out to him. When they came in sight of the place, he caused his servants to wait, lest they should interfere with him when carrying out the command of God. Abraham and his son ascended the mountain where the sacrifice was to be offered. Isaac did not understand what was going to be done— he knew indeed that Abraham was going to offer a burnt offering, for they had the fire and the wood, but he did not know that he was to be the sacrifice. It did not occur to him at all—for he asked where the lamb was that Abraham intended to offer. So calm was Abraham, that Isaac did not notice anything different in his manner; and to the question of his son, Abraham replied, "God will provide himself a lamb for a burnt offering" (Gen. 22:8). When he had prepared the altar, he bound Isaac and laid him on the wood, just as he would have done a lamb. He took the knife and was about to slay him, when God called, "Abraham, Abraham"—repeating his name rapidly, so as to arrest his attention—"lay not thine hand upon the lad, neither do thou any thing unto him: for now I know that thou fearest God, seeing that thou hast not withheld thy son, thine only son from me." And when Abraham lifted up his eyes, he saw a ram caught in a thicket by his horns, and he offered it instead of his son.

God did this to test the implicitness of Abraham's faith. His faith was as plainly manifested as if he had sacrificed his son—for he did do it as far as his mind was concerned. He believed that God would fulfill His promise. Now this was a beautiful exhibition and illustration of faith. But let me say, this was exceedingly calculated to try Abraham, as you will perceive. The manner in which God very often fulfills His promises is to give us a great stumbling block: we are expecting Him to fulfill His promises in one way, and He takes a direct opposite course, which is calculated to subvert all our ideas of things.

Now all such things as these are exceedingly calculated to try our faith in God. But strong faith will not allow itself to stumble at such things. Why should it! Faith embraces at once all the attributes of God; and therefore, has confidence in Him and does not seek to understand everything before yielding the heart to Him. There are, and must be, multitudes of things that we cannot understand, nor would it be useful for us to understand at present.

Walking by Faith Is Reasonable

If God's attributes are what He declares them to be, then there are things that cannot be explained to finite beings. Now, for example, take the doctrine of the Trinity. To be sure, human beings cannot explain that, nor is any explanation called for. God simply announces the fact in the Bible, that the Father, the Son, and the Spirit are God. We find that at one time, before the destruction of Sodom, three individuals appeared to Abraham, and one of them, who is called Jehovah, informed Abraham what they were going to do, and Abraham put up a prayer to have Sodom saved. We learn that there were three men, or apparently so; two of them probably were angels in human form and the other was no less a being than Jehovah himself. Now observe! Who can doubt that God could have assumed the same form in millions of cases at the same time in different parts of the world? There would be nothing contrary to reason in that. There is nothing then unreasonable in the supposition that God should exist in three persons! We say there is nothing *unreasonable* in it. What do people mean when they say that they cannot believe in the Trinity? What do they know about infinity? Can they affirm of the Father, Son, and Holy Spirit that these three cannot exercise and manifest the attributes of God? But since the fact is announced, people of faith need no evidence to convince them. Faith makes no effort to understand it.

If you object to this, let me ask you, "How do you know that you exist?" "Oh yes," you say, "I know that I exist; I believe it." What makes you believe it? Can you explain it? Did you choose your body? Can you tell the connection between matter and spirit? How can you prove what you are?

Some years ago, I was walking with a gentleman in the city of New York, and we were talking about Christianity and the mind. He stopped right short in the street, and said, "You say such and such things about mind; now what is mind?" "If you tell me," I said, "what matter is, I will tell you what mind is." "Why," said he, "matter has the property of extension, solidity, and so forth"; but he did not name the primary attributes of matter. "Well," I replied, "mind wills, thinks, feels, and the like." He looked at me quite astonished. I continued, "you have told me some of the attributes of matter, can you tell what the substance is?" "I do not know," he said. "Neither can I explain what the substance of mind is." If the wisest philosopher in the universe were to stand in my pulpit, a little child might ask him such questions as he could not answer or explain any more than we can explain the doctrine of the Trinity. There is not a single thing in the universe or in all the kingdom of nature, when you dive to the bottom of it, that is not as difficult to explain as any doctrine of the Bible. Why then do you believe in any and all of these things? Why believe in your own existence? The fact is, people do not disbelieve things because they are mysterious until they come to the subject of religion, because the world around them is so deeply mysterious that there is not a single thing that they can understand to the bottom, yet they are enabled to believe in them.

Very frequently, people do not realize that there is a mystery in anything but religion. Now I know that philosophy can in part explain many things, and things that a few years ago were considered mysterious, and even marvelous, are now understood. Science has already placed mankind in a position to explain the theory of many things that were deep mysteries, and spread them out before the minds of the people. But speaking generally, both with regard to the spiritual and the natural world, people have to live by faith. They believe in the various things around them in the natural world although they may not be able to understand them. The same is true of spiritual things. We must receive much on testimony that cannot be explained to us; and, probably in many cases, God would not explain them to us even if we could understand them, because it would not be well for us. He leads us step by step to a correct understanding of things that may be useful and necessary for us to know.

Now in relation to the question of sin, and its necessary attendant misery as it exists in our world; there is a mystery about it. Everyone affirms that where sin is, there misery ought to be. But the questions of wonder are: How did sin come into the world? and Why was it permitted?

No one can doubt that all of creation was very wisely put together. Man was made superior to all the rest of the inhabitants of this globe; and we see his power, sagacity and knowledge. He was designed to be the head of the creation. But mark! Men are in rebellion against God. This is a simple matter of fact: the human race defies God. Now reason affirms that the curse of God should be written upon everything in the universe, in order to testify to God's real character, so it should not be mistaken. But while we see that God does testify against sin, there are also indications that He has a strong disposition to be merciful as far as He wisely can; but the difficulties are many and great in the way of His forgiving sin. But let me say, faith in God does not find it very difficult to remove all these obstructions. Disbelief says, "Sin exists. And looking at God's government as a system of moral law, it does not appear that sin can ever be forgiven. In such a government, pardon is impossible." But faith says at once, "God is kind, wise and good, as well as infinitely powerful. Misery and sin exist, but they are *allowed* to continue in the world only for a wise purpose, to assist in bringing about the end at which God aims. For sin is so great an abomination God will bring good out of it."

Look at the sin of Judas. The devil put it into his heart to betray the Son of God to His enemies, and to his dismay he saw the greatness of his crime; but God overruled their evil intentions. His purpose was that the blood of His dear Son should be shed as an atonement for sin. Now, although we cannot understand the reason why

God should permit the existence of sin in the world at all, faith can easily dispose of the difficulties which may suggest themselves. Faith believes that everything God does must be infinitely good and wise. The fact is, unbelief in such matters is the most unreasonable thing in the world. If you profess not to believe anything until you understand it, why do you believe in your own existence? What do you know of volition? You move your muscles, but *how* you cannot tell. Faith, I say, disposes of all these difficulties, and is not unreasonable in doing so. Take Abraham's case. God promised that Abraham would have a son. "I shall have it," he said. "I am very old, and Sarah is very old, but no matter how old, God is able to give us a son." The child is born and is growing up when God calls to Abraham and tells him to go and offer Isaac in sacrifice. And Abraham said, "I will go. God has a good reason for the requirement. I know He must. He cannot have any other. He is infinitely good and infinitely wise. He cannot make a mistake. The path to duty is plain, and I will walk in it." "Oh," says unbelief, "how will the promise be fulfilled, 'In Isaac shall thy seed be called'?" "I do not know," says Abraham, "but God is able to raise him from the dead." Thus you see his faith very quickly disposes of the difficulty although it was very great. Now is there anything inconsistent with reason in all this? Why, no. Just look at it right in the face.

My own reason tells me that God is infinitely perfect in all His attributes and in everything He does. I find myself in a universe surrounded by a multitude of things that I cannot explain, and that even God himself could not explain to me because of my limited capacity, but these things are true nevertheless. As the law of progression operates, I come to understand many things that before were dark and inexplicable. And does not reason tell us that there must be a vast many things in the government of an infinite God that a finite mind cannot comprehend? But when a man is in a spiritual state of mind, faith takes the place of knowledge. The little child, for instance, lives by faith. Human society exists by faith. Destroy all confidence, all faith, and society could not exist; no business could be transacted. In the spiritual state of man faith is just as necessary.

The Purpose of Trials

Everyone can see that one great object of our trials is to strengthen faith. I have often heard it remarked, by intelligent people too, that in heaven faith will not exist, because there we shall walk by sight. Now there is some truth in that, but much greater error. It is true that many things we merely believe here we shall know there; but there will be much reason to call forth our faith, for there must be in the government of God much that would require millions of ages to understand, and we shall go on acquiring knowledge throughout the immensity of eternity, and thus there will be need of faith in God in eternity as in time; it will be as true in heaven as on earth.

Suppose that the angels did not have faith, the fall of man would have given a shock to the inhabitants of heaven. But they believed that God had some wise design when He permitted man to fall. Now this is the way faith disposes of everything: let what will come because there is no alarm or doubt but all will be right.

There is no hope for those who will not believe God. Suppose you had a family of children, and they should lose confidence in you as a businessman. They would stagger and stumble at every step you took, just because you could not explain to them all your plans. You say to them, "Dear children, I cannot explain these things to you. I am laboring for your good, therefore be quiet, be passive, and have confidence in me, that all will be well." But if they will not, what can you do with them? They must remain in their unbelieving, unconverted state. Now it is the same in God's government. There are many things that cannot be explained, yet some will not exercise faith. If they persist in their unbelief, they will go stumbling and fretting to the gates of hell! Some people will take nothing on trust, they must continually question their Maker; and if He does not explain everything to them they have no confidence in Him. Hence, it is said, that they shall have their part with liars in the lake of fire. My dear readers, the most unreasonable and blasphemous abomination in the world is unbelief.

3

THE INNER AND THE OUTER
REVELATION*

"By manifestation of the truth commending ourselves to every man's conscience in the sight of God" (2 Corinthians 4:2).

There are many who believe that a loose indefinite infidelity has rarely, if ever, been more prevalent in our country than at this time, especially among young men. I am not prepared to say it is an honest infidelity, yet it may very probably be real. Young men may really doubt the inspiration of the Christian Scriptures, not because they have honestly studied those Scriptures and their numerous evidences, but because they have read them little and reasoned legitimately even less. Especially have they almost universally failed to study the intuitive affirmations of their own minds. They have not examined the original revelation that God has made in the human soul to see how far this would carry them, and how wonderfully it opens the way for understanding and indeed for embracing the revelation given in God's Word.

To bring these and kindred points before your minds, I have taken as my text the words of Paul. Paul is speaking of the gospel that he received, and is stating how he fulfilled it. He shows plainly that he sought to preach to the human conscience. He found in each person a conscience to which he could appeal, and to which the manifestation of the truth commended itself.

Probably no thoughtful person has ever read the Bible without noticing that there has been a previous revelation given in some

---

Sermons On Gospel Themes, pp. 231–244.

way to man. The Bible assumes many things are known already. I was studying in my law office when I bought my first Bible to use as one of my law books. No sooner had I opened it than I was struck to see how many things it assumed as known, and therefore states with no attempt at proof. For instance, the first verse in the Bible, "In the beginning God created the heavens and the earth," assumes the existence of God. It does not aim to prove this truth. It goes on the presumption that this revelation—the existence of God—has been made known already to all who are mature enough to understand it.

The Apostle Paul also, in his epistle to the Romans, asserts that the real Godhead and eternal power of the one God, are in a sense "invisible things," yet they are "clearly seen" in the creation of the world "being understood by the things that are made" so that all wicked people are without excuse. His doctrine is that the created universe reveals God. And if this is true of the universe *outside* us, it is no less true of the universe *within* us. Our own minds (their convictions, their necessary affirmations) do truly reveal God and many of the great truths that respect our relation to Him and to His government.

When we read the Bible attentively and notice how many things of the utmost importance it assumes, and bases its precepts upon, we cannot help but inquire, "Are these assumptions properly made?" The answer to this question is found when we turn our eye within and inquire for the intuitive affirmations of our own minds. Then we shall see that we possess an intellectual and moral nature which as truly reveals great truths concerning God and our relation to Him and to law, as the material world reveals His eternal power and Godhead.

For instance, we shall see that people have a moral nature related to spiritual and moral truth, as really as they have a physical nature related to the physical world. As the senses (sight, touch, hearing) intuit certain truths respecting the external world, so does the spiritual nature intuit certain truths respecting the spiritual world. No one can well consider the first class of truths without being forced to consider and believe the second. Let us see if this is true.

Not long ago I had an interview with a young lady of considerable intelligence who was a skeptic. She professed to believe in a God and in those great truths pertaining to His attributes that are embraced in Deism. But, she quite rejected the Bible and all that pertains to a revealed way of salvation. I began by presenting to her mind some of the great truths taught by the mind's own affirmations concerning God, His attributes and government, and then from this I passed on to show her how the Bible came in to make out a system of truth needful to persons who are lost sinners. She admitted the first, of course; and then she saw that the second must be true if the first was, or there could be nothing for mankind but hopeless ruin. Starting back in horror from the gulf of despair, she saw that only her unbelief was ruining her soul, and then renouncing this, she yielded her heart to God and found gospel peace and joy in believing.

I propose now to present much the same course of thought to you as I did to her. And here the first great inquiry is: "What ideas does our own nature—God's first revelation—give us?"

Undoubtedly, the idea of *God*. Our own mind affirms that there is and must be a God, that He must have all power and all knowledge. Our mind also gives us God's moral attributes. No one can doubt that God is good and just. People are never afraid that God will do anything wrong. If they are afraid of God at all, it is because He is good, just and holy.

Man's nature gives him the idea of law: moral law. He can no more doubt the existence of a moral law imposed on himself than he can doubt the existence of his own soul and body. He knows he ought not to be selfish, that he ought to be benevolent. He knows he is bound to love his neighbor as himself, bound to seek the higher good at the sacrifice, if need be, of the lower good. How does man get these ideas? He has them by nature. They are in the mind before any direct instruction from human lips, or else you could never teach a child these ideas any more than you could teach them to a horse. The child knows these things before he is taught, and cannot remember when he first knew them.

Suppose you were to close your Bible and ask, "Now, apart from all this book teaches, how much do I know? How much must I admit?" You would find that your moral nature gives you the idea of a God and affirms His existence. It gives you His attributes, natural and moral, and also your own moral relation to Him and to your fellow beings. In proof of this, I can appeal to you: not one of you can say, "I am under no obligation to love God. I am not bound to love my fellow man." Your moral nature gives you these things. It affirms to you these truths even more directly and undeniably than your senses give you the facts of the external world. Moreover, your moral nature not only gives you the law of supreme love to God, and of love equal and impartial toward your fellow man, but it affirms that you are a sinner, that you have displeased God, have utterly failed to please Him, and of course that you are under condemnation from His righteous law. You know that God's good law must condemn you, because you have not been good in the sense required by that law. Hence, you must know that you are in the position of an *outlaw*, condemned by the law and without hope from the administration of justice.

Another thing it gives you: you know you are still in unrepentance. (I speak to those who know this to be their case, and not to the true Christian.) Your own conscience affirms this to you past all contradiction. It affirms that you are still living in sin, and have not reformed in such a sense that God can accept your reformation. You know that you do violence to your own conscience, and that while you are doing this you can neither respect yourself nor be respected by God. You know that as long as this is the case with you, God cannot forgive you. No, more, if He should forgive you, it would do you no good: you could not be happy; you could not respect yourself even if you were forgiven. Indeed, if your nature spoke out unbiased, it would not allow you to believe yourself really forgiven as long as you were doing violence to your conscience. I can remember when these thoughts were in my mind like fire. I saw that no one could doubt them any more than they could doubt their own existence. So you may see these truths and feel their force.

By your sins, you know that you have forfeited the favor of God, and have no claim on Him at all on the score of justice. You have cast off His authority, have disowned subjection to His law and government. Indeed, you have cast all His precepts beneath your feet. You can no longer come before God and say, "You ought not to cast me off. I do not deserve this at your hand." You can no more say this honestly than you can deny your own existence.

Have you ever tried this? See what you can honestly do and say before God. Have you ever tried to go into God's presence and tell Him solemnly that He has no right to punish you? No one can tell Him this without being conscious of blasphemy. It is a good test, because it may serve to show you how the case really stands. Suppose you try it. See what you can honestly and with an approving conscience say before God, when your soul is deeply impressed with the sense of His presence. I am not asking you if you can harden your heart and violate your conscience enough to curse God to His face, but I am asking you to put the honest convictions of your own conscience to the test and see what they are and what they will allow you to do and to say to God. Can you kneel before God and say, "I have always treated You as a friend. I have never treated You as an enemy"? You know you cannot say this to God without meeting the rebukes of your own mind.

Because of your sins, you can see no reason to hope for forgiveness under the law. With all the light of your Deism, you can discern no ground of pardon. Outside of the Bible's teaching, all is dark as death. There is no hope. If you cherish any hope, it must be directly in the teeth of your own solemn convictions. Why do you think it so difficult to induce a discreet governor to grant a pardon? When Jerome Bonaparte was monarch of Spain, why did Napoleon send him that earnest rebuke for pardoning certain criminals? What were the principles underlying that remarkably able state paper? Have you ever studied those principles as they were grasped and presented so vigorously by the mighty mind of Napoleon?

You can never infer from the goodness of God that He can forgive; much less that He *must*. One of the first Universalist preachers I ever heard announced in the beginning that he inferred from the goodness of God that He would save everyone. I can well remember how perfectly shallow his sophistry appeared to me and how absurd his assumptions. I was no Christian then, but I saw at a glance that he might far better infer from the goodness of God that He would forgive *none* rather than He would forgive *all*. It seemed to me most clear that if God were good and had made a good law, He would sustain it. Why not? I must suppose that His law is a good one. How could a Being of infinite wisdom and love impose any other than a good law? And if it were a good law, it had a good purpose or end in view. And a good God could not allow it to fail to achieve those ends by letting it come to nothing through inefficiency in its administration. I knew enough about law and government then to see that a firm hand in administration is essential to any good results from ever so good a law. Of course I knew that if the law were left to be trampled underfoot by hardened, blasphemous transgressors, and then to cap the climax, an indiscriminate pardon were given and nothing done to sustain the law, there would be an end of all authority and a positive annihilation of all the good hoped for under its administration. What! Shall rational people undertake to infer from God's goodness that He will pardon all sinners?

Suppose the spirit of riot and misrule, now so rampant in some parts of the world, were to go on from bad to worse; that the rioters perpetrate every form of mischief in their power. Suppose they tear up the rails, burn down the bridges, start fires in rail cars, run whole trains off the tracks, and crush the quivering flesh of hundreds en masse into heaps of blood and bones. And by and by, when the guilty are arrested and convicted by due course of law, then the question comes up: "Shall the governor pardon them?" He might be very much inclined to do so, if he wisely could. But the question is: "Can a good governor do it?" Suppose he were purely good and truly wise, what would he do? Will you say, "Oh, he is *too* good to punish. He is so good, he will certainly pardon"? Will you say that pardon indiscriminately given, and given to all, and according to previous assurance, moreover, will secure the highest respect for the law and the best obedience? Everybody knows that this is superlative nonsense. No one who ever had anything to do with the responsibilities of government, or who has ever learned the A B C's of human nature in this relation, can for one moment suppose that pardon—in such ways—can supplant punishment with any other result than utter ruin. No. If the ruler is good, he will surely punish. And all the more surely, by how much the more predominant is the element of goodness in his character. You sinners are under the law. If you sin, you must see great reason why God should punish you and not forgive.

Here is another fact. When you look upon yourself and your moral position, you find yourself twice dead. You are *civilly* dead in the sense of being condemned by the law and outcast from governmental favor. You are also *morally* dead, for you do not love God, do not serve Him, have no tendencies that draw you into sympathy with Him. But, on the other hand, you are dead to all considerations that look in this direction. You are indeed alive to your own low, selfish interests, but dead to God's interests. You care nothing for God, only to avoid Him and escape His judgment. All this you know, beyond all question.

In this condition, without further revelation, where is your hope? You have none, and have no ground for any.

Furthermore, if a future revelation is to be made, revealing some ground of pardon, you can see with the light now before you on what basis it must rest. You can see what more you need from God. The first revelation shuts you up to God—shows you that if help ever comes, it cannot come from yourself, but must come from God. Help cannot come out of His justice, but must come from His mercy; cannot come out of law, but must come from some extra provisions whereby law may have its demands satisfied other than through the execution of its penalty on the offender. Somebody, you can see, must interpose for you, who can take your part and stand in your stead before the offended law.

Did you ever think of this? In the position where you stand, and where your own nature and your own convictions place you, you are compelled to say: "My case is hopeless! I need a double salvation, from condemnation and from sinning; first from the curse, and then from the heart to sin—from the tendency and disposition to commit sin. Inquiring for a revelation to meet these needs of my lost soul, where can I find it? Is it to be found in all the book of nature? Nowhere. Look into the irresistible convictions of your own moral being. They tell you of your needs, but they give you no supply. They show what you lack, but they utterly fail to give it. Your own moral nature shows that you need an atoning Savior and a renewing Spirit. Nothing less can meet the case of a sinner condemned, outlawed, and doubly dead by the moral corruption of all his voluntary powers.

The worst mischief of infidelity is that it ignores all this. It takes no notice of one entire side of our nature, the most important side. Talking largely about philosophy, it primarily restricts itself to the philosophy of the outer world and pays no attention to the inner and higher nature. It ignores the fact that our moral nature affirms one entire class of great truths, with even more force and certainty than the senses affirm the facts of the external world. Verily, this is a grand and a fatal omission!

The Bible Answers Man's Deepest Needs

Without the first revelation the second—the Bible—could not be satisfactorily proved. When the Bible reveals God, it assumes that our minds affirm His existence and that we need no higher proof. When it reveals His law, it presupposes that we are capable of understanding it, and of appreciating its moral claims. When it prescribes duty, it assumes that we ought to feel the force of obligation to obey it.

Now, the fact that the Bible does make many assumptions of this sort establishes an intimate and dependent connection between the Word of God on the one hand and the laws of the human mind on the other. If these assumptions are well and truly made, then the divine authority of the Bible is abundantly sustained by its correspondence and harmony with the intellectual and moral nature of man. The Word of God *fits* the beings to whom it is given.

But, on the other hand, if these assumptions had on examination proved false, then it would be impossible to sustain the credit of the Scriptures as coming from a wise and honest Being.

Having the first revelation, to reject the second is most absurd. To a great extent the second is a reaffirmation of the first, with various important additions of a supplementary sort; for example, the atonement and hence the possibility of pardon, the gift and work of the Holy Spirit and hence the analogous possibility of being saved from sinning.

Now, those things the first revelation affirms and the second reaffirms are so fundamental in any revelation of moral duty to moral beings, that, having them taught so intuitively, so undeniably, we are left self-convicted of extreme absurdity if we then reject the second. Logically, there seems no ground left on which to base a denial of the written revelation. Its supplementary doctrines are not intuitive truths, but they are so related to our needs as lost sinners and so richly supply those needs, so beautifully relate to the needs of God's government and so amply meet them, that no intelligent mind (once apprehending all these things in their actual relationship) can fail to recognize their truthfulness.

The study of the first revelation secures an intellectual reception of the second. I do not believe it possible for a person to read and understand the first thoroughly and then come to the second and fairly apprehend its relationship to his own moral nature, moral convictions, and moral needs, without being compelled to say: "All is true; the Bible is all true!" They coincide so wondrously and the former sustains the latter so admirably and so triumphantly, a person can no more deny the Bible after knowing all his own moral relations than he can deny his own existence.

You see why so many reject the Bible. They have not read *themselves* well. They have not looked within themselves to read carefully the volume God has put on record there. They have contrived to hush and smother down the ever-rising convictions of their own moral nature. They have refused to listen to the cry of want that swells up from their troubled bosom of guilt. Hence, there is yet one whole volume of revelation of which they are strangely ignorant. This ignorance accounts for their rejection of the Bible.

A little attention to the subject will show you that this is the reason the masses in every Christian land place their faith in the Bible. Scarcely one in ten thousand has studied the historical argument for divine revelation extensively and carefully enough to make this a cornerstone for faith. It is not reasonable to demand that they should. There is an argument shorter and infinitely more convincing. It is a simple problem: given—a soul guilty, condemned and undone; required—some adequate relief. The Bible solves the problem. Who will not accept the solution? It answers every condition perfectly; therefore, it must come from God. It is, at least, our highest wisdom to accept it.

If it is replied to this, such a problem meets the case only of those who give their hearts to God, it may be modified for yet another class in this way: given—a moral nature that affirms God, law, obligation, guilt, ruin; required—to know whether a written revelation is reliable, which is built upon the broad basis of man's intuitive affirmations; which gives them the sanction of man's Creator; which appends a system of duty and of salvation of such sort that it interlocks itself inseparably with truth, intuitive to man, and manifestly fills out a complement of moral instructions and agencies in perfect adaptation to both man and his Maker. In the Bible we have the very thing required. A key that threads the countless wards of such a lock must have been made to fit. Each came from the same Author. If you grant to man an origin from God, then you must grant the same origin to the Bible. When I came to examine these things in the light of my own convictions, I wondered why I had not seen them truly before.

Suppose I should stand here and announce to you the two great precepts of the moral law. Would not their obvious nature and bearings enforce on your mind the conviction that these precepts must be true and must be from God? As I should descend to particulars, you would still affirm that these must be true; these must certainly have come down from heaven. If I were even to go back to the Mosaic law (a law many object to, because they do not understand the circumstances that called for such a law) and, if I should explain their peculiar circumstances and the reasons for such statutes, everyone must affirm the rectitude of even those statutes. The Old Testament reveals truth under a veil, the world is not prepared then for its clearer revelation. The veil was taken away when, in the fullness of time, people were prepared for unclouded revealing of God in the flesh.

The reason the masses receive the Bible is not that they are credulous, and hence swallow down absurdities with ease. The reason is that the Bible commends itself so irresistibly to each person's own nature and to his deep and resistless convictions—he is made to receive it—he must do violence to his inner convictions to reject it. Human nature cries out: "This is just what I need!"

The young lady, of whom I spoke earlier, could not help but abandon her infidelity and yield up her heart to God when she received this point. I said, "Do you admit a God?" She answered, "Yes." "Do you admit a law?" "Yes." "Do you admit your personal guilt?" "Yes." "And do you admit your need of salvation?" "Oh, yes." "Can you help yourself?" I inquired further. "Ah, no, indeed. I do not believe that I can ever be saved," she replied. Then I pressed, "But *God* can save you. Surely nothing is too hard for God." "Alas," she replied, "my own nature condemns me. I am in despair. There is no way of escape for me. I don't believe the Bible is from God, and here I am in darkness and despair!"

At this point in our conversation I began to preach the gospel to her, and said, "See there. God has done such and such things as revealed in the gospel. He came down and dwelt in human flesh to meet the case of such sinners as you. He made an ample atonement for sin. There, what do you think of that?" "That is exactly what I need," she said, "if it were only true." "If it is not true, then you are lost beyond hope! Why not believe?" I asked. "I cannot believe it, because it is incredible. It is a great deal too good to be true!" "And is not God *good*, infinitely good? Why do you object that anything He does is too good to be true?" I said. "That is what I need," again she repeated, "but how can it be so?" "Then you cannot give God credit for being so good!" "Alas, I see it is my unbelief. But I cannot believe. It is what I need, I can plainly see. But how can I believe it?"

I then rose up and said to her solemnly, "The crisis has come! There is now only one question for you, *will you believe the gospel?* She raised her eyes, which had been depressed and covered for half an hour or more. Every feature bespoke the most intense agitation while I repeated, *will you believe God?* Will you give Him credit for sincerity? She threw herself upon her knees, and burst into loud weeping. What a scene—to see a skeptic beginning to give God credit for love and truth! To see the door of light and hope opened and heaven's blessed light breaking in upon a desolate soul! Have you ever witnessed such a scene? When she next opened her lips, it was to show forth a Savior's praise!

The Bible assumes that you have light enough to see, and to do your duty, and to find the way to heaven. A great many of you are perhaps bewildered as to your religious opinions, holding loose and skeptical notions. You have not seen that it is the most reasonable thing in the world to admit and embrace this glorious truth. Will you allow yourself to go on, bewildered, without considering that you are yourself a living, walking revelation of truth? Will you refuse to come into such relation to God and Christ as will save your soul?

In my early life, when I was tempted to skepticism, I can well recollect that I said to myself, *It is much more probable that ministers and the multitudes of good people who believe the Bible are right. They have examined the subject, but I have not. It is, therefore, entirely unreasonable for me to doubt.*

Why should you not say, *I know the gospel is suited to my needs. I know I am afloat on the vast ocean of life, and if there is no gospel, there is nothing that can save me. It is, therefore, unreasonable for me to stand here and quibble. I must examine. I must look into this matter. I can at least see that if God offers me mercy, I must not reject it.* Does not this gospel show you how you can be saved from hell and from sin? Oh, then, believe it! Let the blessed truth find a heart open for its admission. When you give God credit for all His love and truth, and when you bring your heart under the power of this truth, and yield yourself up to its blessed sway, that will be the dawn of morning to your soul! Whosoever will, let him come and take of the waters of life, freely.

4

CONSCIENCE AND THE BIBLE IN HARMONY*

"By manifestation of the truth commending ourselves to every man's conscience in the sight of God" (2 Corinthians 4:2).

The context shows that these words of Paul refer to his manner of preaching, and to the aim which he had in those labors.

Conscience is a moral function of the reason or intellect. It is the department of our natural faculties that has to do with moral subjects—with morality and religion. This faculty shows us moral law and obligation. It has the idea of right and wrong, of praise or blameworthiness, of things deserved or retribution. It comprehends all the intuitions of the intellect on moral questions. The term is sometimes used to include those states of the sensibility which are occasioned by and connected with the actions of conscience; yet, strictly speaking, the term is confined to the intellect, and does not embrace the sensibility.

Everyone has a conscience. This is implied in our Scripture text. How could Paul commend himself in presenting the truth to everyone's conscience if every person did *not* have a conscience; that is, if some had no conscience at all? The existence of a conscience in everyone is a fact of consciousness and one of its ultimate facts. Everyone knows that he has a conscience and it is impossible he should know any fact with higher evidence, or with greater certainty, than he knows this. If he had no conscience, it would be impossible for him to have ideas of right and wrong, of reward and

---

Sermons on the Way of Salvation, pp. 112–129.

punishment, of virtue and vice. No one could convey these ideas to his mind, if he did not have a conscience. No language could be of any use to convey such ideas if man had no conscience wherewith to apprehend and appreciate them.

These ideas of God, duty, right, and reward and punishment belong to people—to all people, and cannot be expelled from the human mind.

This faculty of conscience distinguishes people from the lower animals. Obviously, they have some intellect, but whether they know by direct intuition or in some other way it seems impossible for us to determine. For example, we cannot ascertain whether the bee, in constructing his cells on the most perfect mathematical principles, gets his knowledge of this method by intuition or in some other process. Be this as it may, neither the bee nor any other of the lower animals has any moral law, or any ideas of moral character, of right and wrong, of reward or punishment, or of retribution. This is the great characteristic difference between these animals and human beings. Hence, if anyone sets up the claim that he has no conscience, he claims to be a brute, for he denies of himself the great distinction between human beings and brutes.

Metaphysicians are not agreed whether brutes have sensibility and will or not. They do agree that brutes have no conscience and no moral responsibility; so that those who claim this distinction for themselves put themselves at once by that claim on a level with the lower animals.

The Bible and the human conscience are united, agreeing in all their moral decisions and teachings. This fact proves conclusively that they both come from the same author.

Beginning with our Scripture text, I ask, "What can Paul mean by saying that by manifestation of the truth he commends himself to everyone's conscience?" Obviously this: by exhibiting to people the great truths of the gospel and of the law, he made his appeal to everyone's conscience in a way and with sentiments that enforced each one's approval. The truth commended itself as truth; the claims of duty as right. No one who understood this truth could doubt its evidence. No one who understood its moral claims could dispute those claims.

But this point is so important that it should be examined in detail. I therefore remark that conscience reveals the same rules of duty and the same measure of obligation as God's revealed law does. Conscience imposes the same law of love as God's law does: love supreme toward God, love equal and impartial toward our neighbor. Conscience never fails to affirm that each person is bound to love his neighbor as himself. There never was a human being of developed and sane powers whose conscience did not impose this obligation upon him.

Conscience also postulates this law as binding on all moral beings and as extending to all the activities of every moral being. In fact, conscience and reason show that this is the only possible law or rule of duty for moral beings; and the Bible teaches the very same in every particular. Both are entirely at one in all their teachings on this great subject.

Both conscience and the Bible harmonize also in this: man, in his natural state, has entirely fallen from duty. Conscience universally affirms that people do not, apart from grace, love God with all their heart, nor their neighbors as themselves. The human conscience proclaims that man is in a state of total moral depravity; so does the Bible. Conscience affirms that nothing short of full obedience to God is real virtue; and so does the Bible. Conscience presses the sinner with a sense of guilt, and holds him condemned; and so does the Bible. And each decides by the same rule in every respect. You may take each individual precept you find in the law and the gospel, go into the examination ever so minutely, canvas all the teachings of Jesus Christ, all those of the apostles and of the prophets—you will find that conscience says "Amen" to them all.

What a remarkable fact this is! Here is a book containing myriads of precepts; that is, if you enumerate all the specific applications. Yet, they are comprised under two great principles: supreme love to God and equal love to our fellow man. But in all these countless specific applications of these great principles, whatever the Bible affirms conscience endorses. This is a most remarkable fact. It never has been true of any other book, that all its moral precepts without exception are approved and endorsed by the human conscience. This book, so endorsed, must be inspired by God. It is impossible to suppose that a book so accredited of conscience can be uninspired. It is the greatest absurdity to deny its inspiration. A book so perfectly in harmony with conscience must come from the Author of conscience.

People said of Christ when He taught, "Never man spake like this man" (John 7:46). So wonderfully did the truths He taught commend themselves to everyone's conscience that He spoke "with authority" and "not as the scribes" (Matt. 7:29). For every word went home to man's conscience, and every precept revealing duty was recognized and endorsed as right by the hearer's own convictions. This striking feature characterized all His teachings.

Both the Bible and conscience harmonize in respect to the requirement of repentance. Each affirms this to be everyone's duty. Each rests this claim on the same ground, that God is right and the sinner wrong. Therefore, the sinner ought to turn to God in submission, and not God turn to the sinner in a change of His own course.

In a similar manner, both conscience and the Bible harmonize in the requirement of faith and of entire holiness. On all these great gospel precepts, the Bible affirms and conscience responds most fully. As to the demand of entire holiness, it is a clear dictate of our moral sense that we cannot enjoy God without being like Him. When our intelligence apprehends the true character of God and of man, it recognizes at once the necessity that man should be like God in moral character in order to enjoy His presence. Beings possessed of a great moral nature can never be happy together unless their spirits are congenial.

Conscience affirms the position that a sinner is wrong; so does the Bible. It is impossible for a sinner to believe that his sin is right and pleasing to God. This, also, is the doctrine of the Bible.

Conscience affirms the necessity of an atonement. Human beings have always felt this necessity and have manifested this feeling in many ways. Through all ages they have been devising and practicing some form of sacrifice to render it proper for God to forgive the sinner. The idea has been in their mind that God must demand some sacrifice that would honor His law and sustain its injured majesty. That the law has been dishonored by the sinner, all have fully admitted. And obviously, the idea has been in the minds of human beings that it would be dishonorable, degrading, and injurious to God to forgive sin without some atonement. They seem to have apprehended the great truth that before God can forgive sin, He must demand some demonstration that shall sustain law and evince His own position and feelings as a lawgiver. How, but from these universal affirmations of conscience, can you account for the fact that all mankind has felt the necessity for some mediator between God and man? So universal is this felt necessity that when people have had their conscience aroused, and have been in doubt or in darkness as to Christ, the Mediator, they have plunged into despair. If conscience sleeps, the sinner may pass along with little concern, but when it arouses itself like a mighty man, and puts forth its emphatic announcements, then no sinner can resist.

It is a well-known fact that a Unitarian, when thoroughly convicted of sin, can find no rest in his system of religious belief. I am well aware that as long as his conscience is not aroused to its functions, and he is in great darkness, he can say, "Man is pretty good by nature, and I see no need of a vicarious atonement. I accept Christ as a good man, an excellent teacher, and a fine example; but what do I want with an atoning sacrifice?" So he can say till conscience wakes up its voice of seven thunders. Then he cries out, "I am undone. How can I live if there is not some strong sacrifice for my sins?"

There never was a sinner, awakened to see his sins truly, who did not go into despair unless he saw the atonement. I could give you many cases of this sort in which people long denying the need of any atonement, have at length had conscience fully aroused, and have then invariably felt that God could not forgive unless in some way His insulted majesty were vindicated.

Indeed, God might be perfectly ready to forgive, as far as His feelings are concerned. For He is not vindictive; neither is He implacable. But He is a moral governor, and as such He has a character to sustain. The interests of His created universe rest on His administration, and He must take care what impression He makes on the minds of beings who can sin.

In this light, we can appreciate the propensity always felt by the human mind to put some mediator between a holy God and itself. Catholics interpose saints and the Virgin Mary—supposing that these will have a kind of access to God which they, in their guilt, cannot have. Thus conscience recognizes the universal need of an atonement.

Everywhere the Bible reveals the adequacy of the atonement made by Christ. It is remarkable that the human conscience also promptly accepts it as sufficient. You may arouse the conscience as deeply as you please, may set it on fire; and yet, as soon as the atonement of Christ is revealed, and the mind understands what it is, and what relations it sustains to law and government, suddenly conscience is quiet. The sense of condemnation is gone. The assurance of an adequate atonement restores peace to the troubled soul. Conscience fully accepts this atonement as amply sufficient, even as the Bible also does.

Nothing other than this atonement can satisfy conscience: not good works (ever so costly or many), not penance, not any amount of self-imposed suffering and sacrifice. Let a sinner attempt to substitute ever so much prayer and fasting in place of Christ as an atoning sacrifice, and it is of no avail. The more he tries, the more he is dissatisfied. Conscience will not accept it. Neither will the Bible. Most wonderfully, we find it still true that conscience and

48

the Bible bear the same testimony and take the same positions. But how does this happen? Whence comes this universal harmony? This is a problem for those who deny the inspiration of God's Word to solve. Those who admit its inspiration have only to infer both to the same Author. God's voice in the Bible and God's voice in the heart of man utter the same notes, each responsive to the other, and each affirming or denying in perpetual unison.

Both the human conscience and the Bible teach justification by faith. I do not suppose the human conscience could have revealed to us the fact of the death of Christ, but the Bible having revealed it, the conscience can and does appreciate its fitness and adequacy. Therefore, the conscience can and does accept this sacrifice as a ground of justification before God. It recognizes the sinner as brought into a state of acceptance with God on the ground of what Christ has suffered and done. What can be the reason that faith in Christ has such wonderful power to extract the smart of sin, take away the sense of condemnation, and give the consciousness of being accepted by God? The fact we see developed everyday. You cannot make the mind afraid of punishment when once it rests in Jesus Christ. You cannot create a sense of condemnation while your heart has an active faith in the blood of Christ. By no methods you can employ can you force it upon your soul. With faith there will be hope and peace, despite all your efforts to dislodge them. When the soul really embraces Christ, peace will come. The truth is, the provisions of the gospel for the pardon of sin meet the demands of conscience. The conscience affirms that God is just, and therefore, is satisfied, while He justifies the repentant believer in Jesus. It is the province of conscience to affirm the propriety or impropriety of God's moral conduct as well as man's; hence, it moves only within its sphere when it affirms that God can rightly accept such a satisfaction as that made in the atonement of Christ for sin.

Conscience affirms that there can be no other conceivable way of justifying the sinner except by faith in Christ. You may try ever so much to devise some other scheme, yet you cannot. You may try to get peace of mind on any other scheme than this—as some of you have—but all is of no avail. I once said to a Roman Catholic, "When you went to confessional you hoped to be accepted and to get peace?" "Yes." "But did you find it to your full satisfaction?" "Not certainly. I cannot say that I knew I was accepted."

Catholics who have been diligent in all their ceremonies before experiencing the deep peace of the gospel through faith in Christ, will testify of the wide difference between their experiences as

Papists and their experiences as gospel believers. Their consciences completely accept their faith in the latter case, giving them deep assured peace, while in the former case there could be nothing of this sort.

The Bible and conscience agree in affirming the doctrine of endless punishment. Conscience could teach nothing else. At what period would conscience say, "He has suffered enough. The law of God is satisfied; his deserved punishment for sin is now exhausted, and he deserves no more"? Those who know anything about the decisions of conscience on this point know very well that it can conceive of no limitation for punishment of sin. It can see no end to the punishment that sin deserves. It can conceive of the man who has once thus sinned as being nothing else but a sinner before God, since the fact of his having sinned can never cease to be a fact. If you have been a thief, that fact will always be true, and in that sense you must always be a thief in the eye of the law. You cannot make it otherwise. Your suffering can make no sort of satisfaction to an offended law. Conscience will see more and more the guilt in your course of sin, and your sense of guilt must increase to all eternity. You can never reach the point where conscience will say, "This suffering is enough; this sinner ought to suffer no longer." The Bible teaches the same thing. Yet each agree in teaching that God can forgive the repentant sinner through faith in Christ, but can extend forgiveness to no sinner on any other ground.

The Bible Answers the Cry of the Conscience

We see why the Bible is so readily received as being from God. Few have ever read any treatise of argument on this subject. But as soon as one reads those parts that relate to morals, conscience at once affirms and endorses it. You need no higher evidence that He who speaks in the Bible is indeed God himself. The truth commends itself to every man's conscience, and needs no other endorsement of its divine origin.

You see why one who has seen this harmony between conscience and the Bible cannot be reasoned out of his belief in the Bible by any amount of subtle sophistry. Perhaps he will say to his opponent: "I cannot meet your sophistries. I have never speculated in that direction. But I know the Bible is true, and the whole gospel is from God. I know it by an affirmation of my own mind. I know it by its perfect fitness to meet my needs. I know it has told me all I ever felt or have ever needed, and it has brought a perfect supply for all my need." This he can say in reply to sophistry to which he may have no other logic to withstand. And this is amply sufficient.

In my own case, I know it was the beauty and intrinsic evidence of the Bible that kept me from being an infidel. I would have been an infidel if I could, and I would have been a Universalist if I could have been, for I was wicked enough to be either. But I knew the Bible was true, and when I set myself to make out an argument against it, I could not divest myself of an ever present conviction that this was the wrong side. Just as a lawyer who sits down to examine a case and finds at every turn that his evidence is weak or irrelevant, and is troubled with a growing conviction that he is on the wrong side; and the more he examines his case and his law books, the more he sees that he must be wrong—so I found it in my investigations into the evidences of revelation, and in my readings of the Bible. In those times I was wicked enough for anything, and used to go out among the plain Christian people and talk to them about the Bible, and puzzle them with my questions and hard points. I could confound, even though I could not convince them, and then I would try to enjoy my sport at their expense. Sometimes afterward, I would show them how they settled this question of the divine authority of the Bible, although they could not tell me.

I don't believe there ever was, or ever can be, a candid person who shall candidly examine the Bible, compare its teachings with the affirmations of his own conscience, and then deny its authority.

Neither Paul nor Jesus Christ preached sermons on the evidences of a revelation from God. How was it, then, that Christ brought out the truth in such a way as to reach the conscience, wake up its energies, and make it speak out in fearful tones? He manifested the truth in such a way as to commend it to everyone's conscience.

Just in proportion as a person fails to develop his conscience or blinds, abuses, or silences it, can he become skeptical. It will always be so far *only* as his conscience becomes seared and blind; while, on the other hand, as his conscience has free scope and speaks out truthfully, will his conviction become irresistible that the Bible is true and from God.

The Bible is sometimes rejected because it's misunderstood. I once fell in with an infidel who had read much (not in the Bible) and who, after his much reading, settled down upon infidelity. I inquired of him as to his views of the inspiration of the Bible, when he promptly replied, "I know it is not true, and is not from God, for it teaches things contrary to my conscience." "Ah," I said, "and pray tell me in what particulars! What are these things taught in the Bible that are contrary to your conscience?"

He began with these comments:

1. "It teaches the imputation of Adam's sin to his posterity." "But stop," I said, "is that Bible or is it only catechism?" He soon found that he had to look in his catechism to find it, for it was not in his Bible.

2. "It teaches that human nature, as made by God, is itself sinful." I soon showed him that the Bible said no such thing. He declared that this doctrine was contrary to his conscience. I admitted it, but vindicated the Bible from such impiety as ascribing the creation of sin to God.

3. "But the Bible certainly does teach that people are naturally unable to obey God, and especially are unable to repent and believe the gospel." I replied that is neither taught nor implied in the Bible in the sense in which you urge it. But, on the contrary, the Bible both teaches and implies that sinners can obey God and are for that very reason responsible and guilty if they refuse.

4. There was one other point on which all the books were clear and strong, but which was utterly against his conscience, namely, that Christ was *punished* for our sins. "This punishing the innocent instead of the guilty," he said, "was one of the most unjust things that could be imagined." "Well," I said, "that is just what the Bible does *not* teach. It nowhere holds the doctrine that Christ was *punished* as a criminal. Punishment implies guilt, and is inflicted as penalty for crime. Neither of which is true in the case of Christ. He only suffered as an innocent being, and of His own free accord. You cannot say that this is wrong. If one man in his benevolence *chooses* to suffer for another, no principle of justice is violated. This he conceded.

5. "According to the Bible," he said, "none can be saved without having their natures constitutionally changed. But no one can be held responsible for changing his own constitution." Here too I showed him his misapprehension of the Bible. The change is only that which pertains primarily to the voluntary powers and of course is just that which people are capable of doing, and which a person must do himself.

6. He urged but one more point, namely, "that God has elected some to be saved and some to be damned, and that no one can escape their foreordained destiny." To this you know I would reply that the Bible did not teach *such* an election, nor authorize such an inference, but everywhere implies the opposite. Such was our discussion.

You doubtless know that such mistakes as these have led some men to reject the Bible. It is not strange that they should. I could never have received the Bible as from God if I had believed it to teach these things. I had to learn first that those things were not in the Bible, and then I was prepared to accept it in accordance with my conscience and reason as from God.

Skepticism always evinces either great wickedness or great ignorance as to what the Bible teaches, and as to the evidence on which its claims rest. Both the nature of the case and the testimony of observation conspire to prove this.

All the truths of natural religion are taught and affirmed both in the conscience and in the Bible. This is a most remarkable fact; yet easily shown in the fullest detail.

The conscience recognizes the Bible as its own book—the book *of the heart*—a sort of supplement to its own imperfect system—readily answering those questions that lie beyond the range of vision which conscience enjoys. There are questions that conscience must ask, but cannot answer. It must ask whether there is any way in which God can forgive sin, and if so, what it is. Such questions conscience cannot answer without the help from revelation. It is striking to observe how conscience grasps these glorious truths when they are presented, and the heart has come to feel its need of God's light and love. Observe how, when the moral nature of man has sent forth its voice abroad over the universe, far as its notes can reach, imploring light and crying aloud for help, and listening to learn if any response is made; then when it catches these responsive notes from God's written revelation, it shouts "Amen! Amen! that brings me salvation! Let God be praised!"

The skeptic is obliged to ignore the teachings of his own nature, and the voice of his conscience. All those moral affirmations must be kept out of sight, or he could not remain an infidel. It will not do for him to commune with his own heart, and ask what testimony conscience bears as to duty, truth, and his God. All he can do to smother the spontaneous utterance of his conscience, he must do for the sake of peace in his sin and skepticism.

But these efforts must be ultimately vain for sooner or later conscience will speak out. Its voice, long smothered, will break forth with redoubled force, as if in retribution for being abused so long. Many may *live* as skeptics, but few can *die* as such. To that few *you* cannot hope to belong. You already know too much on this subject. You cannot satisfy yourself that the Bible is false and make yourself disbelieve its divine authority so that it will *stay disbelieved*. Such a notion, resting on no valid evidence, but starting up under the stimulus of a corrupt heart, will disappear when moral realities begin to press hard on your soul.

I am aware that in these latter times some young men make the discovery that they know more and are wiser than all the greatest and best men that have ever lived. They think so, but they may in divine mercy live long enough to unlearn this folly, and to lay off this self-conceit. One thing I must tell you: *You cannot die peacefully as skeptics;* you cannot die believing that God can accept you without faith in Christ. Do you ask, "Why?" Because you have heard too much truth. After reading this, you have heard too much truth to allow you to carry such a delusion to your grave. No! You cannot die peacefully in darkness and delusion. I beg you to remember when you come to die that I told you you could not die a skeptic. Mark my words, then, and prove them false if you can. Write it down for a memorandum, and treasure it for a test in the trying hour—that I told you solemnly you could not die peacefully as a skeptic. It will do you no harm to remember this one thing from me, for if you should in that hour find me mistaken, you will still not have comfort in your infidelity.

Every summer since coming here I have had to stand by the deathbed of some young unbeliever. Shall I find you there this year in the dark discomfort of infidelity? There is no happiness in it. Not one of you *can die happy as an infidel!* Dr. Nelson once informed me that he said this same thing to a young infidel. Not long after, this infidel was sick, and thought himself dying. Yet, his infidelity remained unshaken. And when he saw the Doctor next, he cast into his teeth that prediction he thought had been triumphantly disproved. "Dr. Nelson," he said, "I was dying last month, and contrary to your strange prediction my infidelity did not forsake me." "Ah," said the Doctor, "but you were not dying then! And you never can die peacefully as an infidel!" And when that young man came to die, Dr. Nelson was right. The infidel's conscience spoke out in awful thunders, and his soul trembled exceedingly as it passed from this to another world.[1]

But such fears may come too late! The door perhaps is shut and the soul is lost. Alas, that you should lose eternal life for a reason so poor, for a compensation so insignificant!

---

[1] Most probably the Rev. David Nelson, M.D., who wrote the very excellent book, *The Cause and Cure of Infidelity*, New York: The American Tract Society, 1841.

5

MAKING GOD A LIAR*

"He that believeth on the Son of God hath the witness in himself: he that believeth not God hath made him a liar; because he believeth not the record that God gave of his Son" (1 John 5:10).

Multitudes of people speak against unbelief without exactly understanding what it is. Unbelief is not the mere absence of faith, nor is it a mere negative state of mind. Neither is unbelief a mere intellectual attitude, or state, caused by a lack of sufficient evidence. It is also not a state of ignorance of God and His truth, nor does it consist in a state of entire ignorance of the existence and attributes of God. Unbelief is not mere disbelief or belief in the opposite of what the Bible says is true. Unbelief is not an intellectual state at all. The Bible represents unbelief as sin; therefore, it is a choice people make.

What Unbelief Is

Because unbelief is sin, it must be a voluntary state of mind. The Bible complains of unbelief as a spirit that we have no right to indulge, marking it as a great crime for which we are accountable. Now, if this is the fact, it must be a voluntary state of mind; because if we could not help it, the Bible could not denounce it as one of the greatest of sins, and call upon us to cease from it.

Unbelief is really the opposite of faith. What is faith? Faith is not a mere intellectual conviction. We know it cannot be, for if it

---

*The Penny Pulpit, No. 1,544, delivered on May 26, 1850, at the Tabernacle at Moorfields.

were, then the devil has that faith, and so have many wicked people. Their intellects assent to the truth, and that is what often troubles them so much. Faith consists, then, in giving God our confidence, in voluntarily yielding ourselves up to Him, trusting in Him, casting ourselves upon Him, voluntarily receiving His truth and committing ourselves to Him. It is thus that the term *faith* is used in the Bible. The very term that is rendered *commit* is also rendered *faith*. "Let them . . . commit the keeping of their souls to him in well doing, as unto a faithful Creator" (1 Pet. 4:19). And again, "But Jesus did not commit himself unto them, because he knew all men" (John 2:24). In these and other instances, the word here rendered faith is rendered commit.

Now, unbelief is the direct opposite of committal. Unbelief is the withholding of confidence where there is sufficient evidence and sufficient light in the intellect. Withholding of confidence is represented as unbelief of the heart—not merely of the intellect but of the heart. Unbelief implies that the intellect perceives the truth. That which constitutes saving faith is the heart trusting in God, committing itself to the truth, yielding itself up to receive the truth. Unbelief is the opposite of all this; the heart does not commit itself to God and does not yield itself up to receive the truth.

We often see this state of unbelief manifested in relation to this world. You see people withholding their confidence where there is the strongest evidence of the truth of that which they are called upon to believe. Look at that jury box. The prisoner has been tried, the judge has summed up the evidence and put the plain truth before the jury. But some of them will not yield to it, will not give their confidence. This state of mind in religion is unbelief.

Now, we see multitudes of people on every side whose minds are made up concerning the truth of the Bible. They believe it is true, assent to it intellectually, and they call this faith. They say they believe; their opinions are settled. They can argue in defense of their principles, and they say they have faith in them. You call upon them to believe, and they say they *do* believe. While the fact is, when people will not *commit* themselves to the truth, they do not believe to the saving of their souls. Intellectual belief is nothing without confidence. The Bible says, "This is the victory that overcometh the world, even our faith" (1 John 5:4).

How Unbelief Makes God a Liar

The Bible says, "He that believeth not God, hath made him a liar." Withholding confidence is a practical denial that God is worthy of confidence. Now, there is nothing more unreasonable in the universe than unbelief. God has so constituted mankind that by a necessary law of their minds, they affirm that He will not lie. Nobody ever believed that God would lie, everybody knows better. Every intelligent being in earth, hell, or heaven knows that God will not lie. And yet, wherever an individual withholds confidence in God, it is a practical denial of His trustworthiness, a practical denial of what reason and conscience affirm must be true. This is one of the most provoking forms of sin of which a moral agent can be guilty. There is nothing more provoking, even to the greatest liars themselves, than to have their veracity called in question. What an infinitely awful sin it must be to make God a liar! But it is also injurious to yourselves, and ruinous to society.

Who does not know that if a wife should withhold confidence from her husband, she would ruin herself and her husband too? And so, if a husband withholds confidence in his wife, he ruins his own happiness and that of his wife too. Suppose that confidence is withheld without good reason by a husband from his wife. How it ruins her happiness, what a trial it is for her to endure! Suppose that the husband reproaches his wife for having committed some wrong, and withholds his confidence; and suppose the children lose confidence in her, how can she manage to govern them? What wrong is done to the family! Probably the family would be ruined.

Destroy confidence in a government, and unless it is very strong and thus enabled to keep the people in awe, that government will very soon be ruined. So with business transactions. The world has to live by confidence in each other. There is no community whatever that is not ruined if unbelief—lack of confidence—comes to be the law of action. Withholding confidence when there is no reason is the greatest crime a person can commit against society or the family. Everybody must admit this.

You often find people tremblingly, quiveringly, alive to their own reputation for veracity who withhold confidence from God. Some people, who call themselves Christians too, fail to realize the truth of God so as to confide fully in Him. God has said, "All things work together for good to them that love God" (Rom. 8:28). But a great many people have no belief in this! They don't rest in God's words, and they are always in trouble, distress, and tribulation because of their unbelief.

Now, if you should see a man standing on a mountain of granite in the greatest trouble and anguish lest the rock would not be strong enough to hold him, why, you would say the man is deranged; his conduct would be in a high degree ridiculous. Now, the people of God are infinitely more ridiculous, when they withhold confidence in God, than the man on a mountain of granite fearing it might fall. God's promises are infinitely more able to support them than mountains of granite! The strongest rocks in creation are but mere air when compared with the stupendous strength and stability of the promises of Jehovah! "Heaven and earth shall pass away, but the word of the Lord shall stand fast forever" (Matt. 24:35).

Unbelief is the most blasphemous of all forms of sin. Let anyone publicly accuse God of lying, and the law of the land would lay hands on him. He would be indicted for blasphemy. Suppose someone should go through the streets of London, proclaiming aloud that God was a liar, you would very soon find him in Newgate prison, and he would deserve to be there [editor's note: times have now changed]. If anyone should go through the streets, proclaiming that God was a liar, everybody would say it was the most revolting species of blasphemy. They would stop their ears and run in order to get away from him. Nobody would dare to walk in the same street with him, lest a thunderbolt should descend and destroy him, or the earth open and swallow him up. Now, many a person, if his conduct were put into words and he should speak them, would be indicted for blasphemy.

Unbelief accuses God of perjury. God has sworn the greatest oath that He could think of in confirmation of His truth: "Because he could sware by no greater, he sware by himself" (Heb. 6:13). He confirmed His promise "by two immutable things in which it was impossible for God to lie." Now mark! Unbelief accuses God of lying under an oath, of lying under the greatest oath that God could take! Suppose a person should in words accuse God of perjury— that He had not only lied, but sworn to a lie!

The Results of Unbelief

When we are in unbelief we have a lack of rest to our souls. Now, when the soul does not rest on the promises of God—does not believe that "all things work together for good to them that love God"—the soul has no rest in Christ, does not embrace Christ, does not rest in His faithfulness and in His promises.

Now, my readers, let me put one question to you, "Are you guilty of unbelief?" If so, you are the very persons charged with making God a liar!

Another manifestation of unbelief is lack of peace. There is always peace and joy in believing. Now, the lack of peace is an evidence of unbelief. The fact is, where there is real faith, although there may be much to disturb and distress the mind, there is deep peace and joy in God in the midst of it all. But when people do not have peace, real joy and satisfaction in God, in His truth, and in His promises, you may know that there is unbelief. From the very nature of the case, there must be. The mind cannot be reposing in the promises of God, if it has not peace and joy.

When people have not power in prayer, when they have no faith in prayer to prevail with God, it is because of unbelief. In the Bible, we are told that those who have faith have power with God and can prevail with God and receive the spirit of their petitions. Now, let me ask you, do you have this confidence, this faith that makes you mighty in prayer? Or do you lack this power in prayer? If the latter, then you are guilty of unbelief. Now, one of two things must be true, if these things are lacking in your soul. If you have no confidence in the promises, no peace of mind, and no power in prayer, either the Bible is not true or you do not believe the Bible, because the Bible affirms that these are true of those who believe.

Those who live in bondage to any form of sin are in a state of unbelief. "There is therefore now no condemnation to those who are in Christ Jesus, who walk not after the flesh, but after the Spirit" (Rom. 8:1). Now, when people live under any form of worldliness, they are under the condemnation of the law. "This is the victory that overcometh the world, even our faith." Now, if you are living in bondage to sin because of unbelief, you are living in a state of condemnation. Your own conscience condemns you because of your unbelief.

Another evidence of unbelief is the manifestation of a servile spirit in reference to Christianity—the spirit of a servant as distinguished from the spirit of a son. By servant, I mean slave: one who serves his master from fear instead of love. Now, a great many people profess to serve God, but they do not serve Him with the spirit of sons. Although they profess to be children of God, they look upon Christianity as something that must not be neglected. They perform religious duties, not from any love of God, but as the least of two evils; and thus they drag out a painful existence. Christianity, to them, is not a peace-giving religion. It is not their life in which they have supreme delight, loving it for its own sake. It is to them something they must attend to, something they must not neglect, but which they would be very glad to neglect if they dared. They go to meetings, read their Bibles, and pray, but not because their hearts are filled with love to God, love to the Bible, love to their closets—not because they love to have communion with God. No! Their Christian disciplines are regarded as a task, which they must not omit to perform.

Now, remember, that in every instance where people take this view of Christianity and its disciplines, there is unbelief in the heart. Such people go through a form of prayer, not from love to God, but because they think it is their duty to pray. To approach God from such motives is not prayer, but only an indication of a mere servile spirit, an evident manifestation of unbelief.

They don't come to God to get anything. They don't expect to receive anything from God. The Bible has promised them great things in answer to prayer, but they don't expect them. They pray, because it is their duty. They never run to God to make a request, as a child runs to his father for something he wants, holding up his little hands with a smile on his face expecting to get the favor for which he asks. They do nothing of this sort. They say their prayers, or perhaps read them. They go through a form, and do what they call praying, and what for? Many people pray, not because God has given them promises, not because they have something in their hearts that they want God to give and because they expect to get it, but because it is their duty to make a prayer. Now, who does not see that this is a manifestation of unbelief; the evidence of a spirit directly opposite to the spirit of prayer and everything that belongs to true Christianity.

Now, if any of you have been religious because it was your duty, have served God from a servile spirit, and not from spontaneous love, let me urge you, for once, to approach His throne now and pray expecting to receive that for which you seek. I say that now you are an unbeliever. You may call yourself what you please, but as certain as God is true—as certain as God is true—you have no faith!

I remark again, a spirit of worldly-mindedness is an evidence of unbelief. I mean that state in which the mind is given up to worldly pursuits and amusements, minding earthly things—giving up the mind to them—giving the chief attention to them, and being chiefly influenced by worldly considerations. Now observe! This is the very opposite of a state of faith, which, from its very nature precludes this state of mind. If you find that your mind is worldly, that you are engrossed with worldly things, you may be sure that you have no faith. Can you pray with the world in your mind? Can you go to the sanctuary with business engrossing your thoughts? Can you receive God's truth into your mind, if it is given up to other influences? It is naturally impossible for you to serve God and the world! If you are worldly-minded, I say, it is an evidence of unbelief! And unbelief, remember, virtually charges God with being a liar; and the man who is an unbeliever has the hardihood to say in conduct though not in words that God is a perjured being, that He lies under oath!

The spirit of cowardice is also an evidence of unbelief. Those who believe God are not afraid of anybody. Spiritual cowardice is always the result of unbelief. Confidence in God makes the righteous strong as lions. Now, if you are spiritual cowards, if you are afraid to talk to sinners about their souls, if you are afraid to hold up the light, it is because you do not believe.

Neglect of the Bible is also a manifesting of unbelief. Nobody neglects the Bible who believes it. Neglect to use the promises of the Bible—not pleading them in order to receive their fulfillment—is a sure indication of unbelief.

A spirit of indifference in regard to the state of Christianity, blindness in regard to the state of sinners, no compassion for them, a lack of interest in their conversion, are certain indications of unbelief. And I might point out hundreds of others.

But let me ask, who of us are guilty of unbelief? If I am guilty of unbelief, I am the very wretch that stands before you and makes God a liar! If you are guilty of unbelief, you are the wretches who stand before God, and accuse Him of being a liar! Horrible! Horrible! But is it not true? Does not everyone know that if you withhold confidence from God, it is because you regard God as unworthy of confidence; and if unworthy of confidence, it must be that He is not a true being, but a liar!

There are several results of unbelief. Unbelief always produces a heartless religion. Therefore, whenever you find your Christianity is not soul-satisfying, not a living principle in your soul; that your Christianity is not peace and joy in the Holy Spirit, and is not a spontaneous principle of love to God, you may conclude that the reason is because your heart is filled with unbelief.

Again, if you lose faith, your Christianity will be legal. When people lose their faith, they do a great many things without regard to God at all. They cease to have an eye to God's will, pleasure and glory. You cannot distinguish between them and the professedly ungodly. Oftentimes, what they call their religious duties, they perform not out of love to God, supreme regard to Him, but to promote their own selfishness.

Another consequence of unbelief is that it renders salvation naturally impossible. Now, it should always be remembered that the conditions of salvation are not arbitrary; they are natural and necessary conditions. If anybody would go to heaven, he must be prepared for heaven. If an individual does not love God in his heart, it is naturally impossible that he should be happy in heaven. What would there be in heaven to interest him? What would he do in heaven? To enjoy heaven and be happy there, he must be a holy man and this he can only be as he is made so by faith.

Of course, disobedience of heart to God is always a result of unbelief. There is no heart-obedience to any government any further than individuals have confidence in that government. The heart of a person must confide in any system of government in order to have a hearty and true obedience to it. In respect to the governmental consequences, all unbelief entirely rejects the Mediator between God and man—it rejects the office, the authority, and atonement of Christ altogether. The penalty of the law is dead against those who are unbelievers; those who believe not are condemned already, because they have not believed on the name of the only begotten Son of God.

The Early Beginning of Unbelief

The first sin in our world, when we resolve it into its true elements as a particular form of sin, was unbelief. Let us look at it. God had told Adam and Eve that they must not eat of the fruit of the tree of knowledge of good and evil, or by so doing they would die. The tempter told our first parents that they should not die, if they did eat of it and tried to make them believe that God was selfish in the prohibition—that God gave them the injunction from a fear that by their eating of the fruit they should become like himself. Now, what did they do? Why, they dared to withdraw confidence in God. So completely did the insinuation of the tempter take hold of them, that it is said, "When the woman saw that the tree was good for food, and that it was pleasant to the eyes, and a tree to be desired to make one wise, she took of the fruit thereof and did eat, and also gave unto her husband with her; and he did eat" (Gen. 3:6). Now, what was the particular form of sin? Why, it was first withdrawing, and then withholding, faith from God. They refused to confide in what God had said. They did not believe that He considered their good in the prohibition. They listened to the tempter and believed what he told them—that God was jealous of them, that He forbid them to eat of the tree lest they should become gods. And then they withdrew confidence from God and suffered the consequences.

This is the root of sin in man: his withholding confidence in God. All the forms of iniquity in this world took their rise here, and we might, did time permit, trace them by a philosophical method to this source. Withholding confidence in God is one of the worst of evils. Having no confidence in God's wisdom, benevolence, and goodness, leaves the mind a blank. People are drawn aside into vice, because they have lost confidence in God and goodness. If a person yielded his heart to God, could he be carried away with every breath of temptation? No, indeed, he could not. But when he withdraws confidence, his mind is darkened and error exercises its full power in his soul. How remarkable was the effect of unbelief in Adam and Eve! As soon as they withdrew confidence in God, they thought they could hide themselves from Him. So grossly did they fall into darkness by withholding confidence that they thought they could hide themselves among the trees when the Lord God walked in the garden.

Perfect faith would secure entire holiness. Suppose any person has perfect confidence in all that God says, could he sin? What! Have perfect confidence in God's love, God's goodness, God's universal presence, and consent to sin? No more than they do in heaven. For what is the reason they do not sin in heaven but they have such universal confidence in God? If a man had perfect confidence in God, could he sin? Never, never. Where there is any overt act of sin, there is unbelief.

There are a vast number people who profess to be Christians who are grossly guilty of unbelief. They have no peace and joy in God, no power in prayer, are worldly-minded, are "careful and troubled about many things," giving as full evidence of being in a state of unbelief as the world around them. Their lives, words, and actions are just the same as those who make no profession at all. You can hardly distinguish them, unless you see them at the Communion Table. You ask if they are believers, and they say, yes, and persuade themselves that they are Christians. But as certain as God is true, they are unbelievers and will be lost with all their profession! The unbelief manifested by people who profess to be Christians is one of the greatest stumbling blocks in the way of the conversion of the world, and tends to drive their children into infidelity and sin.

Lastly, let me urge upon you to reflect upon the awful wickedness of unbelief. Suppose you have withdrawn confidence from God, what is the state of your hearts? Why, you are playing the hypocrite and concealing the real state of your hearts, and are thus kept from being indicted for blasphemy. Unbelievers, in the sense which I have explained, whether church members or not, if you were to speak out from the real state of your hearts, you would be disgraced before the community and chased from society—if you should venture to persist in this unbelief.

Now, in a few days you and I shall stand before God. What will be our state then? Will we stand before Him as people who have accused Him of lying, who withdrew confidence from Him, and would not believe? May God have mercy on us, and let us ponder these things and turn unto the Lord with full purpose of heart and thus avert His wrath from us!

6

MOCKING GOD*

"Now therefore be ye not mockers, lest your bands be made strong: for I have heard from the Lord God of hosts a consumption, even determined upon the whole earth" (Isaiah 28:22).

The term to mock, in its scriptural sense, means to act hypocritically, to make false pretenses or professions. We sometimes speak of having our hopes mocked, that is, they are disappointed. To be a mocker is to be hypocritical, to make false pretenses, representations that are not true. To mock God is to pretend to love and serve Him when we do not, to act in a false manner, to be insincere and hypocritical in our professions, pretending to obey Him, love, serve, and worship Him when we do not. Anything that amounts to insincerity is mockery, anything that is only pretense, and does not represent the state of the heart. In ordinary language, the term to *mock* means to dishonor. In this sense, God is mocked by not being honored. He is not dishonored really, but only as far as man is concerned. When the Bible says, "God is not mocked" (Gal. 6:7), it means God is not dishonored *really*, although individuals do that which would dishonor Him, if He could be dishonored.

Some of the Ways People Mock God

If there is anything of vital importance to us, it is that we really understand our true position with respect to God; whether we are

---

The Penny Pulpit, No. 1,555, delivered on May 31, 1850, at the Tabernacle at Moorfields.

or are not accepted by Him in the service we profess to render unto Him.

We mock God when we present ourselves in the house of God as His professed servants without the true spirit of obedience, love, worship and faith. Unless we are really in an obedient state of mind, in the true spirit of devotion to His service, we mock Him by the very fact of coming to His house as worshipers. For example, what do we profess in coming before Him as worshipers? It is very important that we should understand what is really implied in coming to God's house, and taking our places before Him as a worshiper of God. Why, in coming to God's house you profess to be devoted to His interests, service and glory, that in your hearts you are really the servants of God, and that you come to His house to express what is in your hearts. You profess by this act to have an obedient spirit, love unfeigned, full confidence in Him, submission to Him, and the spirit of true worship. Now, everyone who goes to the house of God without these sentiments of humility, love and obedience, is a mocker in the biblical sense of the term. And you are sternly asked, "Who hath required this at your hands, that you should tread my courts without the spirit of the true worshiper— the spirit of truth, real obedience, love, faith, repentance, devotion and consecration to me? Why have you come before me as mere mockers, drawing near to me with your lips, while your heart is far from me?" Now, everyone who goes to the house of God as a worshiper professes, by the very act of going, that he possesses the spirit of devotion to God and consecration to His service and glory.

When we go to church, either we already profess to be devoted to Him, or we come to inquire how we may consecrate ourselves to Him and obey Him. The language of the real Christian is, "Let us go up to the house of God and inquire what the will of the Lord is, that we may understand His will, and that we may do it." By the very act of coming to inquire His will, they pledge themselves to obey it when it is made known to them. If this is not the case, what can it mean? For what purpose do you visit God's house? Let me ask those who profess to be Christians, for what end do you come to God's house? Is it to learn His will that you may obey Him and do more to glorify Him? If this is not the disposition of your minds, if this is not what you mean, then you are mockers and you appear before God in the character of hypocrites, virtually saying, "O God, we don't come to obey you, we don't come to inquire about your will concerning us, with the intention of doing it. We only come pretending this, for in our hearts we have no desire to obey your will, and do what you require of us."

Suppose there are some of this class of people in church now. No one can deny that we meet professedly to worship God, and the very fact of coming to such a meeting is surely a declaration that you wish to be instructed in the will of the Lord, that you may obey Him and glorify His Name. Now, is not this true? Why, yes it is! This is a meeting for God's worship, for God to reveal His will to His people in order that they may do it. Now, the very fact that you come together must imply that you have pledged yourselves that when the will of the Lord is made known you will do it. The very fact that we come to God's house must imply that we come to worship God, that we appear before Him as obedient people, with a determination in our hearts to do whatever he may tell us to do. Now, let me ask, is not anything short of complying with the spirit of this pledge, mocking God? Would you not regard yourselves as mocked, if you were served in the same way by your fellow man?

The same would be true if an individual professed great attachment to you, but had no such feeling in his heart. Let it be understood, then, that all who meet for the worship of God, who are really not in a state of heart to do whatever He commands them, are mockers. As far as they are not in a right state of heart they mock God, and all who come to such places and do not honestly intend to apply the truth, and obey it themselves when they return into the world, mock God. The very fact of their appearing before Him implies that they mean to obey Him. If they do not, they are mockers.

Hear what the Lord said by the mouth of the prophet, "[They] speak one to another, every one to his brother saying, Come I pray you, and hear what is the word that cometh forth from the Lord. And they come unto thee as the people cometh, and they sit before thee as my people, and they hear thy words but they will not do them: for with their mouth they shew much love, but their heart goeth after their covetousness. And lo! thou art unto them as a very lovely song of one that hath a pleasant voice, and can play well on an instrument: for they hear thy words but they do them not" (Ezek. 33:30–32). They wanted to make Him believe that they designed to obey Him, and came and sat before the prophet as the people of God, and heard his words with attention, and professed to love and admire them, but would not do them.

Now, let me ask, how is it with you? Do you realize what is implied in your going to church? Are you mocking God, or do you intend to redeem the pledge you make to God by your appearance in His house?

Confessing sin without repentance is mocking God. When people confess sin they profess to be sorry that they have ever committed sin. Surely, then, if there is such a thing as mocking God, it is confessing sin without repentance. When people confess sin without forsaking their sins, they mock God. Who can doubt this? We mock God by confessing sin and professing repentance for sin, without making restitution when we have done wrong. If we confess, without repentance, without forsaking, and without making restitution to those we have injured, of course we are mocking God in all this. I know that people often abound in confession, and then go right on in the same way.

Some people are in the daily habit of confessing their sins, and then suppose that this is all that is required of them. If you tell them that they are sinners and must seek repentance, they tell you, "Remember we confess our sins!" They confess that they are in a bad state of mind, that they do not do their duty, that they have done those things they ought not to have done, and have left undone those things they ought to have done; they confess those things, day after day, and week after week, but never mean to forsake the sins they confess to be guilty of. Now, when people confess sin and do not forsake it, and do not make restitution as far as lies in their power, where they have done wrong, all their confessions only amount to this—mocking God. For what does confession imply? Repentance! What is repentance? Why, repentance is heart rejection of sin; and if the heart turns away from sin the life must also of necessity, for the heart governs the external life. By a necessary law, if a man's heart is right his life will be right. The effect must follow the cause. By a necessary law of man's being this must be so. Now, where people profess repentance for sin, without forsaking sin and turning away from it, by all their confessions they mock God.

Now, from all this you can judge whether you are guilty of mocking God, whether you are hypocritical. As a matter of course, you mock God if you confess sin and do not forsake and resist it, as we have seen. What are your views of sin in general? Do you confess sin in your closets? Confess the sins of the day when you are about to retire for the night? If so, why do you do it? Do you intend to repent of your sins, or do you expect to continue to live just as you have lived? Do you confess your sins because you think it is safe as a matter of form? Now, all such confessions of sin that do not come from the heart, from a repentant heart resolved upon forsaking sin, are not only senseless, they are worse than senseless, much worse. They are downright mocking of God.

All mere formality in prayer, asking for things from mere custom, is mocking God. Some people in their closets, if they are in the habit of closet prayer, will pray for things without thinking what they say. They pray according to custom, they go around in a circle, always asking for much the same things without really considering what they say, or hardly knowing what they do say. They get into the habit of going a certain round, saying certain things from week to week and year to year. They have family worship, or an imitation of it. They keep up the custom, because they have a duty to perform, as they think. It won't do to neglect their prayers, as they call them. They never fail to have these so-called family devotions, but they pray without faith, without deep feeling, and without anything that should characterize prayer. It is all a mere matter of form. Instead of coming from the depths of the heart, it is mere talk and form. Now, of course, such conduct as this amounts only to mockery. People who act this way, instead of praying to God, shamefully mock Him. There is such formality in family worship that every member of the household can tell almost exactly what is going to be prayed for. Sometimes this same thing is seen in the public assembly also. Now, all such things as these are merely mocking God.

All matters of form and stereotyped ways of doing things in public worship, that are done as things of course, because they are accustomed to be done, lack sincerity; and the general state of mind implied in all this is mocking God. For example, congregations are in the habit of doing certain things in a certain order. Sing! Read! Pray! Sing! Preach! Sing! Dismiss! Now, this is all very well if these things are done in the spirit of them. But suppose a congregation got into such a state that they ceased to enter into the spirit of the service. They mock God by this performance! For example, the minister reads the hymn and the people begin to sing. They are emotionally affected by the sound of the music, and in consequence think themselves very Christian. It is a very common thing for individuals to suppose that they are very devotional because they have some sort of emotional feelings when some plaintive hymn is being sung.

For many years, before I was converted, I led the music in a public assembly. I could shed tears in singing; and so deep were my emotions frequently, that I used to take a self-righteous satisfaction in such feelings. But I was an unrepentant sinner and a mocker of God. This is a common thing. Some people who have been living in sin all day, and having no purpose to repent or change, can sit down and sing God's praises. Without being in a state of devotion, and never having given their hearts to God at all, they will sing such lines as these: "Had I a thousand hearts to give, Lord they should all be thine." Indeed! When you have not given Him the one that you have got! They will also sing: "When I survey the wondrous cross on which the Prince of Glory died, My richest gain I count but loss, and pour contempt on all my pride." Who does not know that it is common for people to sing these hymns whose lives tell you that they are not devoted to God? And who will deny that this is dreadful mockery! What can be a more solemn and horrible mockery than for a person with a wicked heart to sing expressions as these.

Now, let me say, there is a vast amount of this in religious assemblies. And there is a vast amount of self-deception. I have observed in many places where I have been since I have been in the ministry that just in proportion as a congregation loses the spirit of true Christianity, the true spirit of prayer, the true spirit of zeal and devotedness, they will spend their time in singing. You appoint a prayer meeting to pray for sinners, but instead of praying they will spend their time in singing. As many long hymns as you please they will sing, but make very short and lifeless prayers. They will amuse themselves by singing hymns, because they can do that and yet go on in their worldly and sinful indulgences. But they have not the heart to pray. Again and again I have known instances in which meetings have been called to pray for sinners, when those who have met to pray have spent nearly the whole time in singing. Instead of considering the guilt and danger of these sinners, and beseeching the throne of God in their behalf, instead of calling mightily upon God to lay hold of them and save them, they have spent their time in singing long hymns.

Indeed, it is universally true, that people who only profess to be Christians will sing in proportion to their lack of spiritual life. Ask them to pray, and they would rather sing, and by so doing frequently deceive themselves. I have seen so much of this mocking God in singing that when I have taken up my hymnal, I have been afraid to read a hymn for the congregation to sing lest they should mock God. When I have known the state in which they were in, and have had reason to believe a great many of them were in a state of spiritual death, I have asked, "Can you sing this? Can you—dare you sing it? Shall we quench the Holy Spirit in our hearts, and drive Him from the assembly?" Now congregations very frequently, and professors of Christianity too, in singing, often grieve and quench the Holy Spirit of God. If the heart does not mean what the lips express, God is mocked.

People often mock God at the Communion Table. What do they profess when they come to the Communion Table? Do they not profess to believe in our Lord Jesus Christ? Do they not profess by this act to pledge themselves afresh to Him? And is this always the temper of mind in which they come? Is it not true that many come to the Table of the Lord as a mere matter of form, because they dare not stay away and thus become mockers of God? Suppose anyone comes with enmity and malignity in their heart toward any of his brethren, or with a consciousness of having oppressed and injured those whom he may have in his employ, without having made restitution, does he not mock God and grieve the Holy Spirit? In this way many mock God and bring leanness into their souls.

People often mock God in professing to give thanks for His mercies. How often is giving of thanks but a mere matter of form? I recollect on one occasion having a note put into my hands by the deacon of a church where I was preaching requesting me to return thanks for some person who had been ill. I found this was a common custom, for the request was partly in print. What was I to do? I did not know that this person was sincere; I did not know that he was a Christian. Must I tell God that this individual came to thank Him for His mercies when it might not be true? What could I do? Was I to do as I was requested because it was a custom? Was I to play the hypocrite in the presence of God and the congregation? And yet how often do ministers conform to this custom when there is reason to believe that the person for whom the thanks are requested has no gratitude to God in his heart at all. Now, it is true a congregation may themselves thank God, although the individual for whom the thanks are returned does not mean it; nevertheless, I have quivered sometimes when such things have been thrown upon me. I have been afraid to return thanks for individuals. I have asked myself, "How shall I dare to appear before God as a mere matter of form or custom?" Now, I am not finding fault with people for returning thanks, for I think it is wise and proper to recognize the hand of God in everything. It is everybody's duty to do so, but let us beware lest we be found lying to the Holy Spirit, who requires truth in the inward parts and abhors that which does not come from the heart.

People often mock God in the public consecration of their children in baptism, and especially in certain forms of consecration. Sponsors, godfathers and godmothers, as they are sometimes called, pledge themselves before high heaven on behalf of the children that they will ensure their being Christians, and perhaps never see them again. What awful and intolerable pretense is this to make before a heart-searching God! If those who do not adhere to these forms profess to bring their children to God and dedicate them to Him in baptism, and yet do not realize what is implied in the act, they are in danger of bringing upon themselves and their children that punishment which God will inflict upon those who mock Him.

All mere compliance with custom in private or public worship, to say and do things because they are customarily said and done, is mocking God. Saying the Lord's Prayer is often a mere mockery, as all of you must be fully aware.

Some Consequences of Mocking God.

The Bible says, in the words of our text, "Be ye not mockers, lest your bands be made strong." What is meant by this?

The fact is, mocking God grieves the Holy Spirit and sears the conscience. And thus the bands of sin become stronger and stronger. The heart becomes gradually hardened by such a process. Why should it not? Why should not the heart become fearfully hardened by such trifling with divine things? When individuals accustom themselves to say things without meaning, the effect must be that they come to disbelieve in them altogether, and their hearts become hard and callous to the invitations of the gospel.

Not only do the bands of sin become strong, but delusion becomes strong. Their minds become so darkened that they lose all sense of what is true, spiritual, and good in relation to Christianity, the Bible, and everything else. I do not doubt that most of you have witnessed the dreadful results of formality in Christianity in hardening the heart, and perverting the mind from a perception of all that is true. Things that would affect the ungodly do not affect them at all. For example, if you can get an infidel to go away by himself and pray, he will find it a very solemn and awful business to speak to God; and will be impressed ten times more than the man who has for years been mocking God by his formality, and pretending to pray all his life. Men become gospel-hardened by mocking God. They mock God until the truth of God ceases to affect them. Their hearts have become so dead and their consciences so stupefied, that when God's voice calls upon them to repent, it passes right by them without affecting them in the least. They will get into such a state, and their darkness becomes so great, that they think and profess they are doing their duty when they are only mocking God by their heartless formality. And, of course, the more such persons abound in their duty, the more they are hardened in sin. Who does not know this? Formalists are the most hardened class, because they mock God the most. It is always so, that just in proportion as people abound in mere form, they become hardened in sin before God.

Stereotyped forms tend to divert the mind from a true idea of Christianity. I have found that all forms of worship, from the very nature of the case, tend to make people formalists and blind their minds to a true idea of the spirituality of religion. For example, what true idea of prayer has the man who reads his prayer from a book? What is prayer? Why, it is the language of the heart coming to God for the supply of its wants, like a little child coming to his parent for something that he wishes for. The child comes to his parent and asks, because he feels that he wants and knows where he can get what he wants. Now, suppose a child, when he wanted a piece of bread, should read a prayer to his parent without the word *bread* being mentioned in it. Or if it was mentioned at the end, he must go right through the whole prayer before he got to it, and thus get his petition before his parent.

Prayer is the language of the heart addressed to God, the language of those who feel that they are in need of something that God can bestow. Now, suppose prayer should be regarded in any other light. The man who begins to use a form of words that he calls prayer, because he thinks it is his duty, why he loses the true idea of prayer altogether. This is how people often lose all true idea of Christianity and spiritual worship. Thus it was with the Jewish nation; they lost the true idea of religion in the multitude of forms and ceremonies.

Without great care we are all liable to fall into the sin of insincerity. Be perfectly upright with God in your closet. I have long been satisfied that much of the backsliding we are called to witness is caused by insincerity in private devotion. If anyone is not honest with God in private, neither will he be honest in public, and thus his mind and soul will become ruined and alienated from God. It is but right and proper that every time we meet together for public worship, the minister should offer public prayer to God, but it never need be insincere prayer, for if the minister lives near to God, as he ought, he will always find enough to say. Yes, more than he could utter if he were to talk from morning till night. And if he does not walk with God, it would be much better to say nothing at all, and not insult and grieve the Spirit of God by using language that is not dictated by the heart. Once more, from what has been said, you see how it is that some leaders in religious services become so excessively hardened. I have known some of this class in the midst of a revival so cold and callous that the truth never served to touch them at all. Now, there is nothing that will so soon blast and destroy the spirituality and prosperity of a church as people of this sort being leaders and *chief* leaders in the church. The Lord deliver us from such!

People should beware of anything like formality in their family worship. I know that some people think forms are better than nothing in a family, but I don't believe it. I am confident that nothing tends so much to ruin a family. It will make the children despise Christianity and become hardened to its influence.

My beloved brethren, how is it with you, you that profess to be Christians? Are you honest with God? Does He know that you are? Do you confess that sometimes you are not, and do you ask what you shall do when you do not feel in the spirit of prayer? Why, begin right there, and tell God that you have not the spirit of prayer. There is something true. Some place where you can begin. Is it that you don't feel right? Then tell God that. Are you not in the spirit of prayer? Tell Him that! If you want the Holy Spirit, tell Him that! If you have sinned, confess that! Be honest, and make no pretense whatever. Let sincerity be the habit of your life, and you will always have something to say to God. Your love, faith and devotion will be strengthened, and your soul blessed. If you are honest with God, you will always find Him honest with you!

Some years ago, I was acquainted with a young man who had been studying for the ministry. This young man, soon after he had completed his college course, became the subject of a very strong conviction that much of his religious profession had been nothing but a mockery. One night he retired to rest, and after having put out the light and laid down to bed, he was very much surprised to see the room re-lighted. He sat up in the bed and looked to see whence the light came. He perceived a person in the room looking very earnestly at him, standing at the foot of his bed. In a few moments the whole light of the room concentrated itself into a single eye, and that eye was fixed intensely upon him. He trembled violently, and was in a state of dreadful agony. The eye continued to glare upon him, looking him through and through, searching his very thoughts. He never forgot this searching. It so completely subdued him that he came to be one of the most holy men and devoted ministers I ever knew. One of the deacons wrote to me a short time ago and said, "Mr. Hopkins is gone to heaven; we want someone to supply his place, but we cannot expect another Mr. Hopkins." Now, he became what he was, because the Holy Spirit searched him and revealed his heart to himself. Oh, for the Holy Spirit to search every one of us! Let Him begin with me! Brethren, pray that my heart may be searched; that the hearts of all your ministers may be searched; that your own hearts may be searched. Pray that God may search us all, that we may be mercifully kept from mocking God, lest our bands be made strong.*

*The trilogy on prayer by Charles G. Finney consists in two devotional books: *Answers To Prayer* and *Principles Of Prayer*; and a collection of sermons on prayer: *Principles Of Devotion*, published by Bethany House Publishers.

7

THE PROMISES OF GOD*

"Whereby are given unto us exceeding great and precious promises: that by these ye might be partakers of the divine nature, having escaped the corruption that is in the world through lust" (2 Peter 1:4).

By a law of our nature we affirm the truthfulness of God. Those who dispute a divine revelation always ask whether God has spoken at all, and never whether what He has spoken is true. The question is whether God has spoken and what He has spoken. When it is once settled that God has spoken and made promises to man, we affirm by a law of our nature that what He has promised must be true. The promises, however, are not to be regarded as the foundation of our confidence in God, for this foundation lies further back in the revelation that He has made in the laws of our own mind. Our confidence in the promise of any being cannot be the result of the promise itself. We have confidence in the promise of any being in proportion as we have confidence in his character. Therefore, our natures affirm that God cannot lie, that He must be a God of truth. No one ever honestly doubted it, no one can honestly doubt it. One of the elements of the idea of God is that of His perfection, His entire truthfulness. The promises, therefore, are to be regarded as the revelation of God's will with respect to granting us certain things.

God might be good and yet not give us many things that He has promised to give us. For example, God might be good and yet

---

The Penny Pulpit, No. 1,522, preached on Friday evening, May 17, 1850, at the Tabernacle, Moorfields.

not pardon our sin—justice is as much an attribute of goodness as mercy is. Unless He had revealed the fact, we could not have known whether perfect goodness would allow Him to forgive us our sins, or to give us the many things that He has promised us. Therefore, His promises are designed to reveal to us His will and to make known to us the fact that His goodness will allow Him to grant us certain favors, that it is in accordance with goodness to give us those things that He has promised. Hence, His promises are given on the condition of our faith and that we pray for forgiveness. These promises are not a ground of faith, but are fulfilled on condition of our faith.

Many of the promises are of a general character, which when you desire and believingly pray for, you shall receive. Under certain circumstances, people may appropriate these general promises to themselves. General promises are ordinarily rendered available to us, as needed by us (when we pray for them understanding what we mean) and by the Holy Spirit of God who leads us to lay hold and appropriate them to ourselves as promises meant to us.

Promises are made to "classes" of people also. It is remarkable to what an extent this is true. There are special promises made to magistrates, ministers, fathers, mothers, widows, orphans, and to all classes of people. With respect to these, when we have ascertained to what class we belong, we may understand that God has promised these things to us by name. There are promises made to people in various states of mind, such as, "Come unto me all ye that labour and are heavy laden, and I will give you rest" (Matt 11:28). If we can say that we belong to that class we may understand the promise, "I will give you rest," as given to us as truly as if it had been first revealed to us, or made for us alone, just the same as if God had called us by name and told us to come to Him. The same with respect to widows and orphans who may appropriate the promises belonging to them without any hesitation, just as if they had for the time been revealed to them by name. It is of great importance for all people to understand this.

The promises are made in and through and for Christ. They are all made for a governmental valuable consideration paid by Christ. In an important sense, God has given the world to Christ and He is represented as having all fullness in Him. As Christ became the Redeemer of mankind, God has given Him "all power in heaven and in earth," to govern it by the use of those means and methods that are essential to secure the great end He has in view. Christ paid for it a governmental valuable consideration. He has done that by making a perfect satisfaction to the government of God.

God's law had been violated, its justice, its equity, and its propriety had been publicly denied and trampled upon by mankind. The majesty of this law must be vindicated, the government of God demanded this. It was unsafe and also unjust for man to be forgiven unless the majesty of the law was asserted. Those who had broken the law could not be forgiven consistently with the rest of the universe, for the law that had been broken was public property. Every moral agent in the universe was interested in the vindication of this law. The strength and efficiency, the power and the glory, should by no means be impaired, for the safety of the universe depended upon its being preserved.

Now Christ came forth and publicly vindicated the honor of this law by paying over to the government of God an equivalent for the offenses and sins that man had committed. He suffered the penalty in order that the guilty might be pardoned. Christ offered to the government of God an equivalent for the execution of the law upon the offender; and in consequence of what He has done, God has promised to bless those who deserved cursing. Now, observe, all the promises of God are represented as being in Christ, and as being in Him; "yes" and in Him, "amen" to the glory of God the Father. Christ magnified the law and made it honorable, so that it consisted with the honor of this law and the justice of God that sinners, rebels against His government, should through Christ be pardoned their offense. These promises are, in the spirit of them, really made to Christ and to Christ's people, to those whom He regards as part of himself, those for whom He came into the world, and those for whom He died.

The promises are, therefore, to be considered something in the light of certificates of deposit; as if Christ had made the deposit for us and allowed us to present our drafts—the promises—and to take away that which God has promised to give, and for which He has received from Christ a valuable consideration. We may regard, then, these promises as drafts or checks that we take and present, and in return receive of the great blessings God has promised by Him, and through Him, and on His account.

With respect to the promises, many of them were made in the time of the Old Testament saints, not for their immediate use— the drafts were not due—but to be believed and pleaded at a future period. Anyone who will take the trouble to examine the Bible in this respect will find this to be the fact, that many of the promises were not in the present tense, but referred to the advent of the

Messiah, and were to become due after His appearing.

Turn to the Book of Jeremiah chapter 31, and read verse 31:

> Behold the days come, saith the Lord, that I will make a new cov-
> enant with the house of Israel, and with the house of Judah: not
> according to the covenant that I made with their fathers in the day
> that I took them by the hand to bring them out of the land of Egypt;
> which my covenant they brake, although I was an husband unto
> them, saith the Lord; but this shall be the covenant that I will
> make with the house of Israel; After those days saith the Lord, I
> will put my law in their inward parts, and write it in their hearts;
> and will be their God, and they shall be my people. And they shall
> teach no more every man his brother, saying, Know the Lord: for
> they shall all know me, from the least of them unto the greatest of
> them, saith the Lord: for I will forgive their iniquity, and I will
> remember their sin no more.

This promise was made to the Church, and of course to each
individual member of it. The promise was not to be pleaded at the
time it was given, but when it became due at a future period. The
apostle who wrote the epistle to the Hebrews quotes this promise
from Jeremiah, and says that the day had come for its fulfillment.
It was made to be believed in its relation to a future time, and the
age of the gospel was the time at which it was to be believed. All
these promises are to be regarded as due in this sense—their fulfillment may be expected in our own days.

With respect to the promises, they have their letter and their
spirit. Many of the promises under the Old Testament dispensation
seem to refer chiefly to temporal blessings, but only in the letter.
For these promises, as applied in the New Testament, have a deep
spiritual meaning. The promises of the Old Testament very commonly speak of worldly prosperity as the reward of the righteous,
when, as it appears from the way in which they are applied in the
New Testament, a great deal more than mere worldly prosperity
and advancement was really meant—spiritual blessings, great and
abundant, were really in the spirit of these promises couched under
language that seemed to promise temporal prosperity only.

Many of the promises of the Old Testament were made to the
Jews—the children of Israel—as if Israelites alone had been
meant; whereas, the New Testament abundantly shows us that
these promises had a very much larger sense—that they also applied to the Gentiles, and to the Church under the Protestant—the
Christian—dispensation. For example, the promise I have just
quoted from Jeremiah, "I will make a new covenant with the house
of Israel and the house of Judah." Now this promise was more

extensive in its application than was at first supposed. It referred to both Jews and Gentiles, to all the spiritual Israel of God, in all ages future from the age in which it was first spoken.

Where promises are made to the Church, people should not overlook the fact that they are also applicable to particular individual members of the Church. Some time ago, conversing with a brother minister respecting the promises, he said that he did not know of any particular promises made to parents on behalf of their children. I quoted some of them, such as, "My Spirit is upon thee, and my words which I have put in thy mouth, shall not depart out of thy mouth, nor out of the mouth of thy seed, nor out of the mouth of thy seed's seed, saith the Lord, from henceforth and for ever" (Isa. 59:21). Again: "I will pour my spirit upon thy seed, and my blessing upon thine offspring: and they shall spring up as among the grass, as willows by the water courses" (Isa. 44:4).

"But," said the minister, "these words were made to the Church and not to individuals." "Well, but brother," I replied, "of what worth are they to the Church if they are not meant for individual members of the Church? If they are meant for the Church in general, they must be meant for every member in particular. Did God intend to trifle with men? He gave promises to His Church to be sure, and any individual of the Church should avail himself of them." God's promises are made to all His children, and to everyone of them in particular, we must not lose ourselves in the mass of people. The feeling is too much abroad among Christians that God's promises are made to everybody in general, but to nobody in particular. Very much of this I have found as I have for many years been passing from place to place. Because the promises are made to masses and classes, they think they are not available to particular individuals. How would this be in any other case?

Suppose, for example, a great famine was in this city, that the people had no provisions. And suppose that the government should issue a proclamation to all persons who were hungry and needy, telling them that they might, by applying at a certain place, secure provisions to supply their wants. Now suppose the proclamation was general in its character, do you think that any individual who was starving would hesitate to go to the store, because the invitation was to everybody, and not addressed to particular individuals? No, indeed. Every individual who was in want would say, "I may go, because I belong to the class intended." Now, if people fail to understand these promises, they may lay and rot in the Bible, and never be of any use to them. How many parents have unconverted children and unruly children, because they neglect to avail themselves of the promises of God.

The promises made to the Patriarchs have a letter and a spirit. They were intended principally to apply to the children of Israel, but now they apply to all, whether Jews or Gentiles.

The Conditions of the Promises

From the very nature of the promises, there must be certain conditions annexed to them all, and when a condition is once expressed it is always implied. For example, when God has promised particular blessings to "His Church," He concludes by saying in one instance, "Nevertheless, I will be inquired of by the house of Israel to do these things for them," and thus in all cases we have conditions annexed to His promises. Unless these conditions are complied with, we cannot obtain the promises, although many of them seem to be given unconditionally. Whenever a condition is not expressed it is implied.

Take another case, when God sent the children of Israel captive into Babylon, He promised them that in seventy years they should find deliverance. Now Daniel understood this! The promise, when taken by itself, would seem to indicate that nothing was to be done by the people in the way of prayer and supplication to effect their deliverance, or as a condition of this promise being fulfilled. But Daniel was led to examine the prophets and to read the promises, and he found that the seventy years were expired but the people were still in bondage. And he found that the reason of this was that the promise had not been fully comprehended. He learned that the promise was made on condition of prayer and supplication being offered to God; consequently, he set himself to confess his own sins and the sins of the people, and to pray, fast, and humble himself before God. This will illustrate what I mean. Now when it has once been said that God will be inquired of to do these things for us, to fulfill His promises, it must be understood as an unalterable condition of His fulfilling the promises that we will ask Him to do so.

We are informed that faith in His promises is a condition of their fulfillment, that no one need expect to receive anything from the Lord unless he asks in faith. This is one of the principles of the government of God: we must ask for those things we need, and we must ask for them in faith; for it is of little use for us to pray without this. God has said that unless we pray in faith, we shall not have the blessing. In all the promises of God, this is implied as a condition on which we are to receive them. Again and again we are told, without faith it is in vain for us to expect the fulfillment of His promises.

There are many conditions which are naturally necessary. For example, suppose God should promise that you should not starve with hunger. Of course it implies that you should be willing to eat the food provided for you; and you would tempt God if you did not, but at the same time kept believing that His promise would be fulfilled. So when He has promised spiritual blessings, the employment of means toward the accomplishment of the end is always implied as a condition of our receiving them. We must appropriate the means and so put ourselves in a position to receive the promises, or we tempt God by expecting their fulfillment.

There are certain conditions that are not only naturally, but governmentally necessary. For example, we are required to offer our petitions in the name of our Lord Jesus Christ. There is, I say, a governmental necessity for God requiring us to recognize Christ as the medium through which we receive these things. It is very easy to see that the same reason that required an atonement be made for sin, required that we should recognize that atonement. The same law that made it necessary that Christ should die for us, required that His death should be recognized by us as the condition of our receiving the blessings promised through this medium. It was governmentally necessary that Christ should die for the safety of the government, that Christ should die to establish God's law as the condition of our receiving the blessing of pardon. Now it is just as governmentally necessary that in our petitions to God we should recognize our governmental relation to Him, that we should remember the sacredness of the divine character, and that we should approach Him solely through Christ, making mention of His name.

God's Promises Are Backed by His Character

In using the promises, regard is always to be given to the attributes of the Promiser. His ability is infinite, and so is His willingness to fulfill them. These things are always to be taken into account. Now if human beings promise us anything, in ever such strong language, we are at liberty to doubt whether we shall ever possess the things promised, having in view the capacity of the promiser. Thus you see we must interpret promises made to us in the light of the attributes of him who promises. It is very common for people to promise in very strong language that which we do not expect them to perform, and which indeed they cannot. Suppose a physician says that he will restore his patient to perfect health; it would be unfair to understand him to mean literally what he says. If the physician should recover the patient from the disease under which he is laboring, and restore him to comfortable health, it is all that can be expected of him. But whatever promise God makes He is perfectly able to perform. We are always, therefore, to have respect to the attributes of Him who makes the promise.

We are to have respect to His relation to us, and our relation to Him. The promises of a father to a child may be construed much more liberally than if they were made to a stranger in whom he had no particular interest, and to whom he sustained no relation. We are to have respect to his interest in us, and God has revealed in many ways His great interest in us. For example, look at the things He has done for His children. The fact that He has given them Christ to die for them, is alone more than sufficient to prove His infinite interest in them.

But in addition to this, on every hand this same fact is revealed—and the great things He has done for us clearly proves that He is able to fulfill all His promises. We are surrounded by innumerable evidences of the highest order of His great interest in us, His great love for us, His great readiness to do for us above all that we can ask or think. Consider what He has already done, when we were enemies to Him He withheld not from us His only and well-beloved Son! Then surely He will not withhold anything else from us. If He freely gave His own Son—the greatest treasure that He had—"shall he not with him also freely give us all things?" (Rom. 8:32). If God gives so great a blessing shall He withhold the less? No, surely, no! In indulging such a thought we do Him wrong and we do ourselves wrong. We must not overlook these facts as the highest possible evidence that all the promises are made in good faith and God's infinite readiness to give the things that He has promised.

It might have appeared incredible if God had told us beforehand that He would give Christ to die for us. It would have appeared extraordinary! We should have exclaimed, can it be possible? Infidels now think it impossible. What? God give His co-equal Son to die for us? We cannot believe it! Now Christians understand it and believe it. And certainly since He has done this, we should look at this fact and never leave it out of view when we come to the promises. All unbelief should vanish when we remember that "While we were yet sinners, Christ died for us" (Rom. 5:8). Shall we not recognize in this fact that He is willing, freely, largely, bountifully, to give us all other things that we want? By this gift of His Son, God has confirmed to us the promises stronger than He could have done by an unsupported oath.

God not only confirmed His promise by an oath, that we might have strong consolation, but by all His conduct He has shown us His entire sincerity in making these promises and His readiness to fulfill them.

We should not forget the design of the promises—that they are intended to meet every demand of our being. We must not forget to construe the language of the promises as meaning as much as the language allows. For example, when it is said in Deuteronomy 30:6, "And the Lord thy God will circumcise thine heart, and the heart of thy seed, to love the Lord thy God with all thine heart, and with all thy soul, that thou mayest live," we are to understand this promise as covering as much ground as a command. We are to construe the language in the promises just the same as the language allows. We cannot suppose that the language means more than it says, but neither are we to regard it as not meaning so much.

It is common in the Church, in writing, printing and conversation to construe language to its widest sense when used in a *command*. "Thou shalt love the Lord thy God with all thy heart, and with all thy soul, and with all thy strength," is made to mean all it can possibly imply—mind I do not find fault with this, for I suppose it is to be so construed—but when the same language is to be found in the *promises*, it is taken to mean much less than the language really implies.

Take another instance. When the apostle says, "I pray God your whole spirit and soul and body be preserved blameless unto the coming of our Lord Jesus Christ. Faithful is he that calleth you, who also will do it" (1 Thess. 5:23–24), we are to interpret this language as liberally as if it had been used in the language of command. We must not trifle with these promises, and so restrict their meaning to imply that they pledge but little, and that little in a most vague and general manner. If we would receive the blessings of the promises, we must understand what it is they promise us.

In using the promises, we should always remember to fulfill the conditions on which they are promised to be granted. If we plead the promises of God, and do not fulfill their conditions, we tempt God. For example, suppose you were to plead the promise that God would forgive sin on the condition of repentance, and you were unrepentant and did not repent, why you tempt God. Suppose a cold-hearted person professing to be a Christian should plead that promise in respect to backsliders, expecting to be forgiven while he continues to go on in worldly-mindedness, why he would be tempting God. Fulfill the conditions first and then plead the promises.

Although conditions may not be expressed in connection with every promise, yet conditions are implied. The promises were made to be used. They were made to be used by God's children, by all who will believe them and appropriate them. They were not made to lay concealed in a gilt-edged Bible, but to be read, understood, and used. The fact is, the Bible is like a book of checks put into the hands of the needy, and we are to use them when we want anything; thus God has given promises to every class and description of persons. And these promises were given not to be hoarded up, but to be used. We are to draw liberally and freely upon the divine bounty for all the blessings that we need.

I became acquainted with one of the most remarkable men that I ever knew in the city of New York. He was forty-five years old, a farmer, and an unlettered man. After his conversion, he had remarkable faith and confidence in God. He sold his farm and took his wife (he had no children), and traveled through various parts of the country, preaching the gospel. He was a man of very humble talents, yet wherever he went there was always a revival. He labored in New Jersey in a most remarkably successful manner.

He labored for many years and once called upon me in the city of New York. After spending a little while in conversation, he proposed to pray. We knelt down together, and he prayed like a little child, "Our Father, thou hast given us great and precious promises, but what are they good for unless they are to be believed?" And so he went on just like a little child, and really it was so perfectly apparent that he believed all the promises that I never forgot the impression his great faith made upon my mind. I could at once comprehend the secret of all his great usefulness. He had such confidence in God's promises, realized to such an extent that God had made all His promises in good faith and on purpose to be used by His children, that he availed himself of them with all freedom and with all boldness. He came to God, as a child would come to its father, fully believing that God would fulfill all His promises.

This was the secret of his usefulness.

If Christians will but understand and get the impression deeply imbedded in their own minds that these promises are regarded by God as their inheritance, given them to be used by them under all the circumstances in which they find themselves placed, they would often much better understand the meaning of the apostle when he says "whereby are given unto us exceeding great and precious promises" (2 Pet. 1:4).

In using the promises, we should never forget that they are given to us in Christ, because He paid for them a governmental valuable consideration and we therefore have a gracious title to them. Don't let me be misunderstood. We had no demand upon God for anything, because we had forfeited His favor by our sins. But it has pleased God to make certain gracious promises to us in regard to what Christ has done, and in Him given us a gracious title to them. Therefore, we can claim them, not in our own name, but in the name of Christ. I love to take this view of the promises of God, that if I am His child, they are all pledged to me in Christ Jesus.

The promises are available to us if we will only comply with the simple condition of believing, and if we will plead them in the name and for the sake of Christ. Every command of God, when properly understood, is to be regarded as implying a promise. If God has required us to do anything whatever, we may always understand the very requirement as implying the promise of sufficient grace to assist us in the performance of the thing required. All needful strength and grace is pledged to us in Christ Jesus. The promises were designed to secure our sanctification, and the will of God is that we should make full, free, and thorough use of them to secure this end. It is very important to notice the manner in which Christ and His apostles quoted the promises of the Old Testament. Take your reference Bibles when you read the New Testament, and see how the promises of the Old Testament were quoted by inspired writers. They will enable you to judge much more properly the real intention and meaning of the promises of God. You will thus be able to see the promises in their fullness and spiritual application.

The promises of God are valued by persons in proportion as they know themselves. They ask in proportion to the sense of their wants. Searching preaching leads men to apply the promises. When the wound is probed, then the plaster is applied. Very much preaching is thrown away upon people who are never sensible of their sins. Suppose an individual should proclaim through the streets that he had found a remedy for the cholera. If the cholera was not here, people would not be very eager in applying for the remedy. They would say they were very glad there was a remedy, because other people might want it, but they did not. The medicine might rot in the shops before the people would avail themselves of it, if they believed there was no danger. Exhibit the gospel, and tell the people of the promises, and they will not let the gospel take hold of them, not apply the promises, because they do not feel their need. You will hear people say, "Yes it is a gracious gospel, I will avail myself of it someday." But sin has taken possession of them, and they never lay hold of this remedy—this great salvation.

If Christians would at once believe, and apply the promises, meet God on the ground that He has promised to meet them, they would find in their own experience how much value there is in prayer, and how powerfully they can prevail with God. They would find that there is a cheerfulness and willingness on God's part to meet them at every point. Many individuals plead the promises without fulfilling their conditions, and then they lose their faith in the promises, because they are not fulfilled in their experiences. The reason for this is because they have not fulfilled the required conditions. I have no doubt but it is a common thing for people to pray themselves out of a confidence in prayer, because they fail to fulfill the conditions on which God has promised them. How general it is that we find people professing to be Christians but who have very little confidence in prayer. And why is this? Because they have come to regard prayer as a duty rather than as something that can prevail with God. Brethren, if you would enjoy communion with God, and prevail with Him, you must look upon prayer as something more than a duty. You must take hold of prayer, as a sure instrument by which you can move God's hand, His arm, and His heart, and then you will do it.

8

PROVING GOD*

"Bring ye all the tithes into the storehouse, that there may be meat in mine house, and prove me now herewith, saith the Lord of hosts, if I will not open you the windows of heaven, and pour you out a blessing, that there shall not be room enough to receive it" (Malachi 3:10).

God manifests His truth to people through His conduct. He has limited His operations. They are controlled by certain laws both of nature and of grace. He has wisely limited himself to a certain order and way of doing things. His heart is greatly set upon the results He has promised—those things that must result from His coming forth and demonstrating His truth. He holds us responsible to be in such a position as to meet the conditions, the fulfillment of which are indispensable to His coming forth in the established and revealed order of things to establish His truth before the world.

We are to put God's truthfulness to the test, to show to ourselves and to everybody else that His promises are true. If we would prove His truthfulness, we must fulfill certain conditions upon which these promises are to be fulfilled. These conditions are expressly revealed or implied in His universal rules in the Bible. It would not manifest His truthfulness to fulfill these promises when the stipulated conditions are not met. It would then rather prove Him untrue. For example, say He has proposed certain conditions, and informed us that unless these conditions have been complied with, He will not fulfill the promises. Then, if He should dispense with

---

*The Penny Pulpit, No. 1,538, delivered on June 19, 1850, preached at the Tabernacle, Moorfields.

the conditions and fulfill the promise without them, instead of proving His truthfulness He would prove that He was a liar. For instance, He has said that He will be inquired of by the house of Israel to do it for them. He will be inquired of in faith, and nothing shall be received without faith. There are multitudes of such declarations in the Bible, which affirm that He will do certain things under certain conditions, otherwise He would prove His own Word to be false.

In the world, to prove himself true, He is obliged to deny us unless we ask in faith. He has told us that certain conditions, such as the use of certain means, are conditions upon which He will do certain things. For example, suppose He commanded us to repent, promised to forgive us if we repented, and then He forgave us without repentance? He who prays for forgiveness without repentance is tempting God—asking Him to do that which He has expressly declared He will not do. People sometimes ask God to break through a revealed condition upon which He has promised to do or not do certain things; but in order to prove His truthfulness, He must refuse to do these things, because the conditions are not fulfilled.

Before I was converted, I had this thought in my mind. I wondered why God did not answer prayer (for I was in the habit of going to prayer meetings as often as I could, even before I was converted—I have no doubt God led me to do so). I heard so much prayer that I wondered why it remained unanswered. I wondered if God's promises were untrue, or whether the people were not Christians. For some time it did not occur to me that by the very truth of these promises, God was pledged not to answer them, unless they were offered upon certain conditions. The very fact their prayers were not being answered proved that they were not offered upon the prescribed conditions. God was not therefore untrue, because the Bible taught that it would be so under circumstances where the conditions were not met.

Under certain circumstances God has promised to withdraw His blessing. Under certain other circumstances, He has promised to give it. Suppose we see Him withhold His blessing, when we have not complied with the prescribed conditions. Suppose that we fulfill the conditions and then see that He fulfills His promise. I do not mean that it is our duty to prove God by disobeying Him, so that we may see Him fulfill His promise by withholding for that reason. But when, as a matter of fact, we fail in our obedience— in the fulfillment of what He requires—He withholds the blessings.

Comply with the conditions, and then see whether He will not fulfill His promise.

We are to prove Him in this sense: we are to use the appointed and revealed means. We should do this even in obtaining our daily bread. Who believes that if he depends on God in the use of the appointed means for procuring his daily bread that he will not get it? If we use the appointed means in the appropriate manner, then we prove God and see whether He will really fulfill His promises. "Trust in the Lord, and do good: so shalt thou dwell in the land, and verily thou shalt be fed" (Ps. 37:3). Now, suppose a person neither "trusted in the Lord," nor "did good," in the sense here meant, who can wonder that he does not "dwell in the land?"

Especially does this apply to spiritual things—the greatest and most important blessings. But let me say again, by the appointed means I mean things to be done which God requires, and done in the manner in which He requires them to be done. Not only is prayer to be made, but made in that spirit that God requires. It is to be such prayer as God has promised to answer. Efforts are to be made in the spirit God requires. Preachers must preach the truth, but they must preach it in a proper manner, in season and out of season, and adapt it to the understanding of the hearers. They must live it, as well as preach it—not contradict it with their lives, while with their lips they declare it. This applies not only to preachers, but to all classes of people. Means are to be used, in faith, and perseveringly. We must do the thing that God has told us to do. But mark the way—see that you do all things according to the spirit and meaning of His Word. Now, certainly, unless people do this, unless they really comply with the spirit as well as the letter of His injunction, how can they expect to obtain the blessing?

We must depend upon God. For example, the Bible plainly presents the subject in this way: everything is to be done with the same heartiness and perseverance and with the same spirit that we would do it if we were expecting to accomplish it ourselves, without God having anything to do with it. The same language is used in precept and requirement throughout the Bible, as is used in this text.

God speaks just as human lawgivers, commanding us to do certain things in a certain manner and with a certain spirit. God everywhere insists upon our obeying Him. We must go about the work *as if* expecting to accomplish it by our own strength. Yet, unless we do it in faith—throwing ourselves upon God—we shall not succeed. These two truths stand out together all through the

Bible. Just as the farmer goes and sows the seed, as if God had nothing to do with it, he understands that without the blessing of God he cannot raise anything. We must be in this state of mind, willing to throw it upon His own blessing, knowing assuredly that unless He makes our efforts succeed, no good will result.

In this respect, the Bible abundantly places things temporal and things spiritual precisely upon the same footing: "Except the Lord keep the city, the watchman waketh but in vain" (Ps. 127:1). Now, the watchman goes about the city, as if God had nothing to do with it. The watchman would tempt God, if he laid down to sleep and left it literally to God. He, therefore, is to keep the city as thoroughly, honestly and earnestly, as if God paid no attention to it. And yet, he must know that unless God watched too, all that he does is in vain. Everything respecting life, health and property—everything worldly and spiritual—is placed by God on the same footing, declaring that without His blessing we can do nothing; yet telling us to do the thing precisely as if we could do it ourselves. Now generally, people do not understand this. They tempt God in these things, for they apply this interposition only to temporal things, and instead of complying with the conditions upon which God offers to bless them, they are laying a stumbling block before their own feet.

In order to prove God, we must abstain from whatever tends to hinder and prevent success. Everybody knows this is true respecting temporal things. They know that if they take poison they may expect sickness. With regard to temporal matters, they understand very well that if they throw obstacles in their own way they may blame themselves for lack of success. In spiritual things it is strange, multitudes throw obstacles in their own way; and yet, how do they account for the lack of success? Rarely do they blame themselves. But they are bound to account for it just as the slothful man in business. They ought to blame themselves just as the man who makes careless calculations in temporal things. The fact is, when people do not abstain from those things that tend to hinder their success, the blame is their own. And if they do not want to tempt God, they must ascribe it to themselves just as much as if they had failed in any earthly scheme by using means to prevent their own efforts.

Suppose parents seek the conversion of their children, and yet place them in such situations in life as almost invariably to ruin them. I knew a gentleman in New York City, who had a son going down to destruction. He had prayed much for him, and entreated me to pray for him for he was getting into such bad company and such dissolute habits that he was afraid he would be ruined. I inquired where the young man was engaged, and was told he was in _____'s store. In _____'s store! Now, I knew the character of that store well. The young man was employed in selling liquor in small quantities! I accordingly gave the father distinctly to understand that unless he removed his son from such temptations, I could not think of praying for him under such circumstances. "Get him out of temptation's way, as much as you can," I said, "and then I will pray for him, but while he is in such a hotbed of temptation I will not tempt God by praying for him." Now, how many of you are doing this? How many of you are sweating over the conversion of your children, and will probably go on to do so until they are plunged into the depths of hell? How many of you are complaining that your children are not converted, while you yourselves are placing stumbling blocks in their way? What does this mean?

I have often questioned people, wives for instance, who wanted their husbands converted. They say their husbands ridicule their Christianity, and so forth. "Well, sister," I said to one of these, "how do you live before your husband? Do you manifest a temper calculated to make him see the true character of Christianity? What are you doing? Do you in your life give evidences of the truth and value of Christian faith as you hold it before his eyes? Or, do you contradict it everyday? Are you a living epistle—an illustration of Christian living before his eyes? Or, are you a living and perpetual denial and contradiction of it?" Now, in multitudes of cases I have found the obstacle to be in the wife. She has been more in the way of the conversion of her husband, perhaps, than the devil himself; for, were she out of the way, or living as she ought, the devil would not find it so easy to persuade the husband that there was no truth in the Christian faith. You cannot help seeing that these very people are often themselves the means of preventing the object they seek after.

I have often had occasion to tell fathers and mothers that they themselves were the obstacles to the conversion of their children. The spirit they manifest, their manner of life, their selfish and worldly motives of action affect their children. While they continue as they are, they need never expect the conversion of their children. They are living denials of the gospel before them. They take the strongest means to prevent their salvation!

I have often thought what wonders we see in society. Look where we will, how many people seem determined to prove that

Christ lied when He told them the solemn truth, "Ye cannot serve God and Mammon" (Matt. 6:24). They profess to serve God; yet on the face of their lives they serve Mammon. Again, Christ has informed us that it is next to impossible for a rich man to enter the kingdom of God. But many seem to read it thus: "How surely shall a rich man enter the kingdom of God," as if salvation depended on their being rich! Again, they seem anxious to get riches for their children, as if it were written, "How surely shall children enter the kingdom of heaven if they get rich." Christ represents the salvation of rich people as next to impossible. And were it not for the wonderful power of God, it would be impossible. He compares it to a camel passing through the eye of a needle, which is certainly marvelously difficult. People who are thus laboring and toiling for riches for their heirs, seem as if they were laboring to send their children to hell, or to prove the Bible untrue—to prove that there was no difficulty in the way of their being rich and saved too.

These are but illustrations. Had I time, I could go into ample details of individual instances in which things are done that stand right in the way. But what I have said will abundantly suffice to show that the difficulty is not with God. He is doing just as He promised under such circumstances to do, and the result will be just what He says it will—they will lie down in sorrow.

I once knew a father who wished to influence his four sons to give up the use of tobacco. He told me that he had always warned them, spoken to them seriously again and again on the subject, but it did not seem to do them any good. His expostulations were all in vain. When speaking to them on one occasion, one of them said, "Father, you have always used it yourself! Example is said to be more forcible than precept." Now, what do you suppose the father said? Why, nothing, of course! He stood terribly rebuked. The same thing in principle, I have seen in a multitude of cases where the people were actually inculcating by their example what they blamed in others. And thus, they placed a formidable obstacle in the way of the conversion of their friends and families, and were nevertheless still expecting that they would be converted.

"If thy right hand offend thee, cut it off" (Matt. 5:30). It is not promised that we shall be saved with it on. We cannot say, "God must save us with our right hand." The idea is this, the most useful thing, things which are important to you, if, after all, they become to you such a stumbling block that you cannot stand, put them away. The right hand is certainly most useful, but even if it were "the right eye," we are told "to pluck it out." What, then, is the principle involved here? We are never to expect God to grant us blessings promised on condition of any sacrifice or self-denial, if we neglect the conditions imposed upon us. "If thy hand or thy foot offend thee, cut them off, and cast them from thee: it is better for thee to enter into life halt or maimed, rather than having two hands or two feet to be cast into everlasting fire" (Matt. 18:8). Now what does this teach? Why, "if even your right hand offend you, cut it off, or I shall let you go to hell; for you need not think that if you refuse to make the self-denial I shall save you notwithstanding." While you hesitate, and will not walk up to the mark, and undertake this self-denial, which God makes the sole condition of blessing you—while you will not do this, you labor in vain. He will not bless you. He will not prosper you.

Now, this may be applied to a thousand things. The fact is, if a Christian or any person would have God's blessing, he must carry out every act of self-denial required as a condition. He must strenuously avoid anything prohibited, in case that would stand in the way of his obtaining the thing promised. And if we do not regard these conditions, the fault is our own if we do not obtain the blessing.

Another condition indispensable to proving God is this: we must really enter into God's motives, and do what we do for the motives from which God acts. We must be benevolent, not selfish. If, for example, we pray for sinners, we must regard sinners as He does and desire their conversions for the same reason that He does. If we seek blessings for ourselves, we must ask them for the same reason for which He would be able to grant them. "Ye ask, and receive not, because ye ask amiss" (James 4:3), that is, your motive is not right. You do not sympathize with God's motives. You do not ask the blessing for a reason for which it would be honorable for God to grant it.

God Wants Your Heart

The prophet asks in the ninth verse, "Will men rob God?" What is the spirit of all this? The Jews had neglected their duty. They had been selfish. They had refused to bring unto God the offerings as He required them to do. They had gone astray, turning away from sympathizing with Him. They had gone in their own ways, and had not brought the offerings to God's house and paid their tithes. In short, they had turned away from His commandments.

This is what they had done. Now, what did He require of them? That they should return to Him, and He would return to them.

Now, a spiritually-minded Jew would have understood these requirements to mean not merely the outward bringing of certain tithes and offerings, but a returning of their hearts to God in the true spirit of obedience, and then they would prove Him and see if He would not be as good as His word, and give them the blessings they sought.

Whatever else you offer, keeping back yourself is an abomination. Yourself is the first great offering. Offer yourself a living sacrifice. By a perpetual offering, offer yourself up to God. What is true devotion? I have often thought that many people entirely mistake the gospel idea of devotion, seeking to be and believing themselves to be devout, without being or pretending to be pious. They work themselves up into an excited frame of mind, till they have produced certain feelings, and this they deem devotion. To be devoted to a thing—what is it? What is it for a man to be devoted to his business? To be diligent, to have his heart in the undertaking, and to give all his energies to the work, this is devotion to business. What is a man's devotion to his wife, a wife's to her husband, a mother's to her children? Now, what would you think of a mother who sat down and neglected her children? Who sat down and worked herself up into a state of devotion to her offspring and allowed them meanwhile to go without their dinner? What would you think of a businessman who let his business go to ruin while he was engaged in these devotional feelings? What would you think of a farmer who indulged in these devotional frames of mind, and neither ploughed his ground, sowed his seed, nor took care of his hedges?

I have known people so infinitely mistaken on this whole question that they have tried to be devotional without possessing a particle of piety. To be devoted is to give the mind up by a voluntary act, and to expend all your energies on any particular thing. To be devoted to God is to give ourselves up to Him, to be devoted to His glory, to give up body and mind and all our energies to the great work to which He calls us. Remember, the first offering is to be yourself; for this is an offering that many have withheld. They have given tithes and all other offerings, but have withheld the offering of themselves.

How many individuals have I known whose reputations, for instance, were not on the altar of God! They would not do anything that would damage them in the eyes of the world. They are unwilling to place themselves in the gap, let men say what they will. They do not come nobly forth, and say, "Lord, here is my reputation. It is of no use to me if it can be of no service to you. If you tell me to do anything for which men will despise me, you know, O my God, I will do it, and leave my reputation to take care of itself or leave it to you." This is the spirit! If God should tell them to do anything that would bring the reproach of mankind upon them, they would do it. If this is not so, it shows the reputation is not given up to God.

Suppose a minister would not preach anything that he knew was so unpopular, that it would bring reproach upon him. I have known individuals who would, if they were about to rebuke any sin which they knew was rife in the community and to which they knew a great many influential men were addicted, either bear silent testimony against them or give notice that they were going to preach about it, and then such persons who felt condemned would naturally stay away. Now, who does not see that when people are afraid to lose their reputation, and refuse to come out and rebuke sin, they can never expect to get rid of it?

Suppose a minister is afraid to rebuke the sin of intemperance. Suppose in America, we should not expose the sin of slavery. Should we ever get rid of it? Never. God commands us to come out and rebuke sin. Suppose a minister has seen things which call for remark, but upon which "the public mind is sensitive," and which he is consequently afraid to rebuke. How could a man, who thus withholds his testimony, ever expect to get rid of that iniquity? Such sins and evils are always likely to exist until their opponents lay their reputations on the altar, and do what God tells them to do irrespective of other's opinions, until they hunt out, expose, and rebuke evil. Do they expect God will get rid of it without their using the revealed and appointed means? He has commanded them everywhere to expose sin, both public and private.

Now suppose there is any sin of so delicate a nature that the ministers and the Church bear no public and pointed testimony against it. Can they expect ever to get rid of it? Never. They must march up, lay their reputations on the altar, and say to God, "If you require me, O Lord, to do that for which all men will curse me, I will do it. If you require me, O Lord, to do that for which men will crucify me, I will do it. If you say, 'Speak, reprove iniquity,' I will do so, if I die for it."

Now, unless the Church does this, the individual membership as well as the pulpit, how can she expect to reform the world? The

Church is the society that God has appointed to reform the world, to take the lead in every reform, and by precept and example to show unto men what they should be. Now, if the Church is afraid to oppose iniquity, can it be wondered that evils great and manifold roll their desolation over generation after generation? Is it not true that the lack of this testimony, both by precept and example, on the part of the Church, accounts for the fact that the world is not converted? The Church tempts God by pretending to find a reason for all this in the sovereignty of God. Why, they might as well neglect every temporal affair, and become paupers, and then trace that to the sovereignty of God. God allows evils to exist and will do so until generation after generation shall have gone to hell, because the appointed means are neglected. There cannot be too much stress laid upon these truths. It is time the Church should understand that unless it devotes itself to the reformation of the world, first reforming itself and giving itself up to every good word and work, things will go on as they have. But upon whose skirts will the blood be? Jehovah has shaken His skirts, and has said, "Bring ye all the tithes into the storehouse, that there may be meat in mine house, and prove me now herewith, saith the Lord of hosts, if I will not open you the windows of heaven, and pour you out a blessing, that there shall not be room enough to receive it."

This language was designed to convey a revealed principle to us that is worthy of all acceptance. In many of the promises, God has revealed the great and fundamental principles of His government. What is true of God under one state of circumstances is always true of Him under similar circumstances. What He will do under one state of circumstances may always be expected of Him under similar circumstances. The principle here revealed is often revealed expressly or impliedly. It is this: *when His requirements and the conditions to which He is pledged are fulfilled, He invariably comes out and fulfills His promises.* "Prove me," etc, is equivalent to saying, "If you prove me, I will surely pour out," etc.

Abound in the Work of the Lord

The common talk with reference to God's sovereignty as applied to the existing evils in the world and the lack of reformation therein—the manner in which this is talked of—is tempting God as manifestly as if the same course were applied to temporal things. God's purposes do not extend more absolutely to spiritual than to temporal things. Divine purposes, foreknowledge, agency, and so forth, extend equally to both. Even the grass will not grow without His blessing. On the subject of Christianity, people are forever applying this talk about Divine sovereignty, election, and such things, as if God had foreordained certain things with respect to Christianity in such a manner as to interfere with the freedom of man. In other words, they say His conduct is different in spiritual matters than it is in temporal; in the former He no longer requires voluntary action, but in the latter He does. Now, this is quite a mistake. The Bible denies it. God does not ordain anything in any such sense. There is not one word in the entire Bible that really favors the idea that any election of God's at all interferes with the liberty and free agency of the creature. I have as strong and as high views of God's sovereignty as any man. I know this, as far as the Divine mind is concerned, there is nothing new or old to Him. The judgment day is as present to God as it ever will be. If a man should ask me, "Do you believe in the sovereignty and foreknowledge of God?" I would reply, "Yes." "Do you believe God knows the very hour I shall die?" "Yes." "Can I alter God's purpose so as to change His foreknowledge?" "Certainly not." "Then I might just as well not take any food, or swallow two ounces of arsenic, as I cannot die before my time." They never will die before their time comes. Nor will they go one moment over it. What, then, has this to do with their own agency? Who does not know that, notwithstanding God has appointed bounds to their habitation, yet all the circumstances must occur to keep them alive, or they would die before their time. They will not die before their time, because they will not reason in this way. But they will use the means and do just as common sense would have them do—just as God foresaw that they would do. They will not leap off a precipice or cast themselves from London Bridge or anything else of the kind, and then say, "I shall not die before my time!" Oh! That men would use their sense in religion as well as in other matters! Men know the human mind is left free, responsible, active; and that, therefore, men are to go on taking care of their property, their health, and their lives, laboring for the results they wish to bring about. But on religious subjects men talk as if they were insane: "If God knows how it will be, what's the use of my doing anything?" Do! Why, act just as you are acting in everything else, or you will go to hell, that's what you will do. Just as a man will die who does not take care of his health; no sovereignty of God in the universe will prevent a man from going to hell who does not repent.

Now, let me ask, "What are you doing to secure the salvation of your souls? Are you using any of the prescribed means? How are you living before your families? Are you doing those things that ought to be done, and must be done, to promote Christianity around you? Do you live, act, and talk, using the means, and in the manner you ought? If not, how do you expect the conversion of the people? Are you endeavoring to remove the evils you see around you? Do you mean to do this? Or are you satisfying yourselves with a merely negative testimony?"

I have known some ministers who would not preach upon slavery except with previous notice, so that those who held erroneous views might remain away; and others who only preach on it once a year, or only once in their life. Now, suppose all the ministers in the United States should simply once come out and preach against slavery, and think that then they had virtually discharged their duty so far, but to say that as to laying themselves on the altar to put it away, why, they are not going to do any such thing. Iniquity must be rebuked through the press, in the pulpit, in the railroad cars, and wherever it may be supported. And unless men will do this, the evils will not be removed.

I ask you before God, have the Christian people in your city taken hold for the removal of the iniquity of your city? Have they borne steady, energetic, yet benevolent testimony against all these evils in every way? Or have they kept silent, and cowered down before the world? Rely upon it, beloved, that if you seek the conversion of your city, every minister must lay his reputation upon the altar—every Christian must put his shoulder to the work, and bid this great iniquity depart in the name of the Lord.

What are you really doing, as individuals? Are there ministers reading this? Brethren, what are you doing? Are you satisfying yourselves with an occasional testimony against such and such an evil without continually pursuing it? If you mean to put them away, you must pursue these evils, or they will pursue you. You must hunt them out, or they will hunt the piety out of you. The natural tendency of things is to get worse instead of better.

And what are you lay people doing in the work? Are you on the altar? Are you personally talking, laboring, and setting a good example—laying your all upon the altar? If you are doing this, we shall soon hear of it; for Jehovah has pledged himself before the universe, that if you do your duty—lay your reputation, time, talents, property, your all, upon the altar—He will pour out His blessings in such a manner that there shall not be room enough to contain them. Yes! The righteousness of your city shall be like the waves of the sea. Do you believe this? He tells you to prove Him. Will you do it?

FAITH AND ITS RELATION TO THE LOVE OF GOD*

"For God so loved the world, that he gave his only begotten Son, that whosoever believeth in him should not perish, but have everlasting life" (John 3:16).

By the term *world* in this passage, John means the human race. The passage affirms God's love for the whole human family. The word *perish* does not mean annihilation nor does the word *life* denote mere existence. Plainly, these terms are contrasted; so if life meant mere existence, then perish would mean, by the force of antithesis, non-existence. But neither of these words can have these meanings in John 3:16. In fact, the words perish and destruction do not primarily denote *annihilation,* but only a change in the *mode* of existence. One of the greatest errors in biblical interpretation is to force upon the word perish the meaning of annihilation. The narrow, short-sighted, view of this interpretation entirely overlooks both the glory of that life which comes to us through Christ and the fearfulness of that woe awaiting the unrepentant.

In the text we are told that God so loved the world He gave His Son for it. Does the emphasis upon the word *so* turn solely upon the degree of this love without respect to its nature? Does the text mean simply to assert that God loved the world *so much* or that His love was moreover *of such a nature* that He could yield up His Son for a lost world? Plainly, the latter comes into consideration, and we are to study the nature as well as the degree of this love.

The Oberlin Evangelist, October 22, 1845.

Directing our attention to this point, it is obvious to remark that this love is not the love of complacency. Complacency is a delight in the character of its object. Now, at the time God so loved us to give His Son, there was nothing in us upon which complacency could rest. God so loved us as to form the purpose of giving up His Son before any soul was converted, while the human race lay before His mind in the attitude of rebels. God commended His love toward us in that while we were yet sinners, Christ died for us. It could, therefore, have been no love of complacency that loved us while we were yet sinners.

God's love is not the love of fondness or natural affection; such love as parents have for their children. Some seem to suppose that this was the love of God, but they utterly mistake its real nature.

Speaking positively, God's love for the world is benevolence, good-willing, a disposition to promote the highest good of beings. Not, as some conceive of it, without regard to their persons as individuals, but with regard to the personal state and needs of individuals. Doubtless, this is the true conception in general.

True love on the part of God is entirely unselfish. This is most fully evident in the fact that God was willing to make personal sacrifices for the end in view. Instead of having any immediate good to himself as the object, the Bible tells us that He so loved the world as to make the greatest possible personal sacrifice—that of giving up His own Son to ignominy, torture, death. What more decided proof could be given of unselfish love than this!

God's love is an impartial love. His love fastened on the human race, on all the individuals of the race, and on all without respect of persons. God has no special favors for certain castes. God does not look at certain classes as such; His love makes no distinction between rich and poor, the free and the slave, the high and the low, the white, red, or black. No, God's love rests impartially and equally on all. He does not look with such an eye as people often cast over their fellows, scorning some and adoring others. No, His love is an eye of pity and love for all. He raises no other question than this: "What is the *value of each person's well-being?*" Then each is appreciated according to his real value.

God's love is a holy love. Intense affection indeed for sinning man; yet, with no delight toward sin. Nothing could be more utterly opposed to sin than God's love which sought the good of sinners. Else, He would never have devised such a plan of salvation, never made a sacrifice of the just for the unjust. Love sought earnestly to save, yet only by putting away all iniquity—only by providing a way of pardon that fully honored the divine law—only by providing such influences as should effectually cleanse the soul from its pollutions.

God's love is just. God could not let His love conflict with justice. He could not allow His throne to suffer by the pardon of sin without an atonement that would fully sustain the dignity of law and effectually secure the interests of other beings who might be tempted to sin. God's love was blended with justice, else He would not have given up His Son.

The love of God for sinners is real. Sometimes people speak of both the love and the wrath of God, as if it had no reality, as if the Bible language on these points were wholly an accommodation to human weaknesses, meaning perhaps that God will act as men do when they love or are angry, while yet no such affections as these really exist in the divine mind. But the truth is that God really feels, yes, really has the very affections and states of mind which these words describe—and in all their most fervid intensity. His love is most intense, most sincere—all-absorbing—self-consuming. If you have experienced it, you know how strong affections sometimes absorb and seem to consume the very vitality of the soul; the physical powers fail under the consuming, exhausting influence of intense mental action.

You know it was said of Christ: "The zeal of thine house hath eaten me up"; as if His very being were consumed by His burning zeal for the house and the cause of God. It seems clear from several intimations in Scripture that our Savior had the appearance of premature old age. "His visage was so marred more than any man, and his form more than the sons of men" (Isa. 52:14), that kings and nations wondered at the strange spectacle. On one occasion the Jews said to him, "Thou art not yet fifty years old" (John 8:57). We may infer from this that He appeared to be nearly fifty years old, though in fact as the Bible shows He was not much over thirty. Hence, we may presume that His physical frame was intensely shattered while yet young in years. He must have used up His vital powers with consuming self-regardless efforts for human well-being and by the intense, burning power of His mental excitement.

So of the love of God. It is not to be supposed that *mind* itself is consumed with intense action, but the body becomes an index of the intense and exhausting action of the soul. The love of God may be seen in the love of Christ. Christ said, "He that hath seen me hath seen the Father" (John 14:9).

This love is great, beyond all finite comprehension. Perhaps we get the most vivid conception of God's love by means of comparisons. See that parent who loves his child most tenderly. His son may be wayward, insolent, ungrateful. Yet, you shall see the father's love unchanging; still he forbears, still he is patient and long-suffering, still he waits and hopes and plans every conceivable method to restore that wayward son. Truly, here is love, but it is only such love as God's love toward us—but infinitely less in degree.

See also that affectionate mother. Her little infant frets and cries, her love endures it patiently. That dear child will not let her sleep, and her nervous system is well nigh prostrated. Still, for her own child, what will a mother's love not endure?

But oh, what is all this compared with the matchless forbearance and long-suffering of the God of Love? We shall never appreciate this until we see in their true colors the sinner's abuse and contempt of God's law and gospel, until we see how God waits on the sinner and how the sinner grows only the more stubborn and insolent; how God sends him repeated tokens of His love and he only mocks God's mercy in return. Such is God's love that He not only forbears to punish, but sends His only begotten Son to save. Yes, He sends His only Son to die that the rebel might live. What a spectacle! There lay spread out before the eye of God a world steeped in wickedness, reeking in its own pollutions, in its own rebellion. Yet, the heart of God pitied—there burned in His bosom the most intense love and from His inmost soul he cried out: "How can I give you up!" Oh, what love was this! Love not only sincere and real, but infinitely great.

We are to think of this as love to enemies, not to friends. It was not such love as husbands have for their wives, or parents for their children. No, but "God commendeth his love toward us, in that, while we were yet sinners, Christ died for us" (Rom. 5:8). This commends and sets off this amazing love of God in a light so glorious. Behold, says another apostle, behold what manner of love the Father hath bestowed upon us that we—that such as we—should be called the sons of God! (1 John 3:1). Well might he say, "What *manner* of love!" Was ever love like this in earth or heaven?

This is a most persevering and efficient love. It is not a mere emotion that flashes and burns itself out without producing action. It is not that sort of good feeling seen among people, that goes off in good wishes and leaves no fruit behind. It is not a love that says, "be ye warmed, and be ye filled," but gives not the things required. Oh, had God's love for mankind been only such as this, how deep and dire the ruin in which we had sunk, hopelessly and forever.

The love of God to mankind is no empty and evanescent emotion. It has continued to sway the attributes of Deity for thousands of years, and will for coming ages, so many may be included in the divine plan for perfecting this glorious scheme of salvation. The love of God to mankind has called forth His infinite wisdom to devise, His omnipotence to execute, and we might perhaps say that this love has employed, not to say, used up, the divine energies since the creation of the world. Oh, who can adequately estimate all that God has done already in devising and carrying into effect this great scheme of human salvation!

God's love moreover is particular and not merely general. By this, I mean that it fastens upon individuals, seeking their good, and does not merely embrace the mass as a whole. We are too apt to conceive of God's love as only general and not as particular at all. We are not inclined to feel that God truly and deeply loves *us*—yes, our own insignificant selves. Yet, this is the *only* right mode of apprehending the love of God. That eye that marks each falling, and counts the hairs of our head, is surely able to notice the lowest of His intelligent creatures and the smallest circumstances that can affect their happiness.

Faith Is More Than a Matter of the Mind

Believing in Christ is something more than to be convinced of the truth of what is said in the Bible. This conviction may be in our minds as firm as the mountains; and yet, we may have no gospel faith. Devils may believe, and in this sense they do. Wicked people may and usually do have this faith of conviction—they may be convinced of the truth respecting Christ, and yet have no more saving faith than devils have.

But positively speaking, faith is trust. Faith is depending upon Christ, relying upon Christ for everything that as a Savior He promises to do for us. The soul, believing, thoroughly commits himself to God, yielding up all his interests to be disposed of according to His wisdom.

Faith implies a realization of our actual dependence upon Christ. This idea of dependence must become a living idea, a practical reality to the mind, or we shall never really depend upon Christ.

This remark applies both to justification and to sanctification. As to justification, we must fully realize that without Christ we never can be pardoned and restored to a state of acceptance and justification before God. We must look to Him in the gospel sense, so as to receive justification unto life. So also with respect to sanctification. Until faith in Christ becomes a reality that the mind deeply feels; that we can be cleansed from sin only through faith in Christ, it is absolutely certain that we shall never by faith take hold of those promises for life.

Faith implies a realizing sense of the nature and extent of our death in sin. We must see and feel that we are really *dead* in sin; for until we see this, we shall naturally be full of self-righteous efforts. No one ever will, or ever can, believe on Christ until he sees this. Why should he? He seems in his own eyes able to help himself, and nothing therefore is more natural than to prosecute self-righteous efforts until the conviction fastens upon the mind that all is hopeless and fruitless until Jesus intervenes. The person must see that he is hopelessly dead in sin—as much lost beyond hope without Christ as if he were already in hell or had been for ages.

Faith implies a penetrating sense of our utter disinclination toward any good. This is indeed the same thing as being dead in sin, and is only another phraseology for the same idea. Many who are not Christians have no just sense of this. Indeed, they have no just view of God and of His law. Perhaps they think they want to be Christians, and are inclined to embrace Christianity, but, oh, how deceived they are! They need to see their utter disinclination toward any good. Then, they would see their dependence upon Christ. They would see that unless Christ interposes while they are in this state of utter disinclination, they are so utterly selfish that they never will embrace Christ for salvation. Let me ask, will an individual ever depend upon Christ, as long as he thinks himself well disposed by nature and has no correct views of his utter death in sin? No; never.

Faith, then, implies that we understand our utter moral impotence and utter disinclination toward God while in an unrenewed state. When one sees this, he is prepared to see that unless a sanctifying Christ undertakes for him, his damnation is certain. He sees that the thing he needs to be saved from is this selfish, morally dead state of mind.

Around this point there hangs in the views of many an unaccountable darkness. They do not see the very reason they need Christ. They are thinking about some particular sins; perhaps lying, theft, or Sabbath-breaking, from which they suppose they need Christ to save them. Yet, what are all these sins, and all such sins, but the mere bubbling up of a certain state of mind—a little of the overflowing water from that deep and vast ocean of iniquity that spreads itself all over their inner moral being? This state of mind, this deep sink of iniquity, the rooted selfishness in which you have accustomed yourself to live and move and have your being; this is what you need to be saved from. This is the great thing that needs to be set right. Do you understand this? What is it that you need when your heart sighs within you for peace, and you look to Christianity for help? What do you need? This only— to have your disposition to sin taken away, and in its place a disposition to serve and please God. When you come to see yourself as you are in all your relations to God and duty, you will see that your own state of mind is the very thing you need to be saved from. You will see that this is really more terrible, and more to be feared than all the devils in hell. You need not fear the mightiest devils if your own state of mind is not radically wrong.

What then are you doing? Groping about to get rid of some one or two sins as if these were all from which you need to be saved? Have you not yet learned that the thing you need first and chiefly is to be saved from a selfish state of mind, a state which is radically averse from or enmity against God?

Another thing implied in Christian faith is a realization that God loves us. I mean just that—that God loves *us*, not the world merely and in general, but *ourselves* in particular. The idea must come to the soul with convincing melting power—*God loves me*. His pity and compassion reach even *me*. Unless you understand this, how can you be penetrated with repentance, gratitude and love? No, until this idea is realized, that God is so infinitely gracious and benevolent that He has set His love on *me*, until this thought comes home, you feel that you do not dare approach Him. This will be the effect just in proportion as the guilt and plague of sin are thoroughly realized. If these are deeply realized, the soul must realize also the great love of God, or it will fly away from the presence of God as if that presence were hell itself.

I have often known people who feel as if they could fly in any direction away from God so deeply did conscious guilt oppress them, and so terrible to their souls was the thought of meeting God. Some of you have heard me say of Father Nash that his sense of God's awful presence was such when under conviction that he would have leaped into a lake of liquid fire at once if he could have thereby escaped the presence of God.

Hence, a realization of God's love to us is essential to real trust. First, you must see your sins; and then to prevent despair and to save you from being repelled by your own conscious guilt from the presence of God, you must apprehend His infinite love. Seeing this, the soul cries out, "After all my guilt and behavior deserving punishment, God does love me. Yes, so much has He loved me as to give His Son to die for me. Now, I see that I may come back at once to my Father."

Without this view of the love of God, you feel as if you could not approach God at all. But when this love is seen and felt, you will come sobbing back with a heart all broken to pieces. When you see not only that God loved the world, but that He even loves you—and so loves you that He gave His own Son to die for you, then you feel yourself aroused by mighty attractions. How can you resist the melting power of such love? "Oh," you say, "what can I do for God? How can I ever praise Him enough?" Such a gospel meets human need and affords an adequate remedy for human selfishness. It presents tangible points of blessed truth upon which a guilty, despairing sinner may take hold.

An apprehension of the nature as well as degree of God's love is essential to and is implied in real Christian faith. The mind must see clearly that this love of God to us is not complacency, but compassionate benevolence.

Finally, Christian faith implies an actual dependence upon Christ in all His offices and relations.[1]

Many people confuse dependence or a *feeling* of dependence with depending upon Christ. They talk about their dependence without really depending upon Christ at all. Now, it is one thing for you to say, "I cannot be saved without Christ"; and quite another thing to say, "I depend on Christ for everything." Father Nash used to say, "I could sometimes see my dependence so clearly that I would gnash my teeth and swear and curse, daring God to do His worst; yet, I was infinitely far from really depending in Christ." Faith always implies a sense of dependence, but this sense of being dependent does not always imply faith. Yet, people often talk much about dependence and have no realizing sense of depending at all. Their talk is really an apology for not doing anything.

---

[1]See Charles G. Finney, *Principles of Union with Christ,* where he discusses how our faith must embrace Christ in all the relations and offices He wishes to have with us as revealed in the Bible.

Many overlook the identity between depending on Christ and true Christian faith. Always remember, depending on Christ is the same thing as real faith. Real faith depends on Christ for justification, and on nothing else. Real faith in the same exclusive sense depends on Christ for sanctification. With regard to both justification and sanctification, real faith is a depending on Christ.

We can easily understand what it is to depend on Christ, for dependence of a similar sort is a perfectly common thing in the ordinary relations of human life. A young person comes to Oberlin to study. He knows that various expenses will be accruing for board, books, clothing, etc. Now, he has no expectation of paying these bills himself—he *depends* on his father to pay them for him. He is not anxious on these points. He knows very well that his father is both able and willing to do all for him that he can need.

But another young student may be here who has no father to depend upon. Perhaps he looks to the church to which he belongs, as they may have pledged themselves to help him. And still another, having neither parents nor pledged supporters to depend on, depends on himself. He expects to labor during the term of study and teach in vacations.

I allude to cases of this sort to show that the idea of depending on others is perfectly familiar to all minds. We are trained into it from the very dawn of life. Such is the Christian's depending on Christ. The Christian looks to Christ for His ceaseless supply of every need. This is faith.

The doctrine of human ability as it lies in many minds produces nothing else than self-confidence and self-dependence as opposed to faith. Many have such an idea of human ability that they suppose they shall readily by dint of their own resolutions and efforts do what God requires of them. Such an idea renders dependence on Christ morally impossible. How can he depend on Christ when he thinks he can just as well depend upon himself? Therefore, it is necessary to true faith that the doctrine of human ability should be taught in such a way as to encourage faith, to enforce the conviction that without aid from Christ obtained by depending on Him, we are certainly undone. In fact, the idea of human ability as often apprehended is nothing but the spirit of the Antichrist. It stands directly and insuperably in the way of the soul's reliance upon Christ for the grace required to save the soul from sin. Faith is forever impossible till this notion of self-sufficiency is utterly put away.

The doctrine of dependence works mischief in some minds when it is misunderstood, for it begets a self-justifying spirit. People get the idea that they are in such a sense naturally unable that God cannot rationally require them to obey Him. In conversation with a lady some time ago, she said, "I believe God was bound in justice to send Christ to die for sinners, and is bound now to do for sinners all that He requires them to be and to do." When she came to explain her views, it appeared that she considered herself as not guilty but only *unfortunate* on account of her sinful nature—unfortunate in having ever sinned at all, so as to need a Savior's atonement; unfortunate in having a state of mind so selfish and averse to God that without gracious aid she never would accept of a Savior already provided. Hence, she thought God would be unjust if He did not help her out of the troubles into which under God's universal agency she had unfortunately fallen.

After I had shown her that she had fundamentally mistaken the nature of sin, and that she could not be innocent in entertaining such views, condemned as they certainly were by her own reason and conscience, her husband said, "I have sometimes thought my wife one of the most pious of women, and other times I have thought that she had no piety at all." The wife rose, and went to her chamber in a dreadful agony and conflict of mind—kept to her room for two days—and then came down all melted, subdued, transformed to the very spirit of a lamb. She no longer held God accountable for her sins, or bound in justice to give her converting grace.

True and deep conviction of sin is the only remedy for either of these errors. In the first case, where the person has high notions of his own ability, only let God show him his own utter wickedness, the deep and fearful depravity of his voluntary selfish heart, and he will see that his ability is only a mountain of lead on his soul to sink it deep in the waves of damnation. Look at that sinner. Suppose God shows him just what he is doing, makes him see his own voluntary agency in sin, makes him see that he might have done good rather than evil, that God endowed him with capacities for doing all his duty. Then, let the Holy Spirit also show him how he resists and fights against God with all his might, and makes him see his own heart to be black and guilty of hell; then see what he will say. "Oh," he cries, "this ability of mine is working out for me the deepest damnation. My whole heart is set upon iniquity. No other being in the universe can be so vile as I am. Oh, surely, I am working my way down to the deepest hell."

When the Lord has thus shown him his amazing guilt, he will

no longer depend on the fact of his being *philosophically* able to repent. He will neither deem this a meritorious thing, nor will he rely upon it for his own salvation. He will see that this ability of his has been the occasion of his meriting a deeper damnation than he otherwise could have done; and that his infatuated abuse of it is always such that he can depend on himself only to work out his own damnation.

So of the other person who makes God responsible for his own sin, for his being unrepentant, and for giving him repentance. Let this person be convicted thoroughly of his own sin, and he will no longer say, "God in justice ought to help me out." Oh, how he will abhor this very thought and the state of mind that can admit it for a moment! Now, his mind turns upon himself in bitter self-execrations. He sees that he has no one to condemn except himself.

God's love to us is entirely consistent with His anger against sin. There is a father who finds it necessary for the best good of his child to punish him. But does this prove that the father does not love his son? By no means. He never gives a more conclusive proof of his love for his son than when his intense desire to secure his highest good is so strong as to overcome all the reluctance a father's heart feels to the infliction of pain upon the child. This is the love of real benevolence.

The same benevolent regard to the good of the rest of the family might constrain a father to punish his son, even though the hope of reclaiming him may be entirely abandoned and form no part of the motive for punishing. So God in love to the universe may punish the sinner after all hope of *his* being thereby reclaimed has past away forever. He may do this for the sake of a public example.

The love of God is of such a kind as to demand that He should abhor the wickedness of man. The reason for this is obvious. This love of God is real benevolence—a sincere desire for the happiness of His creatures. But God knows perfectly well that sin necessarily and fatally destroys happiness. Hence, He cannot but hate it, and hate men and devils too on account of it.

Self-righteous people often mistake the nature of God's love, supposing it to be fondness and that it does not involve a holy and infinite abhorrence of all sin. No mistake could be greater than this.

It is hard for a selfish being to realize the nature of the unselfish love of God. This is one of the most difficult conceptions for the selfish mind to form. The reason for this difficulty is obvious. People are naturally inclined to judge the character and motives of the Deity as they do their own, making God altogether such a being as themselves. Consequently, being supremely selfish themselves, they suppose God is also selfish. When you hear a person denying that God is really benevolent or speaking of Him as if He were as selfish as sinning mortals, you may know that that man is supremely selfish.

Sometimes it seems impossible to make wicked people conceive of God as being truly benevolent. It is so perfectly unlike their own state of mind, they seem almost incapable of apprehending what it is, and withal are by no means very ready to admit that God is so very much better than themselves.

In the same way the sinner is prone to conceive of Christians as feeling toward him as he does toward them. He often has no idea that Christians really love him intensely, and feel the deep yearnings of compassion over him in view of his present wretchedness and coming doom. He seems to have no idea that God, angels, saints, and all the holy in earth or heaven feel utterly different from himself.

Sometimes unrepentant sinners have been broken down completely by kind treatment. Such treatment where they had reason to expect its opposite has sometimes made the idea flash into their mind that there is real benevolence in *other* hearts although there is none in their own.

Many years ago, I knew a man who had abused a Christian in the worst possible way. So outrageous was this abuse that on reflection he felt constrained to go and make some confession to the Christian whom he had abused. What was his amazement to find that this Christian man had not the least ill feeling toward him, had no rebukes or reproaches to utter, that he had cherished no other feelings than compassion. And now, as soon as he saw him, his benevolent heart gushed out in compassion and sympathy. Oh, when the wicked man saw this, it brought before his mind the new and thrilling idea: *It may be that God really loves me. Perhaps God too and all other holy beings are seeking my good and really care for my soul.* This is one of the most important considerations to get before the mind of any class of sinners, whether of backsliders or of those who have never professed repentance. There is a most melting power in the thought: *God, my Maker and my Father, feels real and infinite compassion for me.* Many a heart has bowed before God and been broken in godly sorrow under the power of this consideration.

It is a striking fact that the Bible often presents this feature on the divine character in a strong and most affecting light. "Since I spake against him, I do earnestly remember him still; therefore, my bowels are troubled for him; I will surely have mercy upon him, saith the Lord" (Jer. 31:20). Oh, could you who have wandered and backslidden only get this idea into your mind, could you only see how sincerely and earnestly your Maker is entreating you to return to himself, you could not refuse to come. Hear what the Psalmist said, "Hath God forgotten to be gracious? hath he in anger shut up his tender mercies? And I said, This is my infirmity" (Ps. 77:9–10). Truly so. Is this your infirmity, that you should cherish such thoughts of cold unbelief? Could you but understand how greatly God desires your return, could you see for once how deeply His compassions are awakened toward you and how cordially He would welcome you back to His bosom, it could not fail to break down all your pride and melt your soul in repentance.

There is no danger that this view of the love of God should make people hard-hearted, stupid and reckless. Nothing else has such power as this to soften and melt the hearts of sinful men. Nothing else can be compared with this to subdue rebellion, transform selfishness into benevolence, and regenerate the polluted soul into the image of God.

A realization of the nature and reality of the love of God is indispensable to true Christianity. Without this, all will be hardhearted. Without this, no one can know what it is to have an unction shed over all his soul, drawing it into deep communion with God, and awakening a calm and settled confidence in the Lord of Hosts as his own God and Father.

An apprehension of this needs to become an *omnipresent reality* before people can be *established* in grace. I can testify on this point from experience. Nothing has had such an influence on my mind as this. When I go to God deeply realizing that He loves me more than I love myself, and loves to *give* more than I love to *receive*, then I feel that I *may* be strong in prayer and faith. When I go to pray for my family and can feel that God loves them more than I do, when I pray for my sick wife and can see that God cares for her comfort and usefulness and for the interests of my family more than I possibly can, I then feel that it is cruel unbelief not to trust God for every possible good. So when I pray for Oberlin, it is good to feel that God planted this vine and He can water it at His will, and can defend it so that the "bear out of the wood shall not waste it, nor the wild beast of the field devour it." If this vine is good for anything in His vineyard, He values it more than I do. He loves its prosperity more, and is more ready to make efforts for sustaining and enlarging it.

In short, everything which pertains to His kingdom He loves more than I do. His whole being is awake to these interests. His Word has told me that He feeds even the ravens when they cry, and much more will He feed His little ones.*

A realization of this truth is indispensable to prevailing prayer. In order to prevail in prayer, you need to realize that God loves you infinitely more than you love yourself, that He loves the Church more than you do, and loves to see sinners converted infinitely more than you ever have or ever will. Your heart will then be strong in prayer when you see that He truly cares for you and cares for all human happiness so that you have no need to excite His feelings, for His soul is already on fire, all awake with most intensely glowing emotions of love, with one changeless purpose: to promote the highest happiness of every being in His universe as far as He wisely can. Oh, to have such a God to pray to, and to come before Him with these realizations of His ineffable love—this quickens faith and gives vitality to the soul of prayer. Brethren, do learn how to pray to such a God as this!

---

*For three additional sermons on love, and a comprehensive discussion on the qualities of true love, see Finney's *Principles of Love*, published by Bethany House Publishers. [Finney's wife died two years after he preached this sermon which referred to his sick wife.]

10

TRUSTING IN THE MERCY OF GOD*

"I trust in the mercy of God forever and ever" (Psalm 52:8).

Mercy as an attribute of God is not to be confused with mere goodness. This mistake is often made. That it is a mistake, you will see at once if you consider that mercy is directly opposed to justice, while justice is one of the natural and legitimate developments of goodness. Goodness may demand the exercise of justice. Indeed, goodness often does. But to say that mercy demands the exercise of justice is to use the word without meaning. *Mercy asks that justice be set aside.* Of course, mercy and goodness stand in a very different relations to justice and are very different attributes.

Mercy is a disposition to pardon the guilty. The exercise of mercy consists in arresting and setting aside the penalty of the law, when that penalty has been incurred by transgression. It is, as has been said, directly opposed to justice. Justice treats every person according to what he deserves. Mercy treats every criminal very differently from the way he deserves to be treated.

Mercy is exercised only where there is guilt. Mercy always presupposes guilt. The penalty of the law must have been previously incurred, or else there can be no scope for mercy. Mercy can be exercised no further than one deserves punishment. It may continue its exercise just as long as punishment is deserved, but no longer. If great punishment is deserved, great mercy can be shown. If endless punishment is due, then there is scope for infinite mercy to be shown, but not otherwise.

Sermons on Gospel Themes, pp. 19–36.

The Implications of Trusting in the Mercy of God

A conviction of guilt is implied in trusting in the mercy of God. No one can properly be said to trust in the mercy of God unless he has committed crimes, and is conscious of this fact. Justice protects the innocent, and they may safely appeal to justice for defense or redress. But for the guilty nothing remains but to trust in mercy. Trusting in mercy always implies a deep, heartfelt conviction of personal guilt.

Trust in mercy always implies that we have no hope on the score of justice. If we have anything to expect from justice, then we should not look to mercy. The human heart is too proud to throw itself upon mercy while it presumes itself to have a valid claim to favor on the score of justice. Even more, to appeal to mercy when we might rightfully appeal to justice is never demanded either by God's law or gospel, nor can it be in harmony with our relations to God's government. In fact, the thing is, in the very nature of the mind, impossible.

Trust in mercy implies a just apprehension of what mercy is. On this point many fail, because they confuse mercy with mere goodness, or with grace, considered as mere favor to the undeserving. The latter may be shown where there is no mercy, the term mercy being applied to the pardon of crime. We all know that God shows favor, or grace in the general sense, to all the wicked on earth. He makes His sun to rise on the evil and on the good, and sends His rain on the unjust as well as on the just. But to trust in this general favor shown to the wicked while on trial here is not trusting in the mercy of God. We never trust in mercy till we really understand what it is—pardon for the crimes of the guilty.

Trust in God's mercy implies a belief that He is merciful. We could not trust Him if we had no such belief. This belief must always lie at the foundation of real trust. Indeed, so naturally does this belief beget that outgoing of the soul and resting upon God which we call trust, that in the New Testament sense it commonly includes both. Faith, or belief, includes a hearty committal of the soul to God, and a cordial trust in Him.

"Trusting in the mercy of God forever and ever" implies a conviction of deserving endless punishment. Mercy is co-extensive with deserved severity of punishment, and can in its nature go no further. It is rational to rely upon the exercise of mercy for as long a time as we deserve punishment, but no longer. A prisoner under a three years' sentence to the state prison may ask for the exercise of mercy in the form of a pardon *for so long a time*; but he will not ask a pardon for ten years when he needs it only for three, or ask a pardon after his three years' term has expired. This principle is perfectly obvious; the point at which the deserved punishment ceases, there mercy also ceases and our trust in it. While the potential of punishment continues, so may mercy, and our trust in its exercise. When therefore the Psalmist trusts in the mercy of God forever, he renounces all hope of ever being received to favor on the score of justice.

Trusting in mercy implies a cessation from all excuses and excuse making. The moment you trust in mercy, you give up all apologies and excuses at once and entirely. For these imply a reliance upon God's justice. An excuse or apology is nothing more nor less than an appeal to justice; a plea designed to justify our conduct. Trusting in mercy forever implies that we have ceased from all excuses forever.

Thus a person on trial before a civil court, as long as he pleads justifications and excuses, appeals to justice. But if he goes before the court and pleads guilty, offering no justification or apology whatever, he throws himself upon the clemency of the court. This is quite another thing from self-justification. It sometimes happens that in the same trial, the accused party tries both expedients. He first attempts his own defense; but finding this vain, he shifts his position, confesses his crime and that he deserves punishment, throwing himself upon the mercy of the court. Perhaps he begs the court to commend him to the mercy of the executive in whom is vested the pardoning power.

Now it is always understood that when a man pleads guilty, he desists from making excuses, and appeals only to mercy. So in any private matter with my neighbor. If I justify myself fully, I surely have no confession to make. But if I am conscious of having done him wrong, then I freely confess my wrong and appeal to mercy. Self-justification stands right over against confession.

So in parental discipline. If your child sternly justifies himself, he makes no appeal to mercy. But the moment when he casts himself upon your bosom with tears, and says, "I am all wrong," he ceases to make excuses and trusts himself to mercy. So in the government of God. Trust in mercy is a final giving up of all reliance upon justice. You have no more excuses. You make none.

The Conditions to Trusting in the Mercy of God

Public justice must be appeased. Its demands must be satisfied. God is a great public magistrate, sustaining infinitely responsible relations to the moral universe. He must be careful what He does.

Perhaps no measure of government is more delicate and difficult in its bearings than the exercise of mercy. It is a most critical point. There is eminent danger of making the impression that mercy would trample down law. The very thing that mercy does is to set aside the execution of the *penalty* of law; the danger is lest this should seem to set aside the law itself. The great problem is, "How can the law retain its full majesty, the execution of its penalty being entirely withdrawn?" This is always a difficult and delicate matter.

In human governments, we often see great firmness exercised by the magistrate. During the scenes of the American Revolution, George Washington was earnestly importuned to pardon a certain man. This particular man was eminently an amiable, lovely man. His case excited a deep sympathy in the American army. Numerous and urgent petitions were made to Washington in his behalf; but no, Washington would not yield. They besought him to see the man, in hope that a personal interview might touch his heart; but he refused even to see him. He dared not trust his own feelings. He felt that this was a great crisis, and that a nation's welfare was in peril. Hence, his stern, unyielding decision. It was not that he lacked compassion of soul. He had a heart to feel. But under the circumstances, he knew too well that no scope must be given to the indulgence of his tender sympathies. He dared not gratify these feelings, lest a nation's ruin should be the penalty.

Such cases have often occurred in human governments when every feeling of the soul is on the side of mercy, which makes its strong demand for indulgence; but justice forbids.

Often in family government the parent has an agonizing trial. He would sooner bear the pain himself thrice told than to inflict it upon his child; but interests of perhaps infinite moment are at stake, and must not be put in peril by the indulgence of his compassions.

Now, if the exercise of mercy in such cases is difficult how much more so in the government of God? Hence, the first condition of the exercise of mercy is that something be done to meet the demands of public justice. It is absolutely indispensable that law be sustained. However much disposed God may be to pardon, yet He is too good to exercise mercy on any such conditions or under any such circumstances that will impair the dignity of His law, throw out a license to sin, and open the very floodgates of iniquity. Jehovah never can do this. He knows He never ought to. On this point it only need be said at present that this difficulty is wholly removed by the atonement of Christ.

A second condition is that we repent. Certainly no sinner has the least ground to hope for mercy until he repents. Will God pardon the sinner while he continues to rebel? Never. To do so would be most unjust in God—most ruinous to the universe. It would be virtually proclaiming that sin is less than a trifle—that God cares not how set in wickedness the sinner's heart is, that He is ready to take the most rebellious heart, unhumbled, to His bosom. Before God can do this He must cease to be holy.

Third, we must confess our sins. "Whoso confesseth," and he only, "shall find mercy" (Prov. 28:13). Jehovah sustains such relations to the moral universe that He cannot forgive without the sinner's confession. He must have the sinner's testimony against himself, and in favor of law and obedience.

Suppose a person were convicted and sentenced to be hanged. Suppose he petitioned the governor for a pardon, but was too proud to confess, at least in public. "May it please your Honor," he says, "between you and me, I am willing to say that I committed that crime alleged against me, but you must not ask me to make this confession before the world. You will have some regard to my feelings and to the feelings of my numerous and respectable friends. Before the world, therefore, I shall persist in denying the crime. I trust, however, that you will duly consider all the circumstances and grant me a pardon." "Pardon you!" the governor would say, "Pardon you when you are condemning the whole court and jury of injustice, and the witness of falsehood; pardon you while you set yourself against the whole administration of justice in the State? Never! Never! You are too proud to take your own place and appear in your own character. How can I rely on you to be a good citizen? How can I expect you to be anything better than an arch villain?"

Understand, then, that before we can trust in the mercy of God, we must really repent and make our confession as public as we have made our crime.

Suppose again that a person is convicted and then asks for a pardon, but will not confess at all. "Oh," he says, "I have no crimes to confess. I have done nothing particularly wrong. The reason for my acting as I have is that I have a desperately wicked heart. I cannot repent and never could. I don't know how it happens that I commit murder so easily. It seems to be a second nature to me to kill my neighbor. I can't help it. I am told, governor, that you are very good, very merciful, that you are love itself (and I believe it). Surely, you will grant me a pardon. It will be so easy for you—and it would be so horrible for me to be hanged. You know I have done only a little wrong, and that little only because I could not help it! You certainly cannot insist upon my making any confession. What! Have me hanged because I don't repent? You certainly are too kind to do such a thing." The governor must be indignant and reply, "I don't thank you for your good opinion of me, the law shall take its course. Your path is to the gallows."

See that sinner? Hear him mock God in his prayer: "I trust in the mercy of God, for God is love." Do you repent? "I don't know about repentance—that is not the question. God is love—God is too good to send men to hell." Those who say that God never sends anybody to hell slander Him. Too good! You say; too good! so good that He will forgive whether the sinner repents or not; too good to hold the reins of His government firmly; too good to secure the best interests of His vast kingdom! Sinner, the God you think of is a being of your own crazy imagination, and not the God who built the prison of despair for hardened sinners, not the God who rules the universe by righteous law and our race also on a gospel system that magnifies that law and makes it honorable.

Fourth, we must really make restitution as far as it lies in our power. You may see the bearing of this in the case of a highway robber. He has robbed a traveler of ten thousand dollars, and is sentenced to the state prison for life. He petitions for pardon. Very sorry he is for his crime; will make any confession that can be asked, ever so public; but will he make restitution? Not he; no— he needs that money himself. He will give up half of it, perhaps, to the government; vastly patriotic is he all at once, and liberal withal; ready to make a donation of five thousand dollars for the public good! Ready to consecrate to most benevolent uses a splendid sum of money; but *whose* money? Where is his justice to the man he has robbed? Wretch! Giving to the public what you have stolen from your neighbor and putting it into the treasury of the government! No; such a gift would burn right through the chest! What would you think if the government should connive at such an abomination? You would abhor their execrable corruption.

See that man of the world. His whole business career is a court of overreaching. He slyly thrusts his hands into his neighbor's pockets and thus fills up his own. His rule is uniformly to sell for more than a thing is worth and buy for less. He knows how to monopolize and make high prices and then sell out his accumulated stock. His mind is forever on the stretch to manage and make good bargains. But this man at last must prepare to meet God. So he turns to his money to make it answer all things. He has a large gift for God. Perhaps he will build a church or send out a missionary. Something pretty handsome at least to buy a pardon for a life about which his conscience pierces him. Yes, he has a splendid bribe for God. Ah, but will God take it? Never! God burns with indignation at the thought. Does God want your price of blood, those gains of oppression? Go and give them back to the suffering poor whose cries have gone up to God against you. Oh shame, to think to filch from your brother and give it to God! Not merely rob Peter to pay Paul, but rob man to pay God! The pardon of your soul is not bought so!

Fifth, another condition is that you really reform. Suppose there is a villain in our neighborhood who has become the terror of all the region round about. He has already murdered a score of defenseless women and children; burns down our houses by night; plunders and robs daily; and every day we hear tidings of his crimes at which every ear tingles. None feel safe a moment. He is an arch and bloody villain. At last he is arrested, and we all breathe more easily. Peace is restored. But this miscreant having received the sentence of death, petitions for pardon. He professes no repentance whatever, and makes not even a promise of amendment or reform; yet the governor is about to give him a free pardon. If he does it, who will not say, "He ought to be hanged by the neck till he is dead, dead!" But what does that sinner say? "I trust," says he, "in the great mercy of God. I have nothing to fear." But does he reform? No. What good can the mercy of God do him if he does not reform?

Sixth, you must go the whole length in justifying the law and its penalty. Note the convicted criminal. He doesn't believe that government has any right to take life for any crime. He demurs utterly to the justice of such a proceeding, and on this ground insists that he must have a pardon. Will he get it? Will the governor take a position which is flatly opposed to the very law and constitution that he is sworn to sustain? Will he crush the law to save one criminal, or even a thousand criminals? Not if he has the spirit of a ruler in his soul. That guilty man, if he would have mercy from the executive, must admit the right of the law and of the penalty. Or else he arrays himself against the law and cannot be trusted in the community.

Now hear some sinner. How much he has to say against his impending doom and against the justice of eternal punishment. He denounces the laws of God as cruelly and unrighteously severe. Sinner, do you suppose God can forgive you while you pursue such a course? He would as soon repeal His law and vacate His throne. You make it impossible for God to forgive you.

Seven, no sinner can be a proper object of mercy who is not

entirely submissive to all those measures of the government that have brought him to conviction. Suppose a criminal should plead that there had been a conspiracy to waylay and arrest him; that witnesses had been bribed to give false testimony; that the judge had charged the jury falsely or that the jury had given an unrighteous verdict. Could he hope by such false allegations to get a pardon? Truly, no. Such a man cannot be trusted to sustain law and order in a community under any government, human or divine.

But hear the sinner complain and cavil. "Why," he says, "did God allow sin and temptation to enter this world at all? Why does God let the sinner live at all to incur a doom so dreadful? And why does God block up the sinner's path by His providence, and cut him down in his sins?" Yet this very sinner talks about trusting in God's mercy! Indeed! While all the time he is accusing God of being an infinite tyrant, and of seeking to crush the helpless, unfortunate sinner! What do these cavils mean? What are they but the uplifted voice of a guilty rebel arraigning his Maker for doing good and showing mercy to His own rebellious creatures? For it needs but a moment's thought to see that the temptation complained of is only a good placed before a moral agent to melt his heart by love. Yet, against this the sinner murmurs, and pours out his complaints against God. Be assured that unless you are willing to go the full length of justifying all God does, He never can give you pardon. God has no option to pardon a self-justifying rebel. The interests of myriads of moral beings forbid Him from doing it. When you will take the ground most fully of justifying God and condemning yourself, you place yourself where mercy can reach you, and then it surely will. Not before.

Eighth, you must agree most cordially with the plan of salvation. This plan is based on the assumption that we deserve everlasting death and must be saved, if ever, by sovereign grace and mercy. Nothing can save but mercy—mercy which meets the sinner in the dust, prostrate, without an excuse or an apology, giving to God all the glory and taking to himself all the guilt and shame. There is hope for you, sinner, if you embrace this plan with all your heart.

Several Mistakes Made on This Subject

Many really trust in justice and not in mercy. They say, "God is just—God will do me no injustice—I mean to do as well as I can and then I can safely leave myself in the hands of a just God." True, God will do you no injustice. You never need fear that. But how terrible if God should do you strict justice! How fearful if you get no mercy! If God does not show you infinite mercy, you are forever lost, as surely as you are a sinner! This trusting in God's justice is a fatal rock. The sinner who can do it calmly has never seen God's law and his own heart. The Psalmist did not say, "I trust in the *justice* of God forever and ever."

Many trust professedly in the mercy of God without fulfilling the only conditions on which mercy can be shown. They may hold on in such trusting till they die—but no longer.

Sinners believe that God can dispense with their fulfilling these conditions. But He cannot do so. They spring out of the very constitution of His government, from His very nature, and must therefore be strictly fulfilled. Sooner than dispense with their fulfillment, God would send the whole human race, yes, the whole universe, to hell. If God were to set aside these conditions, and forgive a sinner while unhumbled, unrepentant, and unbelieving, He would upset His kingdom, convulse the moral universe, and kindle another hell in His own bosom.

Many are defeating their own salvation by self-justification. Pleas that excuse self, and cavils that arraign God, stand alike and fatally in the way of pardon. Since the world began, it has not been known that a sinner has found mercy in this state.

Many pretend to trust in mercy who yet profess to be punished for their sins as they go along. They hope for salvation through mercy, and yet they are punished for all their sins in *this* life. Two more absurd and self-contradictory things were never put together. Punished as much as they deserve here, and yet saved through mercy? They are actually praying to be saved after death through justice. Surely, if they are punished all they deserve as they go along, justice will ask no more after death.

People who in the letter plead for mercy, often rely really upon justice. The deep conviction of sin and necessity of punishment does not sink into their soul till they realize what mercy is, and feel that they can rely on nothing else.

Some are covering up their sins, yet dream of going to heaven. Do they think they can hide those sins from the Omniscient Eye? Do they think to cover their sins and yet "prosper," in spite of God's awful word?

We cannot reasonably ask for mercy beyond our acknowledged and felt guilt. They are fatally mistaken who suppose they can. Without a deep conviction of conscious guilt, we cannot be honest or earnest in supplicating mercy. Hear that man pray who thinks sin a trifle and its deserved punishment a small affair. "O Lord, I need a little mercy, only a little. My sins have been few and of small account. Grant me, Lord, exemption from the brief and slight punishment that my few errors and defects may have deserved." Or hear the Universalist pray, "O Lord, You know that I have been punished for my sins as I have passed along. I have had a fit of sickness and various pains and losses, nearly or quite enough, you know, to punish all the sins I have committed. Now, therefore, I pray give me salvation through your great mercy." How astonishing that sane men should hold such nonsense! How can a Universalist pray at all? What should he pray for? Not for pardon, for on their principles they have a valid claim to exemption from punishment on the score of justice, as the criminal has who has served out his sentence in the state prison. The only rational prayer that can be made is that God will do them justice, and let them off, since they have already been punished enough. But why should they pray for this? God may be trusted to do justice without their praying for it. I don't wonder that Universalists pray very little; what have they to pray for? Their daily bread? Very well. But the mercy of God they need not on their scheme, for they suffer all they deserve. Pleasing delusion. Flattering enough to human pride, but strange for rational minds and horribly pernicious!

Restoration takes substantially the same ground, only leaving a part of the penalty to be worked out in purgatory, but claiming salvation on the ground of justice and not mercy. Mercy can have no place in any system of Universalism. Every form of this system arrays God in robes of justice—inflexible, fearful justice—yet these men trust, they say, in the mercy of God! But what have they done with the gospel, with what all the Bible says about free pardon to the guilty? They have thrust it out of the Bible. And what have they given us instead? Only justice. Justice—punishment enough for sin in this world, or at least in a few years of purgatory. Sin a trifle—government a mere farce—God a liar—hell a bugbear and a humbug! What is all this but dire blasphemy as ever came from hell?

If we ask for but little mercy, we shall get none at all. This may seem strange, but is nonetheless true. If we get anything, we must ask for great blessings. Suppose a person deserved to be hanged, and yet asks only for a little favor. Suppose he should say so, can he be forgiven? No. He must confess the whole of his guilt in its full and awful form, and show that he feels it in his very soul. So, sinner, you must come and confess your whole guilt as it is, or have no mercy. Come and get down, low, lower, infinitely low before God, and take mercy there.

Hear the Universalist. All he can say at first is, "I thank God for a thousand things." But he begins to doubt whether this is quite enough. Perhaps he needs a little more punishment than he has suffered in this life; he sees a little more guilt; so he prays that God would let him off from ten years of deserved punishment in hell. And if he sees a little more guilt, he asks for a reprieve from so much more punishment. If truth flashes upon his soul and he sees his own heart and life in the light of Jehovah's law, he gets down lower and lower, as low as he can, and pours out his prayer that God would save him from that eternal hell that he deserves. "Oh," he cries out, "can God forgive so great a sinner!" Yes, and by so much the more readily, by how much the more you humble yourself, and by how much the greater mercy you ask and feel that you need. Only come down and take such a position where God can meet you. Recollect the prodigal son, and that father running, falling on his neck, weeping, welcoming, forgiving! Oh, how that father's heart gushed with tenderness!

It is not the greatness of your sins, but your pride of heart that forbids your salvation. It is not anything in your past life, but it is your present state of mind that makes your salvation impossible. Think of this.

You need not wait to use means with God to persuade Him to save you. He is using means with you to persuade you to be saved. You act as if God could scarcely be moved by any possible entreaties and submissions to exercise mercy. Oh, you do not see how His great heart beats with compassion and presses the streams of mercy forth in all directions, pouring the river of the waters of life at your very feet, creating such a pressure of appeal to your heart that you have to brace yourself against it, lest you should be persuaded to repent. Oh, do you see how God would fain persuade you and break your heart in repentance, that He may bring you where He can reach you with forgiving mercy—where He can come and bless you without resigning His very throne!

To deny you deserve endless punishment is to render your salvation utterly impossible. God never can forgive you on this ground, because you are trying to be saved on the score of justice. You could not make your damnation more certain than you thus make it, if you were to murder every person you meet. You tie up the hands of mercy and will not let her pluck you from the jaws of death. It is as if your house were on fire and you seized your loaded rifle to shoot down everyone who came with his bucket to help you. You stand your ground amid the raging element until you sink beneath the flames.

Who can help you? What is that person doing who is trying to make his family believe Universalism? It is as if he would shoot his rifle at the very heart of Mercy every time she comes in view. He seems determined to drive off Mercy, and for this purpose plies all the enginery of Universalism and throws himself into the citadel of this refuge of lies. Oh! What a work of death this is! Mercy shall not reach him or his family; he seems so determined, and Mercy cannot come. See how she bends from heaven—Jehovah smiles in love—and weeps in pity—and bends from the very clouds and holds out the pierced hand of the crucified One. But no! I don't deserve the punishment. Away with the insult of a pardon offered through mere mercy! What can be more fatal, more damning, more ruinous to the soul?

You see very clearly why all are not saved. It is not because God is not willing to save all, but because they defeat the efforts God makes to save them. They betake themselves to every possible refuge and subterfuge; resist conviction of guilt, and repel every call of mercy. What ails those young men? What are they doing? Has God come down in His red wrath and vengeance, that they should rally all their might to oppose Him? Oh, no, He has only come in mercy—this is all—and they are fighting against His mercy, not His just retribution of vengeance. If this were His awful arm of vengeance you would bow right soon or break beneath its blow. But God's mercy comes in its soft whispers (would you but realize it)—it comes to win your heart; and what are you doing? You band yourselves together to resist its calls—you invent a thousand excuses—you run together to talk, and talk away all solemn thought—you run to some infidel or Universalist to find relief for an uneasy conscience.

Ah, sinner, this can do you no good. You flee away from God—why? What's the matter? Is God pouring down the floods of His great wrath? No, no; but Mercy has come, and would fain gather you under her outspread wings where storms of wrath can never come. But no, the sinner pleads against it—complains, runs, fights, repels the angel of mercy—dashes from his lips the waters of life. Sinner, this scene is soon to close. The time is short. Soon God comes—death shakes his dart—that young man is sick—hear his groans. Are you going to die, my young friend? Are you ready? "Oh, I don't know," he answers. "I am in great pain. Oh! Oh! how can I live so? Alas, how can I die? He answers. I can't attend to it now—too late—too late!" Indeed, young man, you are in weakness now. God's finger has touched you. Oh, if I could only tell you some of the deathbed scenes I have witnessed. If I could make you see them, and hear the deep wailings of unutterable agony as the soul quivered, shuddered, and fain would shrink down swift to hell! Those are the very men who ran away from mercy. Mercy could not reach them, but death can. Death seizes its victim. See, he drags the frightened, shrieking soul to the gateway of hell. How the soul recoils, groans, what an unearthly groan—and he is gone! The sentence of execution has gone out and there is no reprieve. That sinner would not have mercy when he might; now he cannot when he would. All is over now.

Dying sinner, you may just as well have mercy today as not. All your past sins present no obstacle at all if you only repent and take the offered pardon. Your God proffers you life. "As I live," saith the Lord, "I have no pleasure in your death; turn ye, turn ye, for why will ye die?" Why will you reject such offered life? And will you still persist? Be astonished, O ye heavens! Indeed, if there ever was anything that filled the universe with astonishment, it is the sinner's rejection of mercy. Angels were astonished when they saw the Son of God made flesh, and when they saw Him nailed to a tree—how much more now to see the guilty sinner, doomed to hell, yet spurning offered pardon! What do they see! That sinner putting off and still delaying and delaying still, until—what? Until the last curtain falls, and the great bell tolls, tolls, tolls the awful knell of the sinner's death eternal! Where is that sinner? Follow him—down he goes, weeping, wailing, along the sides of the pit— he reaches his own final home; this is "his own place" now and forevermore! Mercy followed him to the last verge of the precipice, and could no longer. She had done her part.

What if a spirit from glory should come and speak to you five minutes—a relative, say—perhaps your mother—what would she say? Or a spirit from that world of despair—Oh, could such a one give utterance to the awful realities of that prison house, what would he say? Would he tell you that the preacher has been telling you lies? Would he say, "Don't be frightened by these made up tales of horror?" Oh no, but that the half has not been told you and never can be. Oh, how he would press you, if he might, to flee from the wrath to come!

11

JUSTIFICATION BY FAITH*

"Knowing that a man is not justified by the works of the law, but by the faith of Jesus Christ, even we have believed in Jesus Christ, that we might be justified by the faith of Christ, and not by the works of the law: for by the works of the law shall no flesh be justified" (Galatians 2:16).

In its general legal sense justification means *not guilty*. To justify an individual in this sense is to declare that he is not guilty of any breach of the law. It is affirming that he has committed no crime. It is pronouncing him innocent.

More technically, legal justification is a form of pleading to a charge of having committed a crime, where the individual who is charged admits the fact, but brings forward an excuse on which he claims that he had a right to do as he did, or that he is not blameworthy. Thus, if a person is charged with murder, the plea of justification admits that he killed the man, but alleges either that it was done in self-defense and he had a right to kill him, or that it was by an unavoidable accident and he could not help it. In either case, the plea of justification admits the fact, but denies the guilt on the ground of a sufficient excuse or reason.

By Deeds of the Law Shall No Flesh Be Justified

In God's court, under the first form of legal justification or the general form of justification mentioned above, no flesh can be jus-

---

Lectures to Professing Christians, pp. 179–193.

tified. In this case, the burden of proof rests with the accuser, who must prove the facts charged. And in this case, he only needs to prove that a crime has been committed *once*. If it is proved once, the person is guilty. He cannot be justified in this way by the law. He is found guilty. It is not appropriate for him to contend that he has done more good than harm, or that he has kept God's law longer than he has broken it. He must contend that he has fulfilled every jot and tittle of the law. Who can be justified by the law in this way? No one.

The same is true under the second sense or technical form of justification: no flesh can be justified. In this case, the burden of proof rests with the person who makes the plea. When he pleads in justification he admits the fact alleged, and therefore he must make good his excuse or fail. There are two points to be regarded. The thing pleaded as an excuse must be *true*, and it must be a good and sufficient excuse or justification, not a frivolous apology or one that does not meet the case. If it is not true or if it is insufficient, and especially if it reflects on the character of the court or government, it is an infamous aggravation of his offense. You will soon see the bearing of this remark.

I will now mention some of the prominent reasons that sinners are in the habit of pleading as a justification for sin, and I will show what is the true nature and bearing of these excuses, the light in which they stand before God. I have not time to name all these pleas, but will only refer to two of each of the classes I have just described, those which are good if true, and those which are true but unavailing.

First, sinners often plead their *sinful nature* as a justification. If it is true, this excuse is a good one. If it is true, as they pretend, that God has given them a nature which is itself sinful, and the *necessary* actings of their nature are sinful, it is a good excuse for sin. If it is true, at the day of judgment it will be a good plea in justification. God would have to annihilate the reason of all rational beings, before any would ever blame you for sin, if God made you sin, or if He gave you a nature that is itself sinful. Nevertheless, how can your *nature* be sinful? What is sin? Sin is a transgression of the law. There is no other sin except this. Now, does the law say you must not have such a nature as you have? Certainly not.

The fact is, the doctrine of a sinful nature overlooks the distinction between sin and the *occasion* of sin. The bodily appetites and constitutional susceptibilities of body and mind, when strongly excited, become the occasion of sin. So it was with Adam. No one will say that Adam had a sinful nature. But he had, by his constitution, an appetite for food and a desire for knowledge. These were not sinful, but were as God made them. These appetites were necessary to fit him to live in this world as a subject of God's moral government. After being strongly excited, as you know, these appetites led to prohibited indulgence, and thus became the occasions of his sinning against God. They were innocent in themselves, but he yielded to them in a sinful manner; that was his sin.

When the sinner talks about his sinful nature as a justification, he confuses these innocent appetites and susceptibilities with sin itself. By so doing, he in fact charges God foolishly and accuses God of giving him a sinful nature. Actually, his nature in all its elements is essential to moral agency, and God has made it as well as it could be made. Man's nature is perfectly adapted to the circumstances in which he lives in this world. The truth is, man's nature is all right, and is as well fitted to love and obey God as to hate and disobey Him.

Sinner! The day is not far off when it will be known whether this is a good excuse or not. Then you will see whether you can face your Maker down in this way, when He charges you with sin. Will you be able to turn around and throw the blame back upon Him?

Now, do you inquire what influence Adam's sin has had in producing the sin of his posterity? I answer, it has subjected them to aggravated temptation, but has by no means rendered their nature in itself sinful.

A second excuse under this same class is inability. If it is true, then it is also a good excuse. If sinners are really unable to obey God, this is a good plea in justification. When you are charged with having committed sin, in not obeying the laws of God, you have only to show by good proof, if you can, that God has required what you were not able to perform. If you can do this, then the whole intelligent universe will resound with the verdict of *not guilty*. If you do not have natural power to obey God, then they must give this verdict or cease to be reasonable beings. For it is a first law of reason that no being has an obligation to do what he has no power to do.

Suppose God required you to undo something that you have done. Everyone should see that this is a natural impossibility. Now, are you to blame for not doing it? God requires repentance of past sins; not that you should undo them. Suppose it were your duty to have warned a certain individual, who is now dead. Are you under obligation to warn that individual now? No. It would be an impossibility. All that God can now require is that you repent. It never can be your duty to warn that sinner now. God may hold you responsible for not doing your duty to him when he was alive and when it was in your power. But it would be absurd to make it your duty to do what is not in your power to do.

Since this plea is false and blames God for tyranny, it is a scandalous aggravation of the crime. If God required you to do what you have no power to do, it would be tyranny. And what God requires, you must do or face the penalty of eternal death. If He were to threaten an infinite penalty for not doing what you have no power to do, then He would be an infinite tyrant. This plea, then, charges God with infinite tyranny, and is not only insufficient for the sinner's justification, but is a horrible aggravation of his crime.

Let us modify the case a little. Suppose God required you to repent for not doing what you never had the natural ability to do. Then, you must either repent of doing what you had no natural power to do or you must go to hell. However, in actuality, you can neither repent of this nor can He make you repent of it. What is repentance? It is to blame yourself and justify God. But if you had no power to obey Him, you can do neither. It is a natural impossibility for a rational being to ever blame himself for not doing what he is conscious he had no power to do. Nor can you justify God. Unless the laws of mind are reversed, the verdict of all intelligent beings must pronounce it infinite tyranny to require that which there is no power to perform.

Suppose God called you to account, and required you to repent for not flying. By what process can He make you blame yourself for not flying, when you are conscious that you have no wings and no power to fly? If He could cheat you into the belief that you had the power, and make you believe a lie, then you might repent. But what sort of a way would that be for God to take with His creatures?

Sinner, what do you mean by bringing such an excuse before God? It is a strange contradiction you make, when you admit that you ought to repent, and in the next breath say you have no power to repent. You ought to take your ground one way or the other. If you mean to rely on this excuse, come out with it in full, and take your ground before God's bar, and say, "Lord I am not going to repent at all. I am not under any obligation to repent, for I have no power to obey your law; therefore, I plead not guilty absolutely, for I have never sinned!" In which of these ways can anyone be justified? Will you take ground on this excuse, and throw back the blame upon God?

Another excuse that sinners offer for their continued unrepentance is their wicked heart. This excuse is true, but it is not sufficient. The first two excuses that I mentioned would have been good, if they had been true, but they were false. The excuse of having a wicked heart is true, but it is not a sufficient excuse. What is a wicked heart? It is not the bodily organ we call the heart, but the affection of the soul, the wicked disposition, the wicked feelings, the actings of the mind. If these will justify you, they will justify the devil himself. Has he not as wicked a heart as you have? Suppose you had committed murder, and you should be put on trial and plead this plea. "It is true," you say, "I killed the man but then I have such a thirst for blood, and such a hatred of mankind, that I cannot help committing murder, whenever I have an opportunity." "Horrible!" the judge would exclaim, "Horrible! Let the gallows be set up immediately, and let this fellow be hanged before I leave the bench. Such a wretch ought not to live an hour. Such a plea! Why, that is the very reason he ought to be hanged. If he has such a thirst for blood, then no man is safe." Such is the sinner's plea of a wicked heart in justification of sin: "Out of thine own mouth will I condemn thee, thou wicked servant."

Another great excuse people make is the conduct of Christians. Ask many a man among your neighbors why he is not a Christian, and he will point you at once to the conduct of Christians as his excuse. "These Christians," he will say, "are no better than anybody else. When I see them live as they profess to believe, then I will think it time for me to attend to Christianity." Thus he is hiding behind the sins of Christians. He shows that he knows how Christians ought to live, and therefore he cannot plead that he has sinned through ignorance. But what does it amount to as a ground of justification? I admit the fact that Christians behave very badly, and do much that is entirely contrary to their profession. But is that a good excuse for you? So far from it, this is itself one of the strongest reasons why you ought to be a Christian. You know so well how Christians ought to live, you are bound to show an example. If you had followed them ignorantly, because you did not know any better, and had fallen into sin in that way, it would be a different case. But the plea, as it stands, shows that you knew they were wrong, which is the very reason why you ought to be right, and exert a better influence than they do. Instead of following them, and doing wrong because they do, you ought to rebuke them, pray for them, and try to lead them in a better way. This excuse, then, is true in fact, but unavailing in justification. You only make it an excuse for charging God foolishly, and instead of clearing you, it only adds to your dreadful, damning guilt. A fine plea this, to get behind some deacon, or some elder in the church, and there shoot your arrows of malice and caviling at God!

Who among you, then, can be justified by the law? Who has kept it? Who has got a good excuse for breaking it? Who dares go to the bar of God on these pleas, and face his Maker with such apologies?

The Meaning of Gospel Justification

First, gospel justification is not the imputed righteousness of Jesus Christ. Under the gospel, sinners are not justified by having the obedience of Jesus Christ set down to their account, as if He had obeyed the law for them or in their place. It is a common mistake to suppose that when sinners are justified under the gospel, they are accounted righteous in the eye of the law by having the obedience or righteousness of Christ imputed to them. This idea is absurd and impossible for this reason: Jesus Christ was bound to obey the law for himself, and could no more perform works of supererogation, or obey on our account, than anybody else. Was it not His duty to love the Lord His God, with all His heart, soul, mind, and strength, and to love His neighbor as himself? Certainly; and if He had not done so, it would have been sin. The only work of supererogation He could perform was to submit to sufferings that were not deserved. This is called His obedience unto death, and this is set down to our account. But if His obedience of the law is set down to our account, why are we called on to repent and obey the law ourselves? Does God exact double service, yes, triple service; first to have the law obeyed by Christ for us, then that Christ must suffer the penalty for us, and then that we must repent and obey ourselves? No such thing is demanded. God does not require that the obedience of another should be imputed to us. All we owe is perpetual obedience to the law of benevolence. And for this there can be no substitute. If we fail of this, we must endure the penalty, or receive a free pardon.

Justification by faith does not mean that faith is accepted as a substitute for personal holiness, or that faith is imputed to us instead of personal obedience to the law. Some suppose that justification is this, that the necessity of personal holiness is set aside, and that God arbitrarily dispenses with the requirement of the law and imputes faith as a substitute. But this is not the way. Faith is accounted for just what it is, and not something else that it is not. Abraham's faith was imputed unto him for righteousness, because it was itself an act of righteousness, and because it worked by love, and thus produced holiness. Justifying faith is holiness, so far as it goes, and produces holiness of heart and life, and is imputed to the believer *as* holiness, not instead of holiness.

Nor does justification by faith imply that a sinner is justified by faith without good works or personal holiness. Some suppose that justification by faith only, is without any regard to good works or holiness. They have understood this from what Paul has said, where he insists so largely on justification by faith. But it should be borne in mind that Paul was combating the error of the Jews, who expected to be justified by obeying the law. In opposition to this error, Paul insists that justification is by faith, without works of law. He does not mean that good works are unnecessary to justification, but that works of law are not good works, because they spring from legal considerations, from hope and fear, and not from faith that works by love. But inasmuch as a false theory had crept into the church on the other side, James took up the matter, and showed them that they had misunderstood Paul. And to show this, he takes the case of Abraham, "Was not Abraham our father justified by works, when he had offered Isaac his son upon the altar? Seest thou how faith wrought with his works, and by works was faith made perfect? And the scripture was fulfilled which saith, Abraham believed God, and it was imputed unto him for righteousness: and he was called the Friend of God. Ye see then how that by works a man is justified, and not by faith only" (James 2:21–24). This epistle was supposed by some to contradict Paul, and some of the ancient churches rejected it on that account. But they overlooked the fact that Paul was speaking of one kind of works, and James of another. Paul was speaking of works performed from legal motives. But he has everywhere insisted on good works springing from faith, or the righteousness of faith, as indispensable to salvation. All that he denies is that works of law, or works grounded on legal motives, have anything to do in the matter of justification. And James teaches the same thing, when he teaches that men are justified, not by works nor by faith alone, but by faith together with the works of faith: or as Paul expresses it, faith that works by love. You will bear in mind that I am speaking of gospel justification, which is very different from legal justification.[1]

Gospel justification, or justification by faith, consists in pardon and acceptance with God. When we say that people are justified by faith and holiness, we do not mean that they are accepted on the ground of law, but that they are treated as if they were righteous on account of their faith and works of faith. This is the method which God takes in justifying a sinner. Not that faith is the foundation of justification. The foundation is in Christ. But this is the manner in which sinners are pardoned, accepted, and justified— that if they repent, believe, and become holy, then their past sins shall be forgiven, for the sake of Christ.

Here it will be seen how justification under the gospel differs from justification under the law. Legal justification is a declaration of actual innocence and freedom from blame. Gospel justification is pardon and acceptance, as if we were righteous, but on grounds other than our own obedience. When the apostle says, "By deeds of law shall no flesh be justified" (Gal. 2:16), he uses justification in a strictly legal sense. But when he speaks of justification by faith, he speaks not of legal justification, but of a person's being treated as if he were righteous.

What Happens When We Are Justified

The first item to be observed is this, when an individual is pardoned, he is no longer under the penalty of the law; the penalty was deserved, but it is set aside. Then, so far as punishment is concerned, the individual has no more to fear from the law, than if he had never transgressed. He is entirely released. Those, then, who are justified by true faith, as soon as they are pardoned, do not need to be influenced by fear of punishment. The penalty is as effectually set aside, as if it had never been incurred.

The next effect of pardon is to remove all the liabilities resulting from the transgression, such as forfeiture of goods, or incapacity for being a witness, or holding any office under government. A real pardon removes all these and restores the individual back to where he was before he transgressed. So, under the government of God, the pardoned sinner is restored to the favor of God. He is brought back into a new relation, and stands before God and is

---

[1]See Charles G. Finney, *Principles of Victory* and *Principles of Liberty* for his exposition of Paul's letter to the Romans, and the difference between works of the law and works of love, works from hope or fear and works from a gospel motive.

treated by Him, so far as the law is concerned, as if he were innocent. It does not suppose or declare him to be *really* innocent, but the pardon restores him to the same state as if he were innocent.

Another operation of pardon under God's government is, the individual is restored to sonship. In other words, it brings him into such a relation to God that he is received and treated as a child of God.

Suppose the son of a sovereign on the throne had committed murder, and was convicted, and condemned to die. A pardon, then, would not only deliver him from death, but restore him to his place in the family. God's children have all gone astray, and entered into the service of the devil; but the moment a pardon issues to them, then they are brought back; they receive a spirit of adoption, are sealed heirs of God, and restored to all the privileges of children of God.

Another thing effected by justification is to secure for pardoned sinners all needed grace to rescue themselves fully out of the snare of the devil, and all the innumerable entanglements in which they are involved by sin. Beloved, if God were merely to pardon you, and then leave you to get out of sin as you could by yourselves, of what use would your pardon be to you? None in the world. If a child runs away from his father's house, and wanders in a forest, and falls into a deep pit, and the father finds him and undertakes to save him; if he merely pardons him for running away, it will be of no use unless he lifts him up from the pit, and leads him out of the forest. So in the scheme of redemption, whatever help and aid you need, all are guaranteed, if you believe. If God undertakes to save you, He pledges all the light and grace and help necessary to break the chains of Satan and the entanglements of sin, and to lead you back to your Father's house.

I know when individuals are first broken down under a sense of sin, and their hearts gush out with tenderness, they look over their past lives and feel condemned and see that it is all wrong, and then they break down at God's feet and give themselves away to Jesus Christ; they rejoice greatly in the idea that they are done with sin. But in a little while they begin to feel the pressure of old habits and former influences, and they see so much to be done before they overcome them all, that they often get discouraged and cry, "Oh, what shall I do, with so many enemies to meet, and so little strength of resolution or firmness of purpose to overcome them?" Let me tell you, beloved, that if God has undertaken to save you, you have only to keep near to Him, and He will carry you through. You need not fear your enemies. Though the heavens should thunder, the earth rock, and the elements melt, you need not tremble, nor fear enemies without or enemies within. God is for you, and who can be against you? "Who is he that condemneth? It is Christ that died, yea, rather, that is risen again, who is even at the right hand of God, who also maketh intercession for us" (Rom. 8:34).

Justification aligns all the divine attributes in your favor, as much as if you had never sinned. See that holy angel, sent on an errand of love to some distant part of the universe. God's eye follows him, and if He sees him likely to be injured in any way, all the divine attributes are enlisted at once to protect and sustain him. Just as absolutely are they all pledged for you, if you are justified, to protect, support, and save you. Even though you are not free from remaining sin, and are so totally unworthy of God's love, yet if you are truly justified, the only wise and eternal God is pledged for your salvation. How can you tremble and be faint-hearted with such support?

If a human government pardons a criminal, it is then pledged to protect him as a subject, as much as if he had never committed a crime. So it is when God justifies a sinner. The apostle says, "Being justified by faith, we have peace with God" (Rom. 5:1). Henceforth, God is on his side, and pledged as his faithful and eternal friend.

Gospel justification differs from legal justification in this respect: If the law justifies an individual, his pardon lasts only as long as his innocence does. As soon as he transgresses once, his justification is of no more avail. But when the gospel justifies a sinner, it is not so; but "if any man sin, we have an advocate with the Father, Jesus Christ the righteous" (1 John 2:1). A new relation is now constituted, entirely peculiar. The sinner is now brought out from under the covenant of works, and placed under the covenant of grace. He no longer retains God's favor by the tenure of absolute and sinless obedience. If he sins now, he is not thrust back again under the law, but receives the benefit of the new covenant. If he is justified by faith and so made a child of God, he receives the treatment of a child and is corrected, chastised, humbled and brought back again. This does not mean that God calls and saves the sinner without his repenting, but that God never changes His mind when once He undertakes the salvation of a soul.

I know this is thought by some to be very dangerous doctrine.

Some say that to teach that believers are perpetually justified will embolden people to sin. Hardly! It is strange logic to believe that a man who has truly repented of sin, heartily renounced sin, sincerely desires to be free from sin, and knows that God will give him victory over sin, will then be emboldened to commit more sin! If this doctrine emboldens anyone to commit sin, it only shows that he never did repent; that he never hated sin and never loved God for His own sake, but only feigned repentance. And if he loved God it was only a selfish love, because he thought God was going to do him a favor. If he truly hated sin, the consideration that notwithstanding all his unworthiness, God had received him as a child, and would give him a child's treatment, is the very thing to break him down and melt his heart in the most godly sorrow. Oh, how often has the child of God melted in adoring wonder at the goodness of God in using means to bring him back, instead of sending him to hell as he deserved! What ridiculousness to think that after all God had done for him, and the gracious help God was always ready to afford him, he should wander away again when his name was written in the Lamb's book of life!

Being justified by faith secures the discipline of the covenant. God has pledged that if anyone who belongs to Christ goes astray, He will use the discipline of the covenant and bring him back. In the eighty-ninth Psalm, God says, putting David for Christ, "If his children forsake my law, and walk not in my judgments: if they break my statutes, and keep not my commandments; then will I visit their transgression with the rod, and their iniquity with stripes. Nevertheless, my lovingkindness will I not utterly take from him, nor suffer my faithfulness to fail. My covenant will I not break, nor alter the thing that is gone out of my lips" (Ps. 89:30–34).

Thus you see that Christians may always expect to be more readily visited with God's judgments, if they get out of line, than the unrepentant. The sinner may grow fat, live in riches, and have no suffering in his death, all according to God's established principles of government. But let a child of God forsake his God, and go after riches or any other worldly object, and as certain as he is a child, God will smite him with His rod. And when he is smitten and brought back, he will say with the Psalmist, "Before I was afflicted, I went astray: but now have I kept thy word" (Ps. 119:67). Perhaps some of you have known what it is to be afflicted in this way, and to feel that it was good.

Another effect of gospel justification is to insure sanctification.

It not only insures all the means of sanctification, but the actual accomplishment of the work, as that the individual who is truly converted will surely persevere in obedience till he is fitted for heaven and actually saved.

Justification by Faith

Faith is the medium by which the blessing is conveyed to the believer. The proof of this is in the Bible. The text declares it expressly: "Knowing that a man is not justified by the works of the law, but by the faith of Jesus Christ, even we have believed in Jesus Christ, that we might be justified by the faith of Christ, and not by the works of the law: for by the works of the law shall no flesh be justified." The subject is too often treated of in the New Testament to be necessary to go into a labored proof. It is obvious, from the necessity of the case, that if people are saved at all, they must be justified in this way, and not by works of the law, for "by the deeds of the law shall no flesh be justified" (Gal. 2:16).

Several Questions That Need to Be Answered

First, "Why is justification said to be by *faith*, rather than by repentance, or love, or any other grace?"

Answer. It is no where said that people are justified or saved *for* faith, as the ground of their pardon, but only that they are justified *by* faith, as the medium or instrument. If you ask why faith is appointed as the instrument, rather than any other exercise of the mind, the answer is because of the nature and effect of faith. No other exercise could be appointed. What is faith? Faith is that confidence in God that leads us to love and obey Him. We are therefore justified by faith *because* we are sanctified by faith. Faith is the appointed instrument of our justification, because it is the natural instrument of sanctification. Faith is the instrument of bringing us back to obedience, and therefore is designated as the means of obtaining the blessings of that return to God. It is not imputed to us, by an arbitrary act, *for* what it is not, but for what it is, as the foundation of all real obedience to God. This is the reason why faith is made the medium through which pardon comes. It is simply set down to us for what it really is because it first leads us to obey God from a principle of love to God. We are forgiven our sins on account of Christ. It is our duty to repent and obey God, and when we do so, this is imputed to us as what it is, holiness or obedience to God. But for the forgiveness of our past sins, we must rely on Christ. And therefore justification is said to be by faith in Jesus Christ.

The second question is of great importance: "What is justifying faith? What must I believe in order to be saved?"

Answer. Justifying faith does not consist in believing that your sins are forgiven. If that were necessary, you would have to believe it before it was done, or to believe a lie. Remember your sins are not forgiven *until* you believe. But if saving faith is believing that they are already forgiven, it is believing a thing before it takes place, which is absurd. You cannot believe your sins are forgiven before you have the evidence that they are forgiven, and you cannot have the evidence that they are forgiven until it is true that they are forgiven, and they cannot be forgiven until you exercise saving faith. Therefore, saving faith must be believing something else.

Saving faith does not consist in believing that you shall be saved at all. You have no right to believe that you shall be saved at all until after you have exercised justifying or saving faith.

Justifying faith consists in believing the atonement of Christ, or believing the record that God has given of His Son. The correctness of this definition has been doubted by some. And I confess my own mind has undergone a change on this point. It is said that Abraham believed God and it was imputed to him for righteousness. But what did Abraham believe? He believed that he should have a son. Was this all? By no means. His faith included the great blessing that depended on that event, that the Messiah, the Savior of the world, should spring from him. This was the great subject of the Abrahamic covenant, and it depended on his having a son. Abraham's faith, then, included the "Desire of all nations," and was faith in Christ. The Apostle Paul has showed this, at full length, in the third chapter of Galatians, that the sum of the covenant was, "In thee shall all nations be blessed." In verse 16, he writes, "Now to Abraham and his seed were the promise made. He saith not, And to seeds, as of many; but as of one, And to thy seed, which is Christ."

It is said in the eleventh chapter of Hebrews, that the saints are not all spoken of as having believed Christ. But if you examine carefully, you will find that in all cases, faith in Christ is either included in what they believe, or fairly implied by it. Take the case of Abel: "By faith Abel offered unto God a more excellent sacrifice than Cain, by which he obtained witness that he was righteous, God testifying of his gifts: and by it he being dead yet speaketh."

Why was his sacrifice more excellent? Because by offering the firstlings of his flock, he recognized the necessity of the atonement, and that without the shedding of blood there is no remission (Heb. 9:22). Cain was a proud infidel, and offered the fruits of the ground as a mere thank offering for the blessings of Providence, without any admission that he was a sinner and needed an atonement as the ground on which he could hope for pardon.

Some suppose that an individual might exercise justifying faith while denying the divinity and atonement of Jesus Christ. I deny this. The whole sum and substance of revelation, like converging rays, centers on Jesus Christ, His divinity and atonement. All that the prophets and other writers of the Old Testament say about salvation comes to Him. The Old Testament and the New, all the types and shadows, point to Him. All the Old Testament saints were saved by faith in Him. Their faith terminated in the coming Messiah, as that of the New Testament saints did in the Messiah already come. In the fifteenth chapter of First Corinthians, the Apostle Paul shows what place he would assign to this doctrine: "For I delivered unto you first of all that which I also received, how that Christ died for our sins according to the scriptures; And that he was buried, and that he rose again the third day according to the scriptures." Mark that expression, "first of all." It proves that Paul preached that Christ died for sinners, as the "first" or primary doctrine of the gospel. And so you will find it, from one end of the Bible to the other, that the attention of people was directed to this new and living way as the only way of salvation. This truth is the only truth that can sanctify people. They may believe a thousand other things, but this is the great source of sanctification, "God was in Christ, reconciling the world unto himself" (2 Cor. 5:19). And this alone can therefore be justifying faith.

There may be many other acts of faith that may be right and acceptable to God. But nothing is justifying faith except believing the record that God has given of His Son. Simply believing what God has revealed on any point is an act of faith, but justifying faith fastens on Christ, takes hold of His atonement, and embraces Him as the only ground of pardon and salvation. There may be faith in prayer, the faith that is in the exercise of offering up prevailing prayer with God. But that is not properly justifying faith.

Third, "When are people justified?"

Answer. Just as soon as they believe in Christ with the faith that works by love. Sinner, you need not go on under the wrath of Almighty God. You may be justified here on the spot, now, if you will only believe in Christ. Your pardon is ready, made out and sealed with the broad seal of heaven; and the blank will be filled up and the gracious pardon delivered as soon as by one act of faith you receive Jesus Christ as He is offered in the gospel.

Fourth, "How can I know whether I am in a state of justification?"

Answer. You can know it in no way except by inference. God has not revealed it in the Scriptures that you or any other individual are justified. But He has set down the characteristics of a justified person, and declared that all who have these characteristics are justified.

1. *Have you the witness of the Spirit?* All who are justified have this. They have communion and fellowship with the Holy Spirit. He explains the Scriptures to them, and leads them to see their meaning. The Holy Spirit leads us to the Son and to the Father, and reveals the Son in the Scriptures, and reveals the Father. Have you this? If you have, you are justified. If not, you are still in your sins.

2. *Have you the fruits of the Spirit?* They are love, joy, peace, and so on. These are matters of human consciousness. Do you have them? If so, you are justified.

3. *Have you peace with God?* The Apostle Paul said, "Being justified by faith, we have peace with God"(Rom. 5:1). Christ says to His disciples, "My peace I give unto you: not as the world giveth, give I unto you" (John 14:27). And again, "Come unto me, all ye that labour and are heavy laden, and I will give you rest" (Matt. 11:28). Do you find *rest* in Christ? Is your peace like a river, flowing gently through your soul and filling you with calm and heavenly delight? Or do you feel a sense of condemnation before God? Do you feel a sense of acceptance with God, of pardoned sin, of communion with God? This must be a matter of experience, if it exists. Don't imagine you *can be in* a justified state and yet have no evidence of it. You may have great peace in reality, filling your soul, and yet not draw the inference that you are justified. I remember the time when my mind was in a state of such sweet peace that it seemed to me as if all nature were listening for God to speak. But yet I was not aware that this was the peace of God, or that it was evidence of my being in a justified state. I thought I had lost all my conviction of sin, and actually undertook to bring back the sense of condemnation that I had before. I did not draw the inference that I was justified until after the love of God was so shed abroad in my soul by the Holy Spirit that I was compelled to cry

out, "Lord, it is enough, I can bear no more."* I do not believe it possible for the sense of condemnation to remain where the act of pardon is already past.

4. *Have you the spirit of adoption?* If you are justified, you are also adopted as one of God's dear children and He has sent forth His Spirit into your heart so that you naturally cry, "Abba, Father!" He seems to you just like a father, and you want to call Him *father*. Do you know anything of this? It is one thing to *call* God your father in heaven, and another thing to *feel* toward Him as a father. This is one evidence of a justified state, when God gives the spirit of adoption.

What Is Your State?

I would like to ask, "Are you in a state of justification? Do you honestly think you are justified?"

I have briefly run over the subject and showed what justification is not, and what it is, how you can be saved and the evidence of justification. Are you saved? Would you dare to die now? Suppose the loud thunders of the last trumpet were now to shake the universe, and you should see the Son of God coming to judgment, are you ready? Could you look up calmly and say, "Father, this is a solemn night, but Christ has died and God has justified me and who is the one who shall condemn me?"

If you think you were ever justified, and yet have not at present the evidence of it, I want to ask you a question: "Are you under the discipline of the covenant?" If not, have you any reason to believe you ever were justified? God's covenant with you, if you belong to Christ, is this: "If they backslide, I will visit their iniquity with the rod and chasten them with stripes." Do you feel the stripes? Is God awakening your mind and convicting your conscience, is He smiting you? If not, where are the evidences that He is dealing with you as a son? If you are not walking with God, and at the same time are not under chastisement, you cannot have any good reason to believe you are God's child.

Those of you who have evidence that you are justified should maintain your relationship with God and live up to your real privileges. This is immensely important. There is no virtue in being distrustful and unbelieving. It is important to your growth in grace. One reason why many Christians do not grow in grace is

---

*See Finney's *Answers Prayer* for a detailed explanation of his conversion to Christ.

they are afraid to claim the privileges of God's children that belong to them. Rely upon it, beloved, this is no virtuous humility but criminal unbelief. If you have the evidence that you are justified, take the occasion from it to press forward to holiness of heart, and come to God with all the boldness that an angel would, and know how near you are to Him. It is your duty to do so. Why should you hold back? Why are you afraid to recognize the covenant of grace in its full extent? Here are the provisions of your Father's house, all ready and free. Are you converted, justified and restored to His favor, and yet afraid to sit down at your Father's table? Do not plead that you are so unworthy. This is nothing except self-righteousness and unbelief. True, you are so unworthy. But if you are justified, then it is your duty to take hold of the promises as belonging to you. Take any promise you can find in the Bible that is applicable, and go with it to your Father, and plead it before Him believing. Do you think He will deny it? These exceeding great and precious promises were given you for this very purpose, that you may become a partaker of the divine nature. Why then should you doubt? Come along, beloved, come along up to the privileges that belong to you, and take hold of the love, peace, and joy offered to you in this holy gospel.

If you are not in a state of justification, however much you have done and prayed and suffered, you are nothing. If you have not believed in Christ, if you have not received and trusted in Him, as He is set forth in the gospel, you are yet in a state of condemnation and wrath. You may have been for weeks and months and even for years groaning with distress, but for all that, you are still in the gall of bitterness. Here you see the line drawn. The moment you pass this, you are in a state of justification.

Dear friend, are you now in a state of wrath? Now believe in Christ. All your waiting and groaning will not bring you any nearer. Do you say you want more conviction? I tell you to come now to Christ. Do you say you must wait till you have prayed more? What is the use of praying in unbelief? Will the prayers of a condemned rebel avail? Do you say you are so unworthy? But Christ died for such as you. He comes right to you now where you are. Where do you sit? Where is that individual I am speaking to? Sinner, you need not wait. You need not go home in your sins with that heavy load on your heart. Now is the day of salvation. Hear the Word of God, "If thou shalt confess with thy mouth the Lord Jesus, and shalt believe in thine heart that God raised him from the dead, thou shalt be saved" (Rom. 10:9).

Do you say, "What must I believe?" Believe just what God says of His Son. Believe any of those great fundamental truths God has revealed respecting the way of salvation, and rest your soul on it, and you shall be saved. Will you now trust Jesus Christ to dispose of you? Have you confidence enough in Christ to leave yourself with Him, to dispose of your body and your soul for time and eternity? Can you say: "Here, Lord, I give myself away; 'Tis all that I can do"?

Perhaps you are trying to pray yourself out of your difficulties before coming to Christ. Sinner, it will do no good. Now, cast yourself down at His feet and leave your soul in His hands. Say to Him, "Lord, I give myself to you, with all my powers of body and mind. Use me and dispose of me as you will, for your own glory. I know you will do right and that is all I desire." Will you do it?

12

NECESSITY OF DIVINE TEACHING*

"Nevertheless I tell you the truth; It is expedient for you that I go away: for if I go not away, the Comforter will not come unto you; but if I depart, I will send him unto you. And when he is come, he will reprove the world of sin, and of righteousness, and of judgment: Of sin, because they believe not on me; Of righteousness, because I go to my Father, and ye see me no more; Of judgment, because the prince of this world is judged. I have yet many things to say unto you, but ye cannot bear them now. Howbeit when he, the Spirit of truth, is come, he will guide you into all truth: for he shall not speak of himself; but whatsoever he shall hear, that shall he speak: and he will shew you things to come" (John 16:7–13).

The doctrine of the necessity of divine influence to enlighten and sanctify the minds of people is very abundantly taught in the Bible, and is generally maintained as a matter of opinion at least in all orthodox churches. But, as a matter of fact, there seems to be very little available knowledge of the gospel among mankind. So little knowledge of the gospel that it exerts comparatively little influence. The great ends of the gospel have hardly begun to be realized in the production of holiness upon the earth. It is a grand question whether we do need divine influence to attain the fullness of the gospel; and if we do need it, then in what degree do we need it and why? If our minds are unsettled on this question, we shall be unsettled on all the subjects that primarily concern our sanctification.

Lectures to Professing Christians, pp. 252–264.

The Pursuit of God Is Reasonable and Spiritual

Our mind is capable of understanding the historical facts of Christianity, just as it comprehends any other historical facts, and is also capable of understanding the doctrinal propositions of the gospel.

Our mind can understand those abstractions making up the skeleton of the gospel, such as, the being and character of God, and the divine authority and inspiration of the Scriptures. That is, the mind can understand them as propositions, and see the evidence that supports them as true, just as it can understand any proposition.

For instance, a person, by his reason, may understand the law of God. He can understand that it requires him to exercise perfect love toward God and all other beings. He can see the ground of his obligation to do this because he is a moral being. He knows by experience what love is for he has exercised love toward different objects. And he can, therefore, form or comprehend the idea of love so far as to see the reasonableness of the requirement. He can understand the foundation and the force of moral obligation, and see, in some measure, the extent of his obligation to love God.

So, likewise, he can see that he is a sinner, and that he cannot be saved by his own works. He has broken the law, so that the law can never justify him. He can see that if he is to ever be saved, he must be justified through mere mercy by an act of pardon.

I might go through the whole circle of theology and show that the human understanding is capable of knowing it, in the abstract, as a system of propositions, to be received and believed, on evidence, like any other science. I do not mean to be understood as saying that unaided reason can attain any available knowledge of the things of Christianity, or any such knowledge as will be effectual to produce a sanctifying change.

The Need for Divine Teaching

At this point it is necessary to distinguish between knowledge which might be available to one who was himself disposed to love and obey God, and what will be available to a sinner wholly indisposed to holiness. It is easy to see that one who is disposed to do right would be influenced to duty by a far less amount of illumination, or a far less clear and vivid view of motives, than one who is disposed to do wrong. What we are now inquiring after respects the matter of fact in this world. Whether the knowledge attainable by our present faculties would be available to influence us to do right, were there no sin in the world, is more than I can say. As a matter of fact, the knowledge Adam had when in a state of innocence did not avail to influence him to do right. But we are now speaking of things as they are in this world, and to show what is the reason why people, as sinners, can have no available knowledge of divine things; no such knowledge as will, as a matter of fact, influence them to love and serve God.

Knowledge, to avail anything toward effecting its object, must be such as will influence the mind. The will must be controlled. And to do this, the mind must have such a view of things as to excite emotion, corresponding to the object in view. Mere intellect never will move the soul to act. A pure scientific abstraction of the intellect, that does not touch the feelings, or excite any emotion, is wholly unavailing to move the will. It is so everywhere. It would be so in heaven. You must bring the mind under a degree of excitement to influence the will in any case. In the case of sinners, to influence sinners to love God, you must have a great degree of light, such as will powerfully excite the mind and produce strong emotions. The reasons for obedience must be made to appear with great strength and vividness, so as to subdue their rebellious hearts and bring them voluntarily to obey God. This is available knowledge. This people never have, and never can have, without the Spirit of God. If people were disposed to do right, I know not how far their knowledge, attainable by unaided reason, might avail. But, as they are universally and totally indisposed to do right, this knowledge will never do it. I will mention some of the reasons.

All the knowledge we can have here of spiritual things is by analogy or comparison. Our minds are here shut up in the body, and we derive all our ideas from external objects through the senses. Now, we never can obtain knowledge of spiritual or eternal things in this way sufficient to rightly influence our wills. Our bodily powers were not created for this. All the ideas we can have of the spiritual world are by analogy, or comparing them with the things around us. It is easily seen that all ideas conveyed to our minds in this way must be extremely imperfect and that we do not after all get the true idea in our minds. The Jewish types were probably the most forcible means that God could then use for giving to the Jews a correct idea of the gospel. Since the eastern nations were accustomed by their education to the use of figures, parables, and types, these were probably the most impressive and happy mode that could be devised to prepare their minds for the truth, and give them a more full idea of the plan of redemption. And yet, it is obvious that the ideas communicated in this way were extremely imperfect; and that without divine illumination to make them see the reality more fully than they could by unaided reason, they never would have gotten any available knowledge in this way.

So words are merely signs of ideas. They are not the ideas, but the representatives of ideas. It is often very difficult and sometimes impossible to convey ideas by words. Take a little child and attempt to talk with him; how difficult it can be on many subjects to get your ideas into his little mind. He must have some experience of the things you are trying to teach before you can convey ideas to him by words.

Suppose your church were made up entirely of people who were blind and had never seen colors. Then suppose that on the wall of the sanctuary hung a most grand and beautiful painting, and the preacher was a perfect master of the subject who tried to describe it to his people. No language could give an idea of the painting as to enable them to form a picture of it in their minds. When, on any subject, we are obliged from the nature of the case to use figurative language, analogies, and resemblances, the knowledge we communicate is necessarily defective and inadequate. Have you ever heard a description of a person or place until you thought you had an accurate knowledge of it, but when you came to see it, you found that you had no true idea of the reality at all?

Suppose an individual were to visit this world from another planet where all things are constituted on the most opposite principles from those adopted here. Suppose he remained here long enough to learn our language, and then undertook to give us a description of the planet he left. We would understand it according to our ideas and experience. Now, if the analogy between the two worlds is imperfect, then it is plain that our knowledge of things there from his description must be imperfect in proportion. So, when we find in the Bible descriptions of heaven and hell, or anything in the invisible world, it is plain that from mere words we can get no true ideas at all adequate to the reality.

The wickedness of our hearts is so great as to pervert our judgment and shut out from our minds much that we might understand of the things of God. When a person's mind is so perverted on any subject that he will not take up the evidence concerning it, he cannot, of course, come to the knowledge of the truth on that subject. This is our case with regard to Christianity. Perverseness of heart so shuts out the light that the intellect does not and from the nature of things *cannot* get even the ideas it might otherwise gain respecting divine things.

Prejudice is a great obstacle to the reception of correct knowledge concerning Christianity. Take the case of the disciples of Jesus Christ. They had strong Jewish prejudices respecting the plan of salvation; so strong that all the instructions of Christ himself could not make them understand the truth. After teaching them personally for three years, with all the talent, simplicity, and skill He was master of, He could never get their minds in possession of the first principles of the gospel. Up to His very death, He could not make them see that He should die and rise from the dead. Therefore, He says in His conversation with them: "If I go not away, the Comforter will not come unto you; but if I depart, I will send him unto you" (John 16:7). This was the very design of His going away from them, that the Spirit of truth might come and show the meaning of all Christ had taught them. The general truth is this: "Without divine illumination people can understand the Bible enough to convict and condemn them, but not enough to sanctify and save them."

Some may ask, "Then what is the use of revelation?" It is of much use. The Bible is as plain as it can be. Who doubts that our Lord Jesus Christ gave instructions to His disciples as plainly as He could? See the pains He took to illustrate His teaching; how simple His language; how He brought His teaching down for the weakest comprehension as a parent would to a little child. And yet, it remains true that without divine illumination the unaided reason of anyone never did (and never will) attain any available knowledge of the gospel. The difficulty lies in the subject. The Bible contains the gospel as plainly as it can be made. That is, it contains the signs of the ideas, as far as language can represent the things of Christianity. Language will forever be inadequate to put our minds in real possession of the things themselves. The difference is in our ignorance and sin, and in the nature of the subject. This is the reason why we need divine illumination to get any available knowledge of the gospel.

Only the Spirit of God Can Supply the Needed Illumination

The Bible says, "No man can say that Jesus is the Lord, but by the Holy Ghost" (1 Cor. 12:3). Now, the abstract proposition of the

Deity of Christ can be proved as a matter of science so as to gain the assent of any unbiased mind to the truth that Jesus is Lord. Nevertheless, no one except the Holy Spirit can lock that teaching in the mind in such a way as to hold the soul and make it available to sanctify the heart.

Christ himself said, "No man can come to me, except the Father which hath sent me draw him: and I will raise him up at the last day. It is written in the prophets, And they shall all be taught of God. Every man therefore that hath heard, and hath learned of the Father, cometh unto me" (John 6:44–45). Here the drawing spoken of is evidently the teaching of the Holy Spirit. They must be taught of God, and learn of the Father, before they can ever come to Christ.

Christ says, "It is expedient for you that I go away: for if I go not away, the Comforter will not come unto you" (John 16:7). The Greek word *Paracletos* is translated here as *Comforter* and properly means "Helper" or "Teacher." "When he is come, he will reprove the world of sin, and of righteousness, and of judgment: Of sin, because they believe not on me; Of righteousness, because I go to my Father, and ye see me no more; Of judgment, because the prince of this world is judged. I have yet many things to say unto you, but ye cannot bear them now. Howbeit, when he, the Spirit of truth, is come, he will guide you into all truth: for he shall not speak of himself; but whatsoever he shall hear, that shall he speak: and he will show you things to come" (John 16:8–13).

So, in the fourteenth chapter the Savior says, "I will pray the Father, and he shall give you another Comforter, that he may abide with you for ever; Even the Spirit of truth, whom the world cannot receive, because it seeth him not, neither knoweth him: but ye know him; for he dwelleth with you, and shall be in you" (John 14:16–17). And again, in the 26th verse, "But the Comforter, which is the Holy Ghost, whom the Father will send in my name, he shall teach you all things, and bring all things to your remembrance, whatsoever I have said unto you." Here you see the office of the Spirit of God is to instruct people with regard to the things of Christianity.

The Spirit of God does what the spoken or written Word cannot. All teaching by words, whether by Jesus Christ, the apostles, or any inspired or uninspired teacher, can never put the mind in possession of the idea of spiritual things. The kind of teaching we need is this: someone to teach us the things of Christianity who is not obliged to depend on words or the medium of the senses. We want some way in which the ideas themselves can be brought to our minds and not merely the signs of the ideas. We want a teacher who can directly approach the mind itself and not through the senses; who can exhibit the ideas of Christianity without being obliged to use words. This the Spirit of God can do.

The manner in which the Spirit of God does this is what we can never know in this world. But the fact is undeniable, that He can reach the mind without the use of words and can put our minds in possession of the ideas themselves, of which the types or figures or words of the human teacher are only the signs or imperfect representatives. The human teacher can only use words to our senses, and finds it impossible to possess us of the ideas of that which we have never experienced. But the Holy Spirit, having direct access to the mind, can, through the outward sign, possess us of the actual idea of things. What Christian does not know this as a matter of fact? What Christian does not know, from his own experience, that the Spirit of God does lead him instantly to see something in a passage of Scripture that all his study and effort of mind to know the meaning of could never have given him in the world?

Take again the case of a painting and a blind congregation. Suppose I was laboring to describe the combinations of colors and their eyes were suddenly opened. They could see for themselves the very things I was vainly trying to describe in words. Now, the office of the Spirit of God is to open the spiritual eye and bring the things we try to describe by analogy and signs before the mind in all their living reality, so as to put the mind in complete possession of the thing as it is. Only the Holy Spirit can do this.

No one but the Spirit of God so knows the things of God as to be able to give us the idea of those things correctly. "What man knoweth the things of a man, save the spirit of man which is in him?" (1 Cor. 2:11). What can a beast know of the things of a man, of a man's character, designs, etc.? I can speak to your consciousness, since we are human beings. But I cannot speak these things to the consciousness of a beast, neither can a beast speak of these things, because he has not the spirit of a person within him. Similarly, "The things of God knoweth no man, but the Spirit of God" (1 Cor. 2:11). The Spirit of God, knowing from consciousness the things of God, possesses a different kind of knowledge of these things from what other beings can possess; therefore, He can give us the kind of instruction we need and such as no other being can give.

Every Person May Be Instructed by the Holy Spirit

Jesus Christ says God is more willing to give His Holy Spirit to them who ask Him, than parents are to give their children bread. "Ask and it shall be given you; seek, and ye shall find; knock, and it shall be opened unto you" (Luke 11:9). "And all things, whatsoever ye shall ask in prayer, believing, ye shall receive" (Matt. 21:22). "Therefore I say unto you, What things soever ye desire, when ye pray, believe that ye receive them, and ye shall have them" (Mark 11:24). James says, "If any of you lack wisdom, let him ask of God, that giveth to all men liberally, and upbraideth not; *and it shall be given him*" (James 1:5). Since God has made these unlimited promises, that *all men*, who will ask of Him may have as much divine illumination as they ask for, then it is true that all men have as much divine illumination as they ask for.

Why Some Have Less Divine Illumination Than Others

They do not ask for it in such a manner or degree as they need it, or they ask amiss or from selfish motives.

The Apostle James says, "Ye ask, and receive not, because ye ask amiss, that ye may consume it upon your lusts" (James 4:3). When a person has a selfish motive for asking or some other reason than a desire to glorify God, he should not expect to receive divine illumination. If his object in asking for the Holy Spirit is that he may always be happy, or that he may be very wise in the Scriptures, or be looked upon as an eminent Christian, or have his experience spoken of as remarkable, or any other selfish view, he will not receive what he asks.

They do not use the proper means to attain what they ask, and therefore, they do not have the divine illumination that they need.

Suppose a person neglects reading his Bible, and yet asks God to give him a knowledge of Christianity. That is tempting God. The manner in which God gives knowledge is through the Bible, and the other appointed means of instruction. If a person will not use these means when they are in his power, however much he may pray, he should not expect divine instruction. "Faith cometh by hearing, and hearing by the word of God" (Rom. 10:17).

There is an important difference between the cases of those who possess these means, and those who do not. I suppose that a person may learn the gospel, and receive all the illumination he needs under any circumstances of privation of means. If he were on a desolate island, or in any other circumstances where he absolutely could not have access to any means of instruction, he might receive direct illumination from the Spirit of God. Some very remarkable cases of this kind have occurred.

I have known one case, which I looked upon at the time as miraculous and for that reason have seldom mentioned it, feeling that even the church was not prepared to receive it. When I was an evangelist, I labored once in a revival in a neighborhood where there were many Germans. They had received but little instruction, and many of them could not read. But when the gospel was preached among them, the Spirit of God was poured out, and a most powerful revival followed. In the midst of the harvest, if a meeting was appointed at any place, the whole neighborhood would come together and fill the house and hang upon the preacher's lips while he tried to possess their minds with the truth of the gospel. One poor German woman naturally intelligent, but who could not read, related her experience (which was certified by her neighbors) in one of these meetings. With many tears and a heart full of joy, she said, "When I loved God, I longed to read the Bible, and I prayed to Jesus Christ. I said and felt, 'O Jesus, Thou can teach me to read thy Holy Bible,' and the Lord taught me to read. There was a Bible in the house, and when I had prayed, I thought I could read the Bible, and I got the book and opened it, and the words were just what I had heard people read. I said 'O Lord Jesus Christ, Thou can teach me to read,' and I believed He could, and I thought I did read, but I went and asked the school teacher if I read, and she said I read it right, and the Lord has taught me to read my Bible, blessed be His name for it." It is possible that the school teacher to whom she referred was in the house and heard her tell this. At all events she was a woman of good character among her neighbors, and some of the most respectable of them afterward told me they did not doubt the truth of what she said. I do not doubt it was true.

At the time I thought it was a miracle, but with the new facts that have been developed respecting the indestructibleness of the memory, I have thought this case might be explained in this way: that she may have been told the names of letters and their powers, when young, and now the Spirit of God in answer to her prayer had quickened her mind, and brought it all to her remembrance so that she could read the Bible.

One evening President Mahan stated here at church something that shows that every impression made on the mind of man remains there forever.[1] One case that he mentioned was that of an old lady, who when she was young, had read some lines of poetry relating a little story; and years later, when old, she wished to tell the story to some children to whom she thought it would be useful. To her surprise every line came up fresh in her memory, and she repeated them word for word, although she had never committed them to memory at all, but only read them when she was young.

Another was the case of an ignorant servant girl. She had once lived with a learned minister who was accustomed to reading aloud the Hebrew Bible in his study, which was in hearing of the place where this girl did her work. Of course, she understood nothing of what the words meant, but heard only the sounds. Years later when she was on her deathbed, she astonished the bystanders by reciting whole chapters of Hebrew and Chaldaic. The neighbors at first thought it was a miracle, but at length learned the explanation. It is plain from this that even unintelligible sounds may be so impressed on the memory that afterward recur with entire distinctness. I suppose that was the case with this poor German woman; that the Spirit of God in answer to her fervent prayer, so refreshed her memory as to recall the sounds and forms of letters she had been told as a child, and thus enabled her at once to read the Bible. I say, therefore, that while those who do not possess any outward means of instruction may obtain directly from the Spirit of God whatever degree or kind of illumination they need in the things of God; those who possess or can obtain the outward means and do not use them, tempt God when they pray for divine illumination and neglect the use of means for obtaining knowledge. To those who have the opportunity, "faith cometh by hearing, and hearing by the word of God." If anyone keeps away from the means within his reach, he can expect illumination in no other way. Whereas, if he is shut out from the use of means, as God is true to His promises, we must believe that he can be illuminated without means to any extent he needs.

Another reason why many do not receive the illumination from the Spirit of God is because they grieve the Spirit in many ways. They live in such a manner as to grieve or offend the Holy Spirit, so that He cannot consistently grant them His illuminating grace.

Another reason is that some *depend* on the instruction of others without divine influence. How many rely on the instruction they

---

[1]President Asa Mahan, who was the first President of Oberlin College while Finney was Professor.

receive from ministers or commentaries or books or their own powers of inquiry, not feeling that all these things, without the Spirit of God, will only kill but can never make alive: can only damn but never save. It seems as though the whole Church is in error on this point, depending on means for divine knowledge without feeling that no means are available without the Spirit of God. Oh! If the Church felt this: if they really felt that all the means in creation are unavailing without the teaching of the Holy Spirit, how they would pray and cleanse their hands, and humble their hearts until the Comforter would descend to teach them all that they need to know of God.

Self-confidence is another reason why so little is experienced of divine illumination. As long as people who profess to be Christians place confidence in learning, or criticism, or their natural ingenuity to learn the ways of God, they are not likely to enjoy much of the illumination of the Spirit of God.

People Are Responsible for All the Light They Have and Could Have.

This is a universal truth acknowledged by all mankind; a man is just as responsible for what light he might have as for that he actually has. The common law, which is the voice of common reason, adopts it as a maxim that no one who breaks the law is to be excused for ignorance of the law, because all are held bound to know what the law is. So it is with your children; in a case where they might know your will, you consider them so much the more blameworthy if they offend. So it is with God; where men have both the outward means of instruction, and the inward teachings of the Holy Spirit absolutely within their reach, and yet they sin ignorantly, they are not only without excuse on that score, but their ignorance is itself a crime, an aggravation of their guilt. All people are plainly without excuse for not possessing all the knowledge that would be available for their perfect and immediate sanctification.

God's People Need God's Teaching

Do you see what the effect is of all other instructions on a congregation where no divine influence is enjoyed? It may convince the church of duty, but will never produce sanctification. It may harden the heart, but will never change it. Without divine influence, it is but a savor of death unto death.

It is important to use all the appropriate means of Christian instruction in our power, as the medium through which the Holy Spirit conveys divine illumination to the mind.

There is no reason why we should not use the means in our power and apply our natural faculties to acquire knowledge of Christianity as faithfully as if we could understand the whole subject without divine influence. If we do not use means when within our power, we have no reason to expect divine aid. When we help ourselves, God helps us. When we use our natural faculties to understand these things, we may expect God will enlighten us. To turn our eyes away from the light, and then pray that we may be made to see is to tempt God.

They are blind leaders of the blind who attempt to teach the things of Christianity without themselves being taught by God. No degree of learning, or power of discrimination as to the didactics of theology will ever make a person a successful teacher of Christianity unless he enjoys the illuminating powers of the Holy Spirit. He is blind if he supposes he understands the Bible without this; and if he undertakes to teach Christianity, he deceives himself, and all who depend on him, and both will fall into the ditch together.

If a person teaches the gospel with the Holy Spirit sent down from heaven, then he will be understood. He may understand the gospel himself, and yet not make his listeners understand it, because the Holy Spirit is not sent on them as well as upon himself. But, if the Spirit of God is on them, precisely in proportion as he understands the real meaning of the gospel he will make his hearers understand it.

In preaching the gospel, ministers should never use texts, the meaning of which they have not been taught by the Spirit of the Lord. They should not attempt to explain passages of which they are not confident they have been taught the meaning by the Holy Spirit. It is presumption. And they need not do it, for they may always have the teachings of the Spirit by asking Him. God is always more ready to bestow divine illumination than an earthly parent is to give bread to his child. And if they ask as a child asks his mother when he is hungry, then they may always receive all the light they need. This is applicable both to preachers and to teachers of Sunday School and Bible Classes. If any of them attempt to teach the Scriptures without themselves being taught by the Holy Spirit, they are no more fit to teach than the most ignorant person in the streets is fit to teach astronomy.

I fear both ministers and teachers generally have understood very little of their need of this divine teaching, and have felt very little of the necessity of praying over their sermons and Bible lessons till they feel confident that the Spirit of God has possessed their minds with the true idea of the Word of God.

If this was done as it ought to be, their instructions would be far more effectual than we now see them. Do you, who are teachers of Bible and Sunday school classes, believe this? Are you in the habit of seeking consciously and uniformly the true idea of every lesson on your knees in prayer? Or do you go to some commentary and then peddle your dry stuff without any of the Holy Spirit in your teaching? If you do this, let me tell you that you had better be doing something else. What would you say of a minister if you knew he never prayed over his texts. You might as well have Balaam's ass for a minister, and even the dumb beast in such a case might speak with man's voice and rebuke the madness of such a man. He could give just as much available instruction to reach the deep fountains of the heart as such a preacher. Well, now, this is just as important for a Sunday school teacher as for a minister. If you do not pray over your lesson until you feel that God has taught you the idea contained in it, *beware*! How dare you go and teach that for Christianity, which you do not honestly suppose you have been taught of God!

It is a vast error in theological students when they study to get the views of all the great teachers, the tomes of the fathers and doctors, and everybody's opinion as to what the Bible means, but ignore the teaching of the Holy Spirit. With hearts as cold as marble, instead of going right to the source of light, they go and gather up the husks of learning and peddle it out among the churches as religious instruction. Horrible! While they do thus, we never shall have an efficient ministry.

It is good to get all the help we can from books to understand the Word of God. But we ought never to rest in anything we get from book learning until we are satisfied that we have been taught the meaning of the text by God himself.

I have tried hard to make this impression, and I believe I have succeeded in some degree on the theological students at Oberlin. And if I had done it more, I have no doubt that I might have succeeded better. And I can say, that when I studied theology I spent many hours on my knees and perhaps I might say weeks, often with the Bible before me, laboring and praying to come at the very mind of the Holy Spirit. I do not say this boastingly, but as a matter of fact, to show that the sentiment here advanced is no recent or novel opinion of mine. And I have always gotten my texts and sermons on my knees. And yet, I am conscious that I have gained very little knowledge in Christianity compared with what I might have had, had I done this right away.

How little knowledge has the great body of the Church respecting the Word of God! Put them, for instance, to read the letters of Paul and Peter and other parts, and probably they will not have knowledge enough to give an opinion as to the real meaning of one-tenth of the Bible. No wonder the Church is not sanctified! They need *more truth*. Our Savior said, "Sanctify them through thy truth" (John 17:17). This grand means of sanctification must be more richly enjoyed before the Church will know what entire sanctification means. The Church does not understand the Bible. And the reason is *they have not gone to the Author* to explain it. Although they have this blessed privilege everyday, and just as often as they choose, of carrying the Book right to the Author for His explanation; yet how little, how very little, does the Church know of the Bible which they are conscious they have been taught to know by the Holy Spirit. Read the text of this sermon again, read other similar passages, and then say if professing Christians are not exceedingly to blame for not understanding the Bible.

Do you see the necessity for giving yourself up to the study of the Bible under divine teaching? I have recently recommended several books to you to read, such as, Wesley's Thoughts on Christian Perfection, the Memoirs of Brainerd Taylor, Payson, Mrs. Rogers, and others. I have found that, in a certain state of mind, such books are useful to read. But I never pretend to make but *one book* my study. I read them occasionally, but have little time or inclination to read other books much while I have so much to learn of my Bible. I find it like a deep mine, the more I work it, the richer it grows. We must read that more than any or all other books. We must pause and pray over it, verse after verse, and compare part with part, dwell on it, digest it, and get it into our minds till we feel that the Spirit of God has filled us with the spirit of holiness.

Will you do it? Will you lay your hearts open to God, and not give Him rest till He has filled you with divine knowledge? Will you *search* the Scriptures? I have often been asked by young converts and young men preparing for the ministry, what they should read. *Read the Bible*. I would give the same answer five hundred times. Over and above all other things, study the Bible. It is a sad fact that most young men, when they enter the ministry, often know less of the Bible than of any other book they study. Alas! Alas! If they had the spirit of James Brainerd Taylor, his love for the Scriptures, his prayer for divine teaching, we should no longer hear the groans of the churches over the barrenness of so many young preachers, who come out of our seminaries full of book learning and almost destitute of the Holy Spirit.

13

CHRIST OUR ADVOCATE*

"And if any man sin, we have an advocate with the Father, Jesus Christ the righteous: and he is the propitiation for our sins: and not for ours only, but also for the sins of the whole world" (1 John 2:1–2).

The Bible abounds with governmental analogies. These are designed for our instruction, but if we receive instruction from them it is because there is a real analogy in many points between the government of God and human government.

An advocate is one who pleads the cause of another. He represents that person, acting in his name. He uses his influence in behalf of another by the other's request, with his purpose being to secure justice.

The advocate may be asked to defend the accused. If one has been accused of committing a crime, an advocate may be employed to represent him during the trial, defending him against the charge and preventing his conviction if possible.

An advocate may be employed to secure a pardon when a criminal has been justly condemned and is under sentence. That is, an advocate may be employed either to secure *justice* for his client, or to obtain *mercy* for him in case he is condemned. He may be employed either to prevent his conviction, or when convicted, he may be employed to set aside the execution of the law upon the criminal.

Sermons on Gospel Themes, pp. 292–306.

Christ Is Our Advocate in the Government of God

Christ is employed to plead the cause of sinners, but not at the bar of justice. He is not to defend them against the charge of sin, because the question of their guilt is already settled. The Bible presents sinners as condemned *already*; and such is the fact, as every sinner knows. Every sinner in the world knows he has sinned, and that consequently he must be condemned by the law of God. The office of advocate, then, is exercised by Christ in respect to sinners; not at the bar of justice, but at the throne of grace, at the footstool of sovereign mercy. He is employed, not to prevent the *conviction* of the sinner, but to prevent his *execution*; not to prevent his being condemned, but since he is already condemned, to prevent his being *damned*.

Being the advocate of sinners implies that Christ is employed at a throne of grace and not at the bar of justice. He is to plead for *sinners* as such. He does not plead for those who are merely *charged* with sin, for those whose charge is not yet established. Being his advocate implies that the guilt of the sinner is already ascertained, the verdict of guilty given, the sentence of the law pronounced, and so the sinner awaits his execution.

Christ was appointed by God as the advocate of sinners and this implies a merciful disposition in God. If God had not been mercifully disposed toward sinners, He would not have appointed an advocate and no question of forgiveness would have been raised.

Since Christ is an advocate, it also implies that the exercise of mercy on certain conditions is *possible*. Not only is God mercifully disposed, but to *reveal* this disposition in the actual pardon of sin is possible. If this had not been the case, then no advocate would have been appointed.

Therefore, the condemned may have hope. Sinners are prisoners, but in this world they are not yet prisoners of despair. They are prisoners of hope.

Appointing Christ as an advocate implies that there is a governmental necessity for the interposition of an advocate; that the sinner's relations are such, and his character such, that he cannot be admitted to plead his own cause in his own name. He is condemned; he is no longer on trial. In this respect he is under sentence for a capital crime; consequently, he is an outlaw, and the government cannot recognize him as being capable of performing any legal act. His relations to the government forbid that in his own name, or in his own person, he could appear before God. So far as his own personal influence with the government is concerned, he is as a dead man: he is *civilly* dead. Therefore, he must appear by his next friend, or by his advocate, if he is heard at all. He may not appear in his own name and in his own person, but must appear by an advocate who is acceptable to the government.

Qualifications of an Advocate

He must be the uncompromising friend of the government. Observe, he appears to pray for mercy to be extended to the guilty party whom he represents. Of course he must not himself be the enemy of the government of whom he asks so great a favor, but he should be known to be the devoted friend of the government whose mercy he prays may be extended to the guilty.

He must be the uncompromising friend of the dishonored law. The sinner has greatly dishonored both the law and the lawgiver by his conduct, and he has publicly denounced both. By his constant disobedience, the sinner has proclaimed, in the most emphatic manner, that the law is not worthy of obedience, and that the lawgiver is a tyrant. Now the advocate must be a *friend* to this law. He must not sell himself to the dishonor of the law nor consent to its dishonor. He must not *second-guess* the law; for in this case he places the lawgiver in a position in which, if he would set aside the penalty and exercise mercy, he would consent to the dishonor of the law, and by a public act himself condemn the law. The advocate seeks to dispense with the execution of the law; but he must not offer, as a reason, that the law is unreasonable and unjust. For in this case he renders it impossible for the lawgiver to set aside the execution without consenting to the assertion that the law is not good. In that case the lawgiver would condemn himself instead of the sinner. Therefore, it is plain that he must be the uncompromising friend of the law, or he can never secure the exercise of mercy without involving the lawgiver himself in the crime of dishonoring the law.

The advocate must be *righteous*; that is, he must be clear of any complicity in the crime of the sinner. He must have no fellowship with his crime. There must be no *charge* or *suspicion* of guilt resting upon the advocate. Unless he himself is clear of the crime of which the criminal is accused, he is not the proper person to represent him before a throne of mercy.

He must be the *compassionate friend* of the sinner—not of his *sins*, but of the sinner himself. This distinction is very plain. Everyone knows that a parent can be greatly opposed to the wickedness of his children, while he has great compassion for them. He is not a true friend to the sinner who really sympathizes with his sins.

I have several times heard sinners say the reason they won't become Christians is that their friends don't want them to; they have a great many "dear" friends who are opposed to their obeying God, desiring them to live on in their sins. They do not want them to change and become holy, but desire them to remain in their worldly-mindedness and sinfulness. I tell such people that these are their friends in the same sense that the devil is their friend. And would they call the devil their good friend, their kind friend, because he sympathized with their sins and wished them not to become Christians? Would you call a man your friend who wished you to commit murder, or robbery, tell a lie, or commit any crime? Suppose this "friend" came and asked you to commit some great crime, would you regard that man as your friend? No!

No man is a true friend of a sinner unless he is desirous that he should abandon his sins. If any person would have you continue in your sins, he is the adversary of your soul. Instead of being in any proper sense your friend, he is playing the devil's part to ruin you.

Now observe: Christ is the compassionate friend of sinners, a friend in the best and truest sense. He does not sympathize with your sins, but His heart is set upon saving you from your sins. I said He must be the *compassionate* friend of sinners; and His compassion must be stronger than death, or He will never meet the necessities of the case.

Another qualification must be that he is able sufficiently to honor the law, which sinners by their transgression have dishonored. He seeks to avoid the execution of the dishonored law of God. The law having been dishonored by sin in the highest degree, must either be honored by its execution on the criminal, or the lawgiver must in some other way bear testimony in favor of the law before He can justly dispense with the execution of its penalty. The law is not to be repealed; the law must not be dishonored. It is the law of God's nature, the unalterable law of His government, the eternal law of heaven, the law for the government of moral agents in all worlds, and in all time, and to all eternity. Sinners have borne their most emphatic testimony against it, by pouring contempt upon it, in utterly refusing to obey it. Now sin must not be treated lightly; God's law must be honored.

God might pour a flash of glory over it by executing its penalty upon the whole race that has despised it. This would be the solemn testimony of God to sustain its authority and vindicate its claims. If our advocate appears before God to ask for the remission of sin, that the penalty of this law may be set aside and not executed, the questions immediately arise, "But how shall the *dishonor* of this law be avoided? What shall compensate for the reckless and blasphemous contempt with which this law has been treated? How shall sin be forgiven without apparently making light of it?"

Plainly, sin has placed the whole question in such a light that God's testimony must in some way be borne in a most emphatic manner against sin, and to sustain the authority of this dishonored law.

It behooves the advocate of sinners to provide himself with a plea that shall meet this difficulty. He must meet this necessity, if He would secure the setting aside of the penalty. He must be able to provide an adequate substitute for its execution. He must be able to do that which will as effectually bear testimony in favor of the law and against sin as the execution of the law upon the criminal would do. In other words, He must be able to meet the demands of public justice.

He must be willing to *volunteer* a *gratuitous* service. He cannot be called upon in *justice* to *volunteer* a service, or suffer for the sake of sinners. He may volunteer his service and it may be accepted; but if he does volunteer his service, he must be able and willing to endure whatever pain or sacrifice is necessary to meet the case.

If the law must be honored by obedience; if, "without the shedding of blood, there can be no remission"; if an emphatic governmental testimony must be borne against sin and the law honored; if he must become the representative of sinners, offering himself before the whole universe as a propitiation for sin, he must be willing to meet the case and make the sacrifice.

He must have a good plea. In other words, when he appears before the mercy seat, he must be able to present such considerations as shall really meet the necessities of the case, and render it safe, proper, honorable, glorious in God to forgive.

Christ's Plea on Behalf of Sinners

Remember that Christ's appeal is not to *justice*. Since the fall of man, God has plainly *suspended* the execution of strict justice upon our race. To us, as a matter of fact, He has sat upon a throne of mercy. Mercy, and not justice, has been the rule of His administration ever since men have been involved in sin.

This is simple fact. Men do sin, and they are *not* cut off immediately and sent to hell. The execution of justice is suspended; and God is represented as seated upon a throne of grace, or upon a mercy seat. It is here at a mercy seat that Christ executes the office of advocate for sinners.

Christ's plea for sinners cannot be that they are not guilty. They are guilty and condemned. No question can be raised respecting their guilt and their deserved punishment; such questions are settled. It has often appeared strange to me that men overlook the fact that they are condemned already. The truth is, no question respecting their guilt or deserved punishment can ever be raised.

Christ as our advocate cannot, and need not, plead for our *justification*. A plea of justification admits the *fact* charged; but asserts that under the circumstances the accused had a right to do as he did. This plea Christ can never make. This is entirely out of place, the case having been already tried, and sentence passed.

He may not plead so as to place the blame upon the law. He cannot plead that the law was too strict in its precept, or too severe in its penalty, for in that case He would not really plead for mercy, but for justice. He would plead in that case that no injustice might be done the criminal. For if He intimates that the law is not just, then the sinner does not deserve the punishment; hence, it would be unjust to punish him, and His plea would amount to this: "The sinner should not be punished, because he does not deserve it." But if this plea should be allowed to prevail, it would be a public acknowledgment on the part of God that His law was unjust. But this may never be.

He may not plead anything that would place the blame upon the *administration of the Lawgiver*. Should He plead that men had been harshly treated by the Lawgiver, either in their creation, or by His providential arrangements, or by allowing them to be so tempted; or if, in any way, He brings forward a plea that blames the Lawgiver, in creation, or in the administration of His government, the Lawgiver cannot listen to His plea and forgive the sinner, without condemning himself. In that case, instead of insisting that the sinner should repent, the Lawgiver would be called upon *himself* to repent.

He may not plead any *excuse whatever* for the sinner in mitigation of his guilt, or in extenuation of his conduct. For if He does, and the Lawgiver should forgive in answer to such a plea, He would confess that He had been wrong, and that the sinner did not deserve the sentence that had been pronounced against him.

He must not plead that the sinner does not deserve the damnation of hell; for, should He urge this plea, it would virtually accuse the justice of God, and would be equivalent to begging that the sinner might not be sent unjustly to hell. This would not be a proper plea for mercy, but rather an issue with justice. It would be asking that the sinner might not be sent to hell, not because of the mercy of God, but because the justice of God forbids it. This will never be.

He cannot plead as our advocate that He has paid our debt, in such a sense that He can demand our discharge on the ground of justice. He has not paid our debt in such a sense that we do not still owe it. He has not atoned for our sins in such a sense that we might not still be justly punished for them. Indeed, such a thing is impossible and absurd. One being cannot suffer for another in such a sense as to remove the guilt of the other being. He may suffer for another's guilt in such a sense that it will be safe to forgive the sinner for whom the suffering has been endured; but the suffering of the substitute can never, in the least degree, diminish the intrinsic guilt of the criminal. Our advocate may urge that He has borne such suffering for us to honor the Law that we had dishonored, that now it is safe to extend mercy to us; but He never can demand our discharge on the ground that we do not *deserve* to be punished. The fact of our intrinsic guilt remains, and must forever remain; our forgiveness is just as much an act of sovereign mercy, as if Christ had never died for us.

But Christ may plead His sin offering to sanction the Law, as fulfilling a condition, upon which we may be forgiven. This offering is not to be regarded as the *ground* upon which justice demands our forgiveness. The appeal of our advocate is not to this offering as payment in such a sense that now in justice He can *demand* that we shall be set free. No. As I said before, it is simply the fulfilling of a condition, upon which it is safe for the mercy of God to arrest and set aside the execution of the law, in the case of the penitent sinner.

Some theologians appear to me to have been unable to see this distinction. They insist that the atonement of Christ is the *ground* of our forgiveness. They seem to assume that He *literally* bore the penalty for us in such a sense that Christ no longer appeals to *mercy*, but demands *justice* for us. To be consistent they must maintain that Christ does not plead at a mercy seat for us, but having paid our debt, appears before a throne of justice, and *demands* our discharge.

I cannot accept this view. I insist that His offering could not touch the question of our intrinsic deserving of damnation. His appeal is to the infinite mercy of God, to His loving disposition to pardon; and He points to His atonement, not as demanding our release, but as fulfilling a condition upon which our release is honorable to God. He may plead as a substitute for the execution of the Law by showing His own obedience to the Law and the shedding of His blood; in short, He may plead the whole of His work as God-man and mediator. Thus He may give us the full benefit of what He has done to sustain the authority of Law and to vindicate the character of the Lawgiver, as fulfilling conditions that have rendered it possible for God to be just and still justify the penitent sinner.

But the plea is directed to the *merciful disposition* of God. He may point to the promise made to Him in Isaiah, chapter 52, from v. 13 to the end, and chapter 53, vs. 1, 2 respectively: "Behold, my servant shall deal prudently, he shall be exalted and extolled, and be very high." And, "As many were astonished at thee; *his visage was so marred more than any man, and his form more than the sons of men:* So shall he sprinkle many nations; the kings shall shut their mouths at him: for *that* which had not been told them shall they see; and *that* which they had not heard shall they consider." "Who hath believed our report? and to whom is the arm of the Lord revealed? For he shall grow up before him as a tender plant, and as a root out of a dry ground: he hath no form nor comeliness; and when we shall see him, *there is* no beauty that we should desire him."

He may plead also that He becomes our surety, that He undertakes for us, that He is our wisdom, and righteousness, and sanctification, and redemption; and point to His official relations, His infinite fullness, willingness, and ability to restore us to obedience, and to fit us for the service, the employments, and enjoyments of heaven. It is said that He is made the surety of a better covenant than the legal one; and a covenant founded upon better promises.

He may urge as a reason for our pardon the great pleasure it will afford to God, to set aside the execution of the Law. "Mercy rejoiceth against judgment" (James 2:13). Judgment is His unpleasant work; but He *delighteth* in mercy.

It is said of Queen Victoria that when her prime minister presented a pardon, and asked her if she would sign a pardon in the case of some individual who was sentenced to death, she seized the pen, and said, "Yes! with all my heart!" Could such an appeal be made to a woman's heart, think you, without its leaping for joy to be placed in a position in which it could save the life of a fellow-being?

It is said that "there is joy in the presence of the angels of God over one sinner that repenteth" (Luke 15:10); and think you not that it affords God the sincerest joy to be able to forgive the wretched sinner, and save him from the doom of hell? He has no pleasure in our death.

It is a grief to Him to be obliged to execute His Law on sinners; and no doubt it affords Him infinitely higher pleasure to forgive us, than it does us to be forgiven. He knows full well what are the unutterable horrors of hell and damnation. He knows the sinner cannot bear it. He says, "Can thine heart endure, or can thine hands be strong in the days that I shall deal with thee?" (Ezek. 22:14). Our advocate knows that to punish the sinner is that in which God has no delight. God will forgive and sign the pardon *with all His heart.*

Do you think such an appeal to the heart of God, to His merciful disposition, will have no avail? It is said of Christ, our advocate, that "for the joy that was set before him endured the cross, and despising the shame" (Heb. 12:2). So great was the love of our advocate for us that He regarded it a pleasure and a joy so great to save us from hell, that He counted the shame and agony of the cross as a mere trifle; *despising* them.

This, then, is a disclosure of the *heart* of our advocate. And how surely may He assume that it will afford God the sincerest joy, *eternal* joy, to be able honorably to seal to us a pardon; and He may urge the glory that will redound to the Son of God, for the part that He has taken in this work.

Will it not be eternally honorable in the Son to have advocated the cause of sinners, to have undertaken at so great expense to himself a cause so desperate, and to have carried it through at the expense of such agony and blood? Will not the universe of creatures forever wonder and adore, as they see this advocate surrounded with the *innumerable* throng of souls, for whom His advocacy has prevailed?

Our advocate has the right to the gratitude of the redeemed, and the profound thanks and praise of all good beings. The whole family of virtuous beings will forever feel obliged for the intervention of Christ as our advocate, and for the mercy, forbearance, and love that has saved our race.

Christ Pleads a Perfect Case

You see what it is to become a Christian. It is to employ Christ as your advocate by committing your cause entirely to Him. You cannot be saved by your works, you cannot be saved by your sufferings or your prayers. You cannot be saved in *any* way except by the intervention of this advocate. "He ever liveth to make intercession for [you]" (Heb. 7:25).

He proposes to undertake your cause. To be a Christian is to at once surrender your whole cause, your whole life and being to Him as your advocate.

He is an advocate who loses no cases. Every one committed to Him, and continued in His hands, is infallibly won. His advocacy is all-prevalent. God has appointed Him as an advocate; and wherever He appears on behalf of any sinner who has committed his case to Him, one word of His is sure to prevail. Hence you see the safety of believers. Christ is always at His post, ever ready to attend to all the concerns of those who have made Him their advocate. He is able to save unto the uttermost all that come unto God by Him; and *abiding* in Him you are *forever* safe.

You see the position of unbelievers. Unbelievers have no advocate. God has *appointed* an advocate, but unbelievers have rejected Him. They try to get along without Him. Are you among them? Some of you know you will be punished for your sins, and won't ask forgiveness. Others of you may think you will approach in your own name; and, without any atonement, or without any advocate, you will plead your own case. But God will not allow it. He has appointed an advocate to act in your behalf, and unless you approach God through Him, God will not hear you.

Apart from Christ, God is to you a consuming fire. When the judgment comes and you appear in your own name, you will surely appear unsanctified and unsaved. You will not be able to lift up your head, and you will be ashamed to look in the face of the advocate, who will then sit both as judge and advocate.

I ask, "Have you *retained* Him? Have you, by your own consent, made Him your advocate? It is not enough that God should have appointed Him to act in this relation. He cannot act for *you* in this relation unless you individually commit yourself and your case to His advocacy. This is done, as I have said, by confiding or committing the whole question of your salvation to Him.

Do any of you say that you are *unable* to employ Him? But remember, the *fee* He requires of you is *your heart*. You *have* a *heart*. It is not *money,* but your *heart* He seeks. The poor, then, may employ Him as well as the rich; the children, who have not a penny of their own, as well as their rich parents. *All* may employ Him, for all have *hearts*. He tenders His services *gratuitously* to all, requiring nothing of them but confidence, gratitude, love, and obedience. This the poor and the rich alike must render; this they are alike *able* to render.

Can any of you do without Him? Have you ever considered how it will be with you? But the question comes now to this, "Will you consent to give up your sins, and trust your souls to the advocacy of Christ, to give Him the fee that He asks—your heart, your confidence, your grateful love, and your obedience?"

Shall He be your advocate or shall He not? Suppose He stood before you, and in His hands were the book of life and a pen dipped in the very light of heaven. Suppose He asked, "Who of you will now consent to make me your advocate?" Suppose He should ask *you,* sinner, "Can I be of any service to you? Can I do anything for you, dying sinner? Can I befriend and help you in any way? Can I speak a good word for you? Can I interpose my blood, my death, my life, my advocacy, to save you from the depths of hell? And will you consent? Shall I take down your name? Shall I write it in the book of life? Shall I tell heaven today that you are saved? And may I report that you have committed your case to me, and thus give joy in heaven? Or will you reject me, because you intend to stand upon your own defense, and attempt to carry your case through at the solemn judgment?"

Sinner, I warn you in the name of Christ not to say "no." Consent *now* and *here*, and let it be written in heaven.

Have any of you made His advocacy sure by committing all to Him? If you have, He has attended to your case because He has secured your pardon; the evidence is in your peace of mind. Has He attended to your case? Have you the inward sense of reconciliation, the inward witness that you believe you are forgiven, that you are accepted, that Christ has undertaken for you, and that He has already prevailed and secured for you pardon, and given in your own soul the peace of God that passeth understanding? It is a striking fact in Christian experience, that whenever we really commit our case to Jesus, He without delay secures our pardon, and in the inward peace that follows, gives us the assurance of our acceptance, that He has interposed His blood, that His blood is accepted for us, that His advocacy has prevailed, and that we are saved.

Do not stop short of this, for if your peace is truly made with God, if you are in fact forgiven, then the sting of remorse is gone; there is no longer any chafing or any irritation between your spirit and the Spirit of God; the sense of condemnation and remorse has given place to the spirit of gospel liberty, peace, and love.

The stony heart is gone; the heart of flesh has taken its place; the dry sensibility is melted, and peace flows like a river. Have you this? Is this a matter of consciousness with you? If so, then leave your cause, by a continual committal of it, to the advocacy of Christ. Abide in Him, and let Him abide in you, and you are safe as the surrounding of Almighty arms can make you.

14

CHRIST THE MEDIATOR*

"For there is one God, and one mediator between God and men, the man Christ Jesus" (1 Timothy 2:5).

A mediator is one who tries to bring a reconciliation between parties who have some matter of difference. The need for a mediator implies that there is some obstacle in the way of their coming together on their own. If there were no obstacle there would be no need for a mediator. The existence of the office in the heavenly government, therefore, implies that there are parties between whom there is some controversy, and some difficulty in the way of their resolving their differences.

The relation of the parties to each other may be the cause of the difficulty. God is a Sovereign, and if His subjects should take up arms against Him, there would be immense impropriety in dealing with them while they continued in this rebellious and hostile position. There is a necessity for some third person to interpose if any reconciliation is ever to be effected. The Sovereign cannot deal with His subjects while they have weapons in their hands. They must first return to their duty and lay down their arms, or He cannot have any fellowship with them. The state of mind in which one or both parties may be, may prevent their coming together. There may be prejudice, misapprehension, or enmity in the minds of one or both parties. And when this is the case, they cannot come together and adjust their matters of difference. This may lay the foundation for the need of a mediator.

---

*The Penny Pulpit, No. 1,537. A sermon delivered on Sunday evening, May 19, 1850, at the Tabernacle, Moorfields, England.

There may be some condition upon which the offended party must insist. These may stem from his relations and the circumstances of the case, conditions which it may be impossible for the offender to fulfill. On this account, it may be necessary for a third person to interpose and fulfill for the offender what he cannot fulfill for himself. Any of these reasons, or all of them, may exist and require the interposition of a mediator.

The Qualifications of a Mediator

The mediator must be the common friend of the parties between whom the controversy exists. By this we mean that he should sustain such a relation to both parties that they can wholly confide in him. He must be able to fulfill any such conditions as are necessary in order to bring about the reconciliation, or he will not meet with success. He must have both willingness and ability to make any personal sacrifice to which the nature of the undertaking calls him. If the nature of the undertaking is such that he cannot bring about an adjustment of the difficulty without making some personal sacrifice, he must be able and willing to make the necessary sacrifice, whatever it may be.

But despite all of the qualifications, his success primarily depends upon the consent of the parties; the mediator can do nothing to bind the parties without their own sanction. A controversy between two parties can only be resolved when the parties agree to go along with any arrangement that may be proposed. The mediator himself may propose some terms to effect an agreement; but only as far as the parties consent to the mediator's terms can he succeed in his object. Just insofar, and no further, as they give the matter up into his hands, can he bring about the reconciliation. This matter of difference cannot be set right by any authority, by any man, or by any means whatever, that shall seek to supersede the consent of the parties themselves.

Christ—the Mediator Between God and Man

The Bible says that Jesus Christ is the mediator between God and man (1 Tim. 2:5). God addresses men in human language. He always uses language we can understand. I once heard someone, who had heard a sermon on the governmental view of the atonement, remark, "Ah, you cannot explain spiritual things by natural things. You cannot explain the government of God by any human government or human transactions." Now, when I heard this remark, I could not forbear saying, "What a pity that God did not know that when He wrote the Bible. God cannot explain spiritual things by natural things! What a pity God did not take that into account when He wrote the Bible, where such illustrations are so abundantly introduced." Surely, if God has seen fit to use such means to illustrate and explain His meaning to us, it is also permitted to us to do the same.

In the text, "For there is one God, and one mediator between God and men, the man Christ Jesus," the opposing parties are shown to be God and man. God is on the one side, and all of the human race is on the other. An obvious fact is that there is a matter in controversy between God and man. The fact is so plain that everyone feels it in his own conscience. And if he is in a right state of mind, he would as soon think of questioning it as he would his own existence. Everyone must be aware of the fact that they do not live in a way that pleases God. What idea should we have of God, if we supposed that He was satisfied and pleased with the conduct of the great mass of humanity? If God is a good being, He must be displeased with their conduct. Who can doubt this? God manifests His displeasure in thousands of ways. To be sure, He tempers His anger with great kindness, and suffers long with the perversities, follies, and sins of mankind. Yet, very often this world's history has shown that God is angry with its inhabitants. How often has He swept over the world with His arm of destruction! At one time, all the inhabitants of the earth were swept away by a flood of waters, with the exception of only one family. And on the other hand, we see that people are everywhere doing what they can to repudiate God's authority and claims to love and obedience, and are making war on His throne and government. In all this we can plainly see that there is a controversy between God and man. Man opposes God, and God is continually, by many ways, showing His displeasure with mankind.

But I also said that the existence of the office of mediator implied that there was some obstacle in the way of their coming together and reconciling their differences, and that this might arise, first, from the relation which the parties sustained to each other. Now, anyone who has ever considered what government is, or has had anything to do with administering the law, can understand the sacredness of government, and the difficulty there is in the way of exercising mercy to the rebellious. Can rebels approach offended majesty in their own name? What have rebels to say in their own name? They cannot come near to deal with God in their own name, for God has, "purer eyes than to behold iniquity" (Hab. 1:13). It is of no use for rebels to attempt to approach Him in their own name, for He will not look at them.

The difficulty may arise out of a state of mind of the parties concerned. To be sure, God is disposed to do humanity good, in spite of their rebellion, and there is no state of mind that would not allow Him to exercise compassion and mercy where sinners will repent, but His governmental relations are such as to prevent His having any fellowship with those who continue in a state of hostility. The sinner's state of mind renders it indispensable for some third person to interpose in order to reconcile them to God. Hence, Christ is represented as reconciling the world unto himself, not imputing their trespasses unto them. But I said further, that the existence of the office of mediator implied that there might be some conditions, the fulfillment of which it might be necessary for the offended party to insist upon, but which it was impossible for the offending party to fulfill or cause to be fulfilled.

Now, here I suppose was the great difficulty which stood in the way of God's showing mercy to sinners, even if His own disposition disposed Him to be merciful. The law had been violated and dishonored, and God *must* insist upon its being honored and public justice satisfied. Here I must notice a distinction between *public* and *retributive* justice. *Retributive justice* has to do with the individual, one person against another. Now, *public justice* respects public interests; the laws of a country are public property, and when they are violated, all the subjects of the government are interested in having the law executed, that its authority might not in any way be weakened; for when the laws are violated with impunity, they are of no weight, and the government which cannot enforce them is despised.

Let me observe, also, that in establishing a government of law, the lawgiver pledges himself to punish the guilty, and protect and reward the innocent; the public interests demand this. The criminal must be made a public example, or the authority and intention of law cannot be maintained. *No lawgiver, in heaven or on earth, has any right to compromise the claims of public justice.* Now, observe, God has expressly or impliedly pledged himself to sustain His government and maintain the authority of His law. Man has dishonored and violated it, and public rights will be compromised unless something is done to assert and sustain the authority of the law. Here is the difficulty; what shall be done? Shall the execution of the law be dispensed with, and thus be rendered void?

Now, public justice required that law should be vindicated by its penalties being executed upon the offending parties, or something be done to secure reverence for the law and the lawgiver. Now, observe, God himself says that Christ is sent to be a propitiation for our sins, that He may be just, and yet the justifier of those who believe in Jesus. God cannot set aside the execution of the penalty. Here is the great difficulty: God's relations and character are such, and man's relations and character are such, that something must be done that men could not do as the condition of their being forgiven—the requirement is that they must make satisfaction to public justice. Why, to be sure, public justice required every offender to be punished. What, then, shall be done to meet the demands of public justice, and yet the offender be spared the infliction of the penalty? God's government is perfect; no compromise must be made which shall set aside the true spirit of the law. God could not dispense with the *spirit* of the law. All that the spirit of the law required, was simply this: not that the letter of the law should in every instance be fulfilled, that every individual who violated the law should be punished without any reserve, but that ways should be adopted to secure obedience to the law. The offender must receive the punishment, unless something else could be done that would as truly and effectually honor the insulted law, and make a deep public impression of God's regard for it and His determination to sustain it, and as thoroughly serve to promote holiness and rebuke sin. This would be the fulfilling of the spirit of the law. Here would be no compromise of its claims, neither a literal execution of its penalty; but it would be a full satisfaction made to the spirit of its claims.

Were God to execute the law upon sinners, the result would be a deep public impression of His abhorrence of sin and His determination to maintain the law inviolate, to honor it at all hazards. The execution of the penalty would teach the universe certain great lessons in respect to God's character and government. Now, suppose that the lawgiver himself should teach these lessons in some other way that would be as effective, as impressive, and as influential as would be the execution of the penalty of the law upon sinners. The result would be the same: the spirit of the law would be effectively honored and sustained. But suppose, to show His great regard for it, He should yield implicit obedience to it himself, and become the representative of man, as it is said He did: "He hath made him to be sin for us, who knew no sin; that we might be made the righteousness of God in him" (2 Cor. 5:21). Now, in order to do this, in order to make an offer of pardon to the poor guilty sinner, there must be a public demonstration made to the whole universe; the law must be honored as widely as it had been broken.

How was this demonstration to be made? How was the law to be honored? Who was to do it? See, God's own Son, closely associated with Him, one with Him in the formation and government of the universe, takes upon himself human nature, and represents the race. He undertakes to be the impersonation and representative of sin. God is about to show how He regards sin by inflicting the penalty due man upon one who has come forth to be a mediator between the sinner and the insulted majesty of the law. God is about to make a terrible demonstration, and show to the whole universe His deep and eternal abhorrence of iniquity. Now, this will fulfill the law even more thoroughly than if the consequences of sin had been visited upon the heads of the guilty themselves. "The Lord hath laid upon him the iniquity of us all" (Isa. 53:6). What a wonderful demonstration was this!

It is plain that this condition was indispensably necessary. God, as the governor of the universe, must insist upon something being done to meet the claims of public justice. The dishonored law must be restored, public justice must be appeased. The spirit of the law must be maintained in all its integrity. Now, there was only one being in the universe qualified to sustain the office. The Lord Jesus Christ was both God and man; He sustained such a relation to both the parties as to be in a position to "magnify the law" and make it even more honorable than it would have been made by its execution upon mankind. Christ satisfied the claims of public justice, and hence it is said, "[he] gave himself a ransom for all" (1 Tim. 2:6). Christ, by His atonement, testified to the manner in which God regarded the sins of man.

Our Lord Jesus Christ knew well what it would cost Him. As I pointed out before, one of the conditions of a mediator's office is that if there is a call for any sacrifice on his part, he must be fully willing to make it. He must be willing to make any sacrifice, or undergo any degree of self-denial, which may be requisite in the nature of the case. Now, the Lord Jesus Christ knew well what it would cost Him. It was no part of His business to compromise the claims of public justice; no part of His business to justify iniquity or let down the authority of the law. He knew better what He had to do than to act thus, and He was willing to do what the office required of Him. The circumstances of Christ's death were such as could never be accounted for except upon the supposition that He suffered not as a mere mortal, but as the representative of a race of sinners. The circumstances of His death were of a very peculiar nature. He died not as martyrs generally die; when they have been tied to the stake, the words of gladness and triumph have burst from their lips and they have passed from earth shouting and singing glory to God. Christ did not die so. How was this? Is it true that Christ was more afraid to die than martyrs are? What was it extorted from Him that cry: "My God, my God, why hast thou forsaken me?" (Matt. 27:46). How was that? Is God prone to forsake even the lowliest of His saints in their hour of trial?

Let me ask those who have been in the habit of visiting the deathbeds of the saints. How many, when the last enemy was approaching and the clammy sweat was upon their brow, have you heard speak in the language and with the accents of despair? Did they cry out, "My God, my God, why hast thou forsaken me?" No, indeed! Their language is that of peace, serenity, triumph, and when their voice has been gone, they would give you a quivering grasp of the hand to indicate that the light of God's countenance was upon them. The fact, then, is plain: Christ died not as a martyr, but as the representative of a sinful race. Although God loved Him infinitely, still, as the representative of a sinful race, in His displeasure He poured down upon Him the vials of His indignation. The death of Christ was intended to make an impression upon the universe, and all the circumstances attending it show what a wonderful effect it had. When He was nailed to the cross, the sun refused to look on and the heavens were clothed in sackcloth; the whole universe seemed shaking to its foundations. Heathen philosophers observed it, and said, "Either nature is being dissolved, or the god of nature is dying." The dead could not sleep in their graves, the earth trembled, the tombs opened, and those who had been dead came forth, and walked into the city. The veil of the temple was rent in two. God made a mighty impression upon the entire universe. In order that sinners might be pardoned, He thus made a fearful demonstration of His hatred against sin.

Now Is the Day of Salvation

You recollect that the success of the mediator must depend upon the consent of the parties. Now, it is for us, on our part, as one of the parties, to consent to receive Christ as the mediator in the relation in which He is proposed to us. The divine government has given to Christ the adjustment of this difficulty, so that as parties in this controversy we must give ourselves up to the will of the mediator. The sacrifice He has made has satisfied the claims of justice. But this will affect us, and prevail in our favor, no further than we ourselves approach Him as the mediator between God and man.

Man can be reconciled to God only in one way, and that is by faith in Christ. When people believe in Him, the matter is at once adjusted between them and the divine government. They are reconciled to God through Christ. Now, we have only to leave this matter in the hands of Christ, and He will set us free from the penalty of sin.

With respect to those who decline to accept this mediator, the matter is not only not adjusted, but greatly aggravated. If they will "not have this man to reign over [them]," (Luke 19:14), they will never be reconciled to God and their guilt and consequent punishment is greatly magnified and aggravated. Remember that all those resist this arrangement who do not most cordially embrace it by believing on the Lord Jesus Christ.

This leads me to say again that you are not to understand by faith in the Lord Jesus Christ merely as an intellectual assent to the truths which He taught—and to the fact that He sustains the office of mediator. The devil knows this, and believes it, but he does not have saving faith. You may have no more doubt of the historical fact that Christ died for the sins of mankind, than you have of any other historical facts, but this is not faith in Him as a Savior. You must embrace the method of salvation with all your heart. This is the way in which God purposes to save you, and when you have done this, you can enter the door of mercy that Christ has opened for your reception.

Understand, then, what it is to be a Christian. It is not mere intellectual assent to the truth of the gospel, or that you outwardly appear to be religious, but it is with the heart that you must believe unto righteousness. You must yield up your whole being to Christ, and rely not upon your own goodness as a ground of acceptance, but upon Jesus Christ, the mediator between God and man, who has magnified the law, and made it honorable (Isa. 42:21). God requires us to approach Him in Christ's name, or He cannot deal with us or make us any offer of pardon.

Suppose that the inhabitants of London, or any other city, should rise up in rebellion against the government. It might be quite impossible to make a general offer of pardon without endangering the safety of that government. It would be very unwise to do so. It would be the way to encourage other cities to rebel—taking refuge under the precedent the government had established. The way to make a government strong is by asserting a principle and adhering to it, making the people understand the inviolability of the law, and that it is not to be broken with impunity, and that rebellion cannot be connived at.

Now, it may be safe sometimes for a government to exercise pardon, but not unless the exercise of mercy will tend more than the infliction of the penalty toward reverence for the law and government. Rebels against the law and government of God could never have been forgiven unless an atonement had been made. God's law is inviolable, and therefore cannot be transgressed without the penalty being inflicted somewhere; and God, by accepting the sacrifice of Christ as an atonement for sin, at once showed His love for man and testified to the goodness of His law. Christ magnified the broken law, and rendered to it a governmental equivalent.

Before a rebel can entreat God for mercy, he must lay down his weapons of rebellion. He cannot make terms with God with his weapons still in his hands. He must repent before he can hope for mercy. Every human government demands this, and so does the government of God. No government can stand on any other principle. Those entirely misunderstand this subject who think and say that it is an easy thing for God to show mercy. It cost Him more than the creation of the world. But the work is done: Christ has thrown the doors of mercy wide open. "Behold," He says, "I have set before [you] an open door" (Rev. 3:8).

Love to mankind caused Him to make such a sacrifice. The atonement was not demanded in a malignant spirit, but as a necessary condition to salvation. God himself proposed the plan. God saw no other eye to pity and no other arm to save. His own eye pitied and His own arm brought salvation. His heart yearned over *you* and over *me*. "[He] loved *me*," says the apostle, "and gave himself for *me*" (Gal. 2:20). Can you apply this language to yourself? Have you committed yourself to Him? Is Christ your mediator in this great controversy?

Now, I come as the servant of Christ, to ask you whether you will receive this mediator—whether you will repent and renounce your sin, and commit yourself to the hands of Christ as the great mediator between God and man. Do you reply that you do not want a mediator? The minds of many are so dark that they are foolish and absurd enough to think they can approach God and get salvation from Him without a mediator.

The following fact was communicated to me some time ago. The sister of a minister's wife who had imbibed Unitarian principles always used to resist the idea of the necessity of a mediator. She would say, "If God is disposed to be merciful, He can exercise mercy without any reference to the death of His Son. I want no mediator. I am not conscious of needing one. Is not God my Father—my heavenly Father? Can I not have fellowship with my Father? I know no necessity for a mediator." In this way she used to talk, with that kind of sentimentalism that is common to Unitarians. A great revival took place in the congregation, and one evening this lady returned home and went direct to her chamber. The family, who was below, presently heard her shriek out in great agony, and at the top of her voice. They rushed to her room and saw her standing there in a great fright, with her arms extended, and her eyes starting from their sockets. With much alarm they cried out, "What is the matter? What is the matter?" "Oh!" said she, "God is looking right at me, and there is no mediator. There, can't you see, right opposite there?" And she shrieked again in fearful agony, "God is looking right at me, and there is no mediator." In this state of mind she continued for some time, but eventually Christ was revealed to her, and she was led to embrace the truth. She never realized before what it was to stand before the Judge of all the earth without a mediator; but when she felt the eye of God blazing upon her, and searching into her heart, she felt then the necessity of "a mediator between God and man."

Oh sinner, let me tell you that without a mediator you are undone; but there is one provided, and He is offered for you to embrace. It will not take you long to embrace Christ if you are disposed to do it. You can do it now—even now. If you will not accept Him into your hearts, His blood for you has been shed in vain. There is no middle course: you must be either the friend of Christ, or His enemy. God offers mercy now, but He has not promised that He will ever offer it again! Remember that! There is no angel in heaven, or minister upon earth, who is authorized to say that salvation will ever be offered to you again.

Suppose that Christ himself should now come and take His stand with the Book of Life in His hand, and should say, *"Whose name shall I write in this book? Whoso will accept of me as a Mediator? Who will give me his heart?"* Would you respond, "I will! I will! I will! O Lord Jesus, take my unworthy name, take my heart; I renounce my sin, and gladly give all my being to thee"? Would you reply thus to the personal invitation of the Savior? Why not do it now? God invites you! Jesus invites you! The Bible invites you! The Spirit invites you! The preacher invites you! Will you come to Jesus, and come now? Why not? Are you not prepared? What preparation do you want? Can you not get your own consent? This is the difficulty—the great and only difficulty! If you can get your own consent, there is no one in the universe who can stand in the way of your salvation. But may you not obtain your own consent if you so will it? What say you? Will you consent? Will you allow Christ to have your name? Will you give Him your heart? This is a momentous question. Will you decide to have salvation now? Those who are willing to accept Christ as their mediator, bend their hearts at a throne of grace; and, Christians, let us seek to get the arms of our prayer round every unrepentant sinner and bring them to Jesus.

15

RELATIONS OF CHRIST TO THE BELIEVER*

"But of him are ye in Christ Jesus, who of God is made unto us wisdom, and righteousness, and sanctification, and redemption" (1 Corinthians 1:30).

Wisdom is a comprehensive term often used in the Scriptures to denote true religion. Perhaps no other more strictly philosophical definition of true religion can be given than this: it is *wisdom*, acting wisely in view of all known truth which is important to our welfare. All who are truly wise will reverence and obey God.

Some commentators believe that wisdom is mentioned first because it covers the whole ground, being a comprehensive term that may include all that pertains to human salvation. Such would read the next word, "and" as "*even*"; thus: "Christ is made unto us wisdom, yes, even righteousness, sanctification and redemption. All these are comprehended in His being our wisdom." Or the meaning may be according to the common interpretation: "Christ imparts to us each moment the wisdom we need in daily life." As His own word says, "If any [man] lack wisdom, let him ask of God, that giveth to all men liberally" (James 1:5). Righteousness denotes justification, acceptance with God. This is the meaning of the term as often used in the Bible.

Sanctification means *holiness*; being made pure from sin, and becoming holy as God is holy. Redemption, as a part of the scheme of salvation, stands intimately connected with our being justified

---

*The Oberlin Evangelist, July 30, 1845.

and sanctified. Its figure supposes us to have been slaves of sin, and to be bought off from this state of slavery by Jesus. Henceforth, we are no longer held under either the curse of the law or the control of sin.

Thus, these various terms, when all employed as in our text, denote salvation from sin itself and from all its penal consequences.

Man's Sinfulness; Christ's Perfection

1 Cor. 1:30 implies our own fallen and helpless state. Christ would not be our wisdom if we were wise enough ourselves. He never would become our righteousness, if we could be righteous before God without Him. Nor would He be our sanctification if we were not so wholly polluted as to need divine cleansing. We are so hopelessly unclean that no efforts of our own either would be made or could be made to transform us from utter pollution to intrinsic purity of heart. He would not have given himself for our redemption if we had not been fearfully enslaved past the power of self-effected emancipation. Thus all just views of Christ's work serve to abase us, for they show that Christ becomes everything to us because we are nothing and less than nothing in ourselves.

This Scripture also implies that we have in Christ a perfect wisdom, a perfect righteousness, sanctification, and redemption. If God presents us His own eternal Son as a supply for some specific need of ours, we may rest assured that the supply is perfect. The source is exhaustless. It is both adapted to meet the existing need and is amply adequate. If God should raise up to any one of us a Socrates or a Solomon to be our wisdom, the supply might be valuable to the extent of their ability to teach us—but no further. If God gives us Christ, the supply must be just as perfect as Christ's own ability. So also, if Christ should give us some heavenly-minded saint, say from the upper world, to stand by us and come into the closest relation possible for a heavenly and an earthly saint to sustain in order that this heavenly saint might be our sanctification—then he would be worth just as much to us as he could do. His ability to effect our sanctification would be the measure of his value to us. So of Christ. He is a perfect sanctifier, because He is able to "keep [us] from falling, and to present [us] faultless before the presence of his glory with exceeding joy" (Jude 24), because He gave himself for the Church "that he might sanctify and cleanse it with the washing of water by the word, that he might present it to himself a glorious church, not having spot or wrinkle, or any such thing; but that it should be holy and without blemish" (Eph. 5:26–27). This last passage shows that this cleansing is effected by means of "the washing of water by the word," agencies pertaining to the present state. Of course, the present is the state in which the sanctifying work takes place; unless it is already effected, none can see God in heaven. So also is Christ a perfect Redeemer. All that redemption can do for enslaved and accursed man—all that it needs to do is fully done by Christ.

This Scripture implies that the wisdom, righteousness, sanctification, and redemption provided for us by Christ is something God can accept. If we become righteous through Christ's righteousness, God will accept us. If sanctified through Christ, our sanctification will be acceptable to God. If redeemed through Christ, God endorses the redemptive act and we are held slaves to sin no longer. This must logically follow. The scheme of God's own providing, when legitimately received by us according to the true intent of the provision, God cannot disown and reject. God cannot accept our own righteousness, but will accept Christ's righteousness. Our own self-made sanctification can never be worthy of His acceptance, but that wrought in us by an indwelling Christ, the Father can and will approve.

Never forget that God has *made Christ* our wisdom, righteousness, sanctification, and redemption, and that Christ has accepted the office; Christ has undertaken the work. Of course, nothing less than perfectly ample provisions are afforded for our being wise, righteous, sanctified and redeemed.

It is obviously one thing for God to set Christ apart to be our wisdom, righteousness, sanctification, and redemption, and another thing for Christ to be willing to undertake the work His Father has given Him. And it is yet another thing for Him actually to become these things to any individual of the human race.

Christ does not become these things to us by *imputation*. Many have supposed, strangely enough, that Christ works out a perfect righteousness in himself and not in us, and then transfers it over to us so that by imputation His righteousness becomes ours. He first becomes holy, wise, and righteous himself, and then accounts this holiness, wisdom, and righteousness as ours by some process of transfer, which however, makes it ours not by causing us to be holy, wise, or righteous, but only by causing us to be regarded so by God His Father.

This view seems to be exceedingly unlike the gospel of Jesus

Christ. The gospel scheme of salvation clearly contemplates a real change wrought in us from folly to wisdom, from sin to holiness, from unrighteousness to righteousness.

Christ does become our wisdom and righteousness *by uniting himself with us*. It is not merely by entering into a covenant relation as some have supposed, but by entering into an actual relation of the most intimate sort; as the Bible often expresses it, by entering *into* us and dwelling *in us* so that we are *in Christ* and Christ is *in us*.

Having really entered into us in this spiritual union, Christ works in us by the influence of His Spirit through His truth, thus enlightening our intelligence, molding our hearts, chastening our temper, and transforming us into His own image. In the language of the Bible, Christ works in us "both to will and to do of his good pleasure" (Phil. 2:13). It is not strange that by such a union, and by means of such influences exerted upon our souls, Christ should become our wisdom, righteousness, sanctification and redemption.

Contemplating righteousness and redemption in their strictly technical meaning, Christ becomes our righteousness and redemption by presenting us to the Father as redeemed through His blood and thus made *right* in the eye of the law, the punishment due for our sins being set aside in consideration of Christ having suffered enough to answer all the goals of public justice under the government of God. Consequently, we appear before the great King of the universe, not as self-redeemed, but as redeemed by Christ; not as self-justified, but as justified only through the righteousness of Christ.

In this spiritual union formed between Christ and the believer, Christ takes possession of our faculties and so controls them with His gracious influences that He rescues us from the power of temptation, and delivers us from the law of sin which is in our members. The Bible represents our very bodies as being emancipated from the thraldom of sin and Satan. We become temples of the Holy Spirit, and so united to Christ that Scripture says, "We are members of his body, of his flesh and of his bones" (Eph. 5:30).

Such is our relation to the Lord Jesus Christ that is it any wonder we are accepted by the Father? We are accepted for Christ's sake, and not for our own. We are accepted for His righteousness and not for our own. We are not accepted for anything in us that is primarily ours, but we are accepted for everything in Him.

Now, however curiously we may inquire about the philosophy of our union with Christ, however we may push our inquiries to learn how one mind can dwell in and thus control another, however we may wonder how the vicarious death of one being may avail for the pardon and life of another; there may still remain points about the subject to us that are inexplicable. However, we should not, therefore, doubt the reality of these doctrines. There may be realities in the spiritual world and in the vast government of God that our short vision cannot fathom. The strong presumption is that there should be more in the universe than we can fully know today.[1]

Self Must Be Renounced Before Christ Can Be Received

A full renunciation of ourselves must be a condition for Christ becoming our wisdom, righteousness, sanctification and redemption. While we are trying to gain access to God and acceptance by ourselves, we are rejecting Christ and He will of course reject us. It is all vain to expect success while rejecting Christ. Our works and our persons will be rejected if we disown Christ, cleaving to our own merits and righteousness. How could it be any different? Our own works, outside of Christ, are worthless. They are never right in themselves except as Christ works in us to make us do right. And as for pardon, there is nothing we can do that comes close to making an atonement for our sin.

Therefore, any effort to merit pardon or to make ourselves so holy without Christ as to be accepted by God, will utterly fail. We must become quite empty of ourselves, if we would be filled with Christ and surely we must be filled with Christ if we would be right with God.

It is essential that we apprehend Christ as being our wisdom, righteousness, sanctification and redemption, and understand what is meant by these precious words. We must know in some good degree what is meant by the often recurring language of the Bible that represents Christ as being our Life, our Light, our All, which affirms that Christ is *in* us, dwells in us and is our sanctification.[2] Until we understand these passages intellectually, we cannot believe in Christ and receive Him in these relations. Faith begins with the intelligence; hence, the idea must be in some measure developed in our minds before we can put forth moral efforts to realize this state in our own experience. There must be a hun-

---

[1]See Finney's *Principles of Union with Christ* for the union Christ has with the believer and the other relations He has with the believer.
[2]*Ibid.* for Christ as our Life, Light, and All.

gering and thirsting after Christ, a state of mind ripe for giving up everything that stands in the way of receiving Christ. We must be ready to renounce self altogether and put the Lord Jesus Christ on the vacant throne. Christ must take the place so long held by self.

During my ministry I have seen striking cases of people who have groped a long time after Christ as if they were ready to embrace Him, if they might find Him; but yet, when the idea of embracing Christ came to be fully developed, and they saw what it really was, they drew suddenly back and would not embrace such a Savior on such conditions. Before, they thought themselves quite ready and anxious to get such a Savior as they supposed Christ to be. But when they saw how much self-denial and self-renunciation were implied in receiving Christ, they turned away like the young man in the gospel history—"sorrowful: for he had great possessions" (Matt. 19:22). How could he make up his mind to give them all away?

Thus many are very often deceived. They think themselves quite ready to receive Christ. They suppose themselves really to thirst for the gospel salvation. They think that surely if they could see it and find it they would embrace it; but let me tell you, my own experience testifies that this is not always the case. I know that some may be greatly anxious for relief and apparently most ready to receive it; and yet, when they come to see how much self-renunciation Christ demands, they draw back. A positive readiness to welcome Christ at the utter sacrifice of self and of all that is dear to self is an *indispensable* condition of receiving Him.

If Christ is received at all by us in all these relations, it must be as a *whole*—a whole Savior, one who delivers from *all sin*, one who demands absolute and universal self-renunciation. You must understand that every sinful indulgence must be crucified, and Christ become all in all to our life and happiness.

The great comprehensive condition is *faith*—that act of the mind that receives Christ for all that He is offered—as our wisdom, righteousness, sanctification, and redemption. It is faith on our part that consummates this blessed union between our soul and Christ. Christ has of a long time been ready to enter into this relation to us. And now, the moment the soul commits itself to Him, and truly yields up to receive Christ in all His relations, the thing is done: Christ is of God made unto us wisdom, righteousness, sanctification, and redemption. It is impossible that this union of our soul with Christ should take place without faith on our part.

Christ may be at hand—may reveal himself to the soul and show us what He stands ready to do for us; yet, if we do not voluntarily receive Him, He does not become our wisdom, righteousness, sanctification, and redemption.

In order for Christ to become our wisdom, we must receive Him for *all* that He is. We must really cease to trust in our own wisdom and practically rely entirely upon Him. So we must receive Him as our righteousness, sanctification, and redemption, taking Him alone for the full supply of every need in all these respects, and recognizing ourselves as incapable of doing what Christ is provided to do for us.

No Man Comes to the Father but by the Son

It may be proper to present in a few words the true idea of salvation through Christ; namely, Christ living and reigning in the soul; a vital union between a living God and the very soul of the believer. This is the very thing that Christ so beautifully and forcibly illustrated by the figure of the vine and its branches. As the branch is in the vine and cannot live and be fruitful unless it is, so no more can we unless we abide in Christ.

It is remarkable to see to what an extent the Church has lost the true idea of faith and union with Christ, and how nearly Christians have lost sight of that which is the very soul of the whole gospel. The Old School theologians hold that Christ's salvation is something imputed to us, not a living union effected by Christ's dwelling within us but something made and done by Christ and reckoned ours by imputation; that is, by being so regarded.

The New School theologians hold no such idea, but hold simply that we are forgiven through the atonement of Christ and then as to salvation from sin, we must work that out ourselves. Yes, some of their great leaders say that if you want to become free from sin, then you must work for it. This is the very language of Dr. Chalmers in his commentary on Romans. After arguing forcibly and at length the doctrine of imputed holiness and righteousness, he asks: "How shall we get personal holiness and righteousness?" He answers, "I tell you, *you must work for it.*"

Precisely the same answer was given by the Synod of New York and New Jersey. They maintained strenuously that personal sanctification must be got simply by working for it; they use the very language of Dr. Chalmers.

What a development this is in the Church! Instead of receiving

Christ for holiness, they put our own works in His place. Nothing is said, apparently nothing is believed, concerning a living union between the soul and God whereby a mighty transformation is wrought and fruit brought forth to God; this view seems to be entirely lost, or overlooked. Imputed righteousness is made to answer for pardon, and then as for personal holiness, "you must work for it."

A full salvation is equally open to all of every grade and in all ranks in society. A door is set wide open, and whoever will may rise and enter. The whole of this salvation is open to each and all. When self is rejected and Christ received, you have the whole of it—nothing more remains. The rich and the poor, the free and the bond, may have it all only on these conditions.

This great and full salvation may be received by any and all, *now*, at this very moment. Let me ask the unrepentant sinner: "Do you suppose that it is possible for you to be really saved and blessed today as the purest soul on earth? Do you suppose that the work is too difficult and the time required for doing it so long that you must naturally delay till some more convenient time—till some season less filled with studies, business, etc? Do you suppose it possible to be fully saved from sin and death at once?" But you say, "Must I not work? Must I not be convicted and thus get ready for a work of grace?" Oh, sinner; you do not understand the great simplicity of the gospel system. But you must understand it, or never come to Christ at all. You think you must work much and long; but no mistake can be greater. God wants not those works of yours; He will accept Christ's but not yours. You might go about until doomsday to get ready, and not even approach the subject. In this way you never begin, you make not the least advance.

God does not ask of you any of these works. He can receive nothing but Christ, and He offers you Christ today. Christ on the cross is your pardon; Christ in your soul is your sanctification. When you accept Him in all His relations, the work is done; until you do, nothing is done at all. God will no sooner accept you outside of Christ, than He would accept the devil. Outside of Christ, He will no sooner accept at your hands one thing than another: your prayers no sooner than your curses; your reading the Bible no sooner than your reading Tom Thumb; your going to church no sooner than your going to a brothel—all is odious, abominable, shocking to Him. Abandon, then, forever the idea that you must make these preparations. All are of no use, only that you may thus use up all your own efforts and learn that you must renounce them all, utterly and forever. Will you push your prayers and your self-righteousness into the very face of God! Will you set yourself up to merit His favor? Horrible!

"O my God," said a sister who had long been fasting and praying and had worn herself out; "O, Lord, I give it all up. I leave it all; I cast it all away. Jesus is my salvation: this is enough. I want nothing more. I put away all things but Christ. Let me have Christ only and forever!"

But perhaps some sinner will say, "Must I not first be converted? You are urging Christ on me before I am converted." Sinner, what is it to begin? What is it to be converted? Conversion is the very thing I am talking about. Paul did not say to the Jailer, "Go and pray, go and read the Bible, do penance." Paul said, "Believe on the Lord Jesus Christ, and thou shalt be saved" (Acts 16:31). So sinner, God says to you now: "All the things you would do before you come to Christ are of no use. You might work hard, but like the boatman in the rapids of Niagara, despite your hard rowing you will go over the falls."

From what has been said, it can be easily seen why so few embrace the gospel. If this entire self-renunciation is an indispensable condition of receiving Christ, then the reception of Christ has met with two obstacles. Often this condition has not been thoroughly preached and insisted upon; and again, when it has been, many have stumbled upon it and could not receive Christ on such terms.

The true and glorious idea of the gospel being left out, people have of course been left in bondage to sin. How could they be saved when they were not told that they must receive Christ as of God made unto us wisdom, righteousness, sanctification and redemption?

This view of the subject presents the most adequate remedy for our necessities: the only thing that can really save souls. Have you made great efforts to be saved? Did not those efforts leave you in a yet more wretched state, except when Christ was with you and led you to receive Him alone? What did all your other efforts avail? "Oh!" some of you can say, "I know what this fruitless toil means. I have tried it all, and gotten into the experience described in the seventh chapter of Romans. And there I groaned out, 'O wretched man that I am'; and there I found nothing but wretchedness and fruitless struggles till I went forward and found peace, and no condemnation in Christ Jesus."

Hitherto, the mass of those in the Church have gone only into the seventh chapter of Romans, and then have floundered along plunging deep in the mire like Bunyan's pilgrim in the slough of despond, toiling and agonizing. Oh, what cases of agony you would find if you were to go about the churches. I cannot tell you how much my soul has been agonized as I have found such multitudes confused, agonized, crying out, "O wretched man," and all this time supposing that this is the highest attainable state of experience in this present world, and the very state in which Paul was when he wrote the epistle to the Romans.[3] Alas, if God had really doomed the Church to such a life till death comes for their relief! Alas, yet more if the Church dooms herself to such a living death, when God has provided so simple and immediate a deliverance through Jesus Christ our Lord!

It is infinitely dangerous to mistake the true idea of the gospel. The more I see the real state of the Church, the more I am perplexed to conceive how the Church can be saved in such a state of darkness and unbelief.

How infinitely important that a ministry be raised up to go out and preach the truth, and a whole gospel. Oh, how much good one such minister may do! Let him go where he will, he will find not a few who are crying out in agony, "O wretched man!" If he can only reveal to them a living, redeeming Savior, what work he may achieve! Oh, is it not time, young person, to be awake to these things! Will you not get hold of this glorious gospel for yourselves, and then go out and tell the Church its glories and its power to save? But, alas, there is a young student, yes, perhaps a theological student. He goes out and lectures not on the glorious gospel of Jesus Christ but on Mesmerism and Phrenology! Horrible! Instead of preaching to the churches a full salvation and leading forth her desponding sons and daughters into glorious liberty, he goes about manipulating minds and working upon the nerves of some pale invalid.

Alas, I cannot tell you how much my soul has been agonized to think that there ever could be a theological student at Oberlin who could do this! Let him only be full of Christ, so full of Christ that he can think and talk of nothing else, and he will lecture on something very different from Mesmerism and Phrenology. Let all these young people be filled with Christ and this institution can shake the world! When every student is full of this one great idea, and

---

[3]See Finney's *Principles of Victory* and *Principles of Liberty* for an exposition of the seventh chapter of Romans and the experience he is speaking of here.

every professor, and every Christian in this church; then we will pour forth abroad like waves of light and glory over all the land. Oh, haste that day of salvation!

Many have put faith in the soul in the place of Christ in the soul. Now, Christ is received by faith, but Christ in the soul and faith in the soul are very different things. We never should rest till our faith is such as really receives Christ into the soul; then we shall have Christ there and not faith only.

We may see the relation of faith to sanctification. Faith must take the lead in all truly gospel experiences. Faith receives Christ; and then, Christ becomes our sanctification. Christ once received in the soul then works in us to will and to do, develops every grace and leads us along to the stature of perfect people.

Let no one stumble at the mystery of Christ in the soul, achieving there the work of salvation. I have often injured my own soul by philosophizing about the work of faith; but now, I have learned that Christ is my all, that Christ received within us works in us and effects all that need be wrought.

It is easy to see why this doctrine is regarded by many in the Church as so mysterious. It is because they still hold on to the notion of self-sanctification; sanctification by faith or by works, without Christ. They are in great agony, they toil hard; and no wonder. They have not the true gospel. They are working out their salvation without Christ.

It is a present and universal duty to receive Christ as your wisdom, righteousness, sanctification, and redemption. All who do not do so are living in sin. Whatever they may think of themselves, they are in bondage to the flesh and to Satan.

Beloved, if you live in sin, you will die in sin, and wherever Christ goes you cannot go. You are rejecting Christ, and you can have no salvation outside of Him. Truly, there can be no salvation without receiving Christ into the soul as our wisdom, righteousness, sanctification, and redemption.

Now, if this is so, what is the state of many professing Christians? Many of you have not received Christ by a living faith. You have no peace and rest in Christ. You have no rest anywhere. Until you find Christ, you have not found the true gospel nor its salvation. You are living, not in Christ, but in yourself. You are not conscious of having eternal life actually in your possession. You do not realize its vital, sin-subduing, soul-purifying power. And will you rest there? Can you?

I am afraid that very many in the churches have not the power of the gospel within them. That young person who can go out and preach nothing better than Mesmerism and Phrenology, is his soul running over with the flood tides of the gospel? Do you think that young people, if their souls were filled with the love of Christ, could go about and lecture on politics? No, truly. Could they go out and tell people how to vote for President, if their own souls were full of Christ, and they knew that hundreds and thousands abroad in the land are strangers to the glorious gospel of a full salvation?

Oh, it does seem to me that we are crazy if we will not wake up to the fact that the Church knows not Christ, and that Christ must be held forth in His fullness before His gospel can become truly the power of God unto salvation to the souls of the Church.

I am constrained to believe that very many in the churches do not know this glorious gospel yet! Their souls do not teem with the subject. Oh, how I want to see every student, and every man and woman in a blaze for Jesus Christ! Then might the Church begin to be the light of the world. Who will not pray God that His own mighty power may come down and abide upon the Church?

16

THE SAVIOR LIFTED UP, AND THE LOOK OF FAITH*

"As Moses lifted up the serpent in the wilderness, even so must the Son of man be lifted up: That whosoever believeth in him should not perish, but have eternal life" (John 3:14–15).

"And I, if I be lifted up from the earth, will draw all men unto me. This he said, signifying what death he should die" (John 12:32–33).

The passage Jesus referred to is found in the Book of Numbers:

And the Lord sent fiery serpents among the people, and they bit the people; and much people of Israel died. Therefore the people came to Moses, and said, We have sinned, for we have spoken against the Lord, and against thee; pray unto the Lord, that He take away the serpents from us. And Moses prayed for the people. And the Lord said unto Moses, Make thee a fiery serpent, and set it upon a pole: and it shall come to pass, that every one that is bitten, when he looketh upon it shall live. And Moses made a serpent of brass, and put it upon a pole, and it came to pass, that if a serpent had bitten any man, when he beheld the serpent of brass, he lived. (Numbers 21:6–9)

This is the transaction to which Christ alluded in the texts. The object in both cases was to save men from perishing. The bite of the serpent, its influence being unchecked, is the death of the body;

Sermons on Gospel Themes, pp. 57–71.

the effects of sin, unpardoned and uncleansed from the heart, are the ruin of the soul. Christ is lifted up, to the end that sinners, believing in Him, may not perish, but may have eternal life. In such a connection, to "perish" cannot mean annihilation, for it must be the antithesis of eternal life, and this is plainly much more than eternal existence. Eternal life must be eternal happiness— real life in the sense of exquisite enjoyment. The counterpoint of this, eternal misery, is presented under the term "perish." It is common in the Scriptures to find a state of endless misery contrasted with one of endless happiness. We may observe two points of analogy between the brazen serpent and Christ. First, Christ must be lifted up as the serpent was in the wilderness. From the passage quoted above, it is plain that this refers to His being raised up from the earth upon His cross at His crucifixion. Second, Christ must be held up as a remedy for sin, even as the brazen serpent was a remedy for a poison.

The Bible commonly represents sin as a malady. For this malady, Christ had healing power. He professed to be able to forgive sin and to cleanse the soul from its moral pollution. He claimed continually to have this power and encouraged people to rely upon Him and to resort to Him for its application. In all His personal instructions He was careful to hold up himself as having this power, and as capable of affording a remedy for sin.

In this respect the serpent of brass was a type of Christ. Whoever looked upon this serpent was healed. So Christ heals not from punishment only, for to this the analogy of healing is less pertinent; but He heals especially from sinning, from the heart of sin. He heals the soul and restores it to health. The announcing angel said, "Thou shalt call His name Jesus, for He shall save His people from their sins" (Matt. 1:21). His power avails to cleanse and purify the soul.

Both Christ and the serpent were held up to be a remedy. Especially note they were a full and adequate remedy. The ancient Hebrews, bitten by fiery serpents, were not to mix up nostrums of their own devising to help out the cure: it was totally sufficient for them to look up to the remedy of God's own providing. God wanted them to understand that the healing was altogether His own work. The serpent on a pole was the only external object connected with their cure. They were to look at the serpent, and in this most simple way—only by an expecting look, indicative of simple faith, they received their cure.

Christ is to be lifted up as a *present* remedy. So was the serpent.

The cure wrought then was present, immediate. It involved no delay. This serpent was God's appointed remedy. So is Christ. Christ is a remedy appointed of God, sent down from heaven for this express purpose. It was indeed very wonderful that God should appoint a brazen serpent for such a purpose—such a remedy for such a malady. And it is just as wonderful that Christ should be lifted up in agony and blood, as a remedy for both the punishment and the power of sin.

The brazen serpent was a divinely certified remedy; not a nostrum gotten up as thousands are, under high-sounding names and flaming testimonials; but a remedy prepared and brought forth by God himself, under His own certificate of its ample healing virtues. So was Christ. The Father testifies to the perfect adequacy of Jesus Christ as a remedy for sin.

Jesus Christ must now be held up from the pulpit as one crucified for the sins of people. His great power to save lay in His atoning death. He must not only be held up from the pulpit, but this exhibition of His person and work must be endorsed, and not contradicted by the experience of those who behold Him.

Suppose that in Moses' time many who looked were seen to be still dying. Who could have believed the unqualified declaration of Moses, that "every one that is bitten, when he looketh upon it shall live"? The same applies here in the gospel and its subjects. Doubtless the Hebrews had before their eyes many living witnesses who had been bitten and yet bore the scars of those wounds, but who, by looking, had been healed. Every such case would go to confirm the faith of the people in God's Word and in His own power to save. So Christ must be represented in His fullness and this representation should be powerfully endorsed by the experience of His friends. Christ represents himself as one ready and willing to save. This, therefore, is the thing to be shown. This must be sustained by the testimony of His living witnesses.

The first point of analogy is the lifting up of the object to be looked upon, the second is this very looking itself.

Men looked upon the serpent, expecting divine power to heal them. Even those ancient men, in that comparatively dark age, understood that the serpent was only a type, not the very cause in itself of salvation. So is there something very remarkable in the relation of faith to healing. Take, for illustration, the case of the woman who had an issue of blood. She had heard something about Jesus, and somehow had caught the idea that if she could but touch the hem of His garment, she should be made whole. See her pressing her way along through the crowd, faint with weakness, pale, and trembling. If you had seen her you would perhaps have cried out, "What will this poor dying woman do?"

She knew what she was trying to do. Unnoticed, she reached the spot where the Holy One stood and put forth her feeble hand and touched His garment. Suddenly He turned and asked, "Who was it that touched me?" The disciples, astonished at such a question, put under such circumstances, replied, "The multitude throng thee and press thee, and sayest thou, 'Who touched me?' " (Luke 8:45).

The fact was, somebody had touched Him with faith to be healed thereby, and He knew that the healing virtue had gone forth from himself to some believing heart. How beautiful an illustration of simple faith! And how wonderful the connection between the faith and the healing!

Just so the Hebrews received that wonderful healing power by simply looking toward the brazen serpent. No doubt this was a great mystery to them. Yet it was nonetheless a fact. Let them look. The looking brings the cure, although not one of them can tell how the healing virtue comes. So we are really to look to Christ, and in looking receive the healing power. It matters not how little we understand the mode in which the looking operates to give us the remedy for sin.

Looking to Jesus implies that we look away from ourselves. There is to be no mixing up of quack medicines along with the great remedy. Such a course is always sure to fail. Thousands fail in just this way: forever trying to be healed partly by their own stupid, self-willed works, as well as partly by Jesus Christ. There must be no looking to man or to any man's doings or man's help. All dependence must be on Christ alone. As this is true in reference to pardon, so is it also in reference to sanctification. This is done by faith in Christ. Only through and by faith can you receive that divine influence that sanctifies the soul—the Spirit of God; and this in some of its forms of action was the power that healed the Hebrews in the wilderness.

Looking to Christ implies looking away from ourselves in the sense of not relying at all on our own works for the cure desired, not even in works of faith. The looking is toward Christ alone as our all-prevalent, all-sufficient and present remedy. There is a constant tendency in Christians to depend on their own doings, and not on simple faith in Christ. The woman of the blood-issue seems to have toiled many years to find relief before she came to Christ.

She had no doubt tried everybody's prescriptions, and taxed her own ingenuity to its utmost capacity, but all was of no avail. At last she heard of Jesus. He was said to do many wonderful works. She thought to herself, *This must be the promised Messiah; who is to "bear our sicknesses" and heal all our maladies. Oh, let me rush to Him, for if I may but touch the hem of His garment, I shall be whole.* She did not stop to philosophize upon the mode of the cure. She leaned on no one's philosophy, and had none of her own. She simply thought, *I have heard of one who is mighty to save, and I will flee to Him.* To be healed of our sins, we must despair of all help in ourselves or in any other name than Christ's. Assured there is virtue in Him to work out the cure, we must expect to be cured by Him and come to Him to obtain it.

Several times within the last few years, when people have come to me with the question, "Can I be saved from my sins—actually saved, so as not to fall again into the same sins, and under the same temptations?" I have said, "Have you ever tried looking to Jesus?" "O, yes," they have replied. "But have you *expected* that you should be actually saved from sin by looking to Jesus, and be filled with faith, love, and holiness?" "No; I did not expect that."

Now, suppose a person had looked at the brazen serpent for the purpose of speculation. He had no faith in what God said about being cured by looking, but was inclined to try it. He would look a little and watch his feelings to see how it affected him. He did not believe God's Word, but since he did not absolutely know whether it was true or not, he condescended to try it. This is not looking in faith at all in the sense of our text. It would not have cured the bitten Israelite; it cannot heal the poor sinner. There is no faith in it.

Sinners must look to Christ with both desire and design to be saved. Salvation is the object for which they look. Suppose one had looked toward the brazen serpent, but with no willingness or purpose to be cured. This could do him no good. Nor can it do sinners any good to think of Christ otherwise than as a Savior, and a Savior for their own sins.

Sinners must look to Christ as a remedy for *all* sin. To wish to make some exception, sparing some sins, but consenting to abandon others, indicates rank rebellion of heart, and can never impose on the all-seeing God. There cannot be honesty in the heart that proposes to itself to seek deliverance from sin only in part.

Sinners may look to Christ at once—without the least delay. They need not wait till they are almost dead under their malady.

For the bitten Israelite, it was of no use to wait and defer his looking to the serpent till he found himself in the jaws of death. He might have said, "I am wounded plainly enough, but it does not swell much yet. I do not feel the poison spreading through my system. I cannot look at the serpent yet, for my case is not yet desperate enough. I could not hope to excite the pity of the Lord in my present condition; therefore I must wait." I say, there was no need of such delay then, and no use of it. Nor is there any more need or use for it in the sinner's case now.

We must look to Christ for blessings promised; not to our works, but to faith. Many mistakes are made on this point. Many people believe that there must be great mental agony, long fasting, many bitter tears and strong crying for mercy before deliverance can be looked for. But all these manifestations of grief and distress are not of the least avail, because they are not simple faith, nor any part of faith, nor indeed any help toward faith. They are not needed to act on the sympathies of the Savior. If under the serpent-plague of the wilderness, people had set their wits at work to get up quack remedies, such as fixing up plasters, ointments, and plying the system with depletions, cathartics and purifiers of the blood, all this treatment could avail nothing. There was but one effective cure: looking as directed.

Similarly, look at the case of the sinner. If he is a sinner and knows it, he is already prepared to come to Jesus. He should not go about preparing quack prescriptions, and mixing up remedies of his own devising to go along with the great remedy God has provided. Yet there is a constant tendency in religious efforts toward this very thing, toward fixing up and relying upon an indefinite multitude and variety of spiritual quack remedies. See that sinner. How he toils and agonizes. He would compass heaven and earth to work out his own salvation, in his own way, to his own credit, by his own works. See how he worries himself in the multitude of his own devisings! Commonly before he arrives at simple faith, he finds himself in the deep mire of despair. Alas he cries, "There can be no hope for me! Oh! My soul is lost!" But at last the gleam of a thought breaks through the thick darkness, "Possibly Jesus can help me! If He can, then I shall live, but not otherwise, for surely there is no help for me except in Him." There he is in despair, bowed in weariness of soul, and worn out with his vain endeavors to help himself in other ways. He now thinks of help from above: *There is nothing else I can do but cast myself utterly in all my hopelessness upon Jesus Christ. Will He receive me? Perhaps*

He will, and that is enough for me to know. He thinks on a little further: *Perhaps, yes, perhaps He will—no, I think He will, for they tell me He has done so for other sinners. I think He will. Yes, I know He will. Here's my guilty heart! I will trust Him. Yes, though He slay me, I will trust in Him.*

Have any of you experienced anything like that? Have you said, "Perhaps He will admit my plea. Perhaps will hear my prayer"? This is as far as the sinner can dare to go at first. But soon you will hear him crying out, "He says He will; I must believe Him!" Then faith gets hold and rests on promised faithfulness, and before he is aware, his soul is "like the chariots of Amminadib" (Song of Sol. 6:12), and he finds his bosom full of peace and joy as one on the borders of heaven.

Look to Christ and Be Saved

When Jesus said in John 12, "If I be lifted up from the earth, [I] will draw all men unto me," the language is indeed universal in form, but cannot be construed as strictly universal without being brought into conflict with Bible truth and known facts. It is indeed only a common mode of speaking to denote a great multitude. I will draw great numbers—a vast "multitude that no man can number." There is nothing here in the context or in the subject to require the strictly universal interpretation.

This expedient of the brazen serpent was no doubt designed to try the faith of the Israelites. God often put their faith to the test, and often adapted His providences to educate their faith—to draw it out and develop it. Many things did He do to prove them. So now. They had sinned. Fiery serpents came among them and many were poisoned and dying on every hand. God said, "Make a brazen serpent, and set it upon a pole, and raise it high before the eyes of all the people. Now let the sufferers look on this serpent and they shall live." This put their faith to the test.

Conceivably, many perished through mere unbelief, although the provisions for their salvation were most abundant. "We look at a serpent of brass," they might say scornfully, "as if there were not humbugs enough among the rabble, but Moses must give us yet another!" Perhaps some set themselves to philosophizing on the matter. "We," they say, "will much sooner trust our tried physicians than these 'old wives' fables. What philosophical connection can anyone see between looking upon a piece of brass and being healed of a serpent's bite?"

Just so, many now mock at the gospel. They wonder how any healing power can come of gospel faith. True, they hear some say they are healed, and that they know the healing power has gone to their very soul, and they cry, "I looked to Jesus and I was healed and made whole from that very hour." But they count all this as mere fanatical delusion. They can see none of their philosophy in it.

But is this fanaticism? Is it any more strange than a man bitten of poisonous serpents being healed by obeying God's command and looking on a brazen serpent?

Many stumble at the simplicity of the gospel. They want something more intelligible! They want to see through it. They will not trust what they cannot explain. On this ground many stumble at the doctrine of sanctification by faith in Christ. It is so simple their philosophy cannot see through it.

Yet the analogy afforded in our text is complete. People are to look to Jesus that they may not perish, but may have eternal life. And who does not know that eternal life involves entire sanctification?

The natural man always seeks for some way of salvation that shall be altogether creditable to himself. He wants to work out some form of self-righteousness and does not know about trusting in Christ alone. It does not seem to him natural or philosophical.

There is an amazing and most alarming state of things in many churches: almost no Christ in their experience. It is most evident that He holds an exceedingly small space in their hearts. So far from knowing what salvation is as a thing to be attained by simply believing in Christ, they can only give you an experience of this sort. "How did you become a Christian?" "I just made up my mind to serve the Lord." "Is that all?" "That's all." "Do you know what it is to receive eternal life by simply looking to Jesus?" "Don't know as I understand that." "Then you are not a Christian. Christianity, from beginning to end, is received from Christ by simple faith. Thus, and only thus, does the pardon of sin come to the soul, and thus only can come that peace of God, passing all understanding, which lives in the soul with faith and love. Thus sanctification comes through faith in Christ."

What, then, shall we think of that religion which leaves Christ out of view?

Many are looking for some wonderful sign or token, not understanding that it is by faith they are to be brought completely into sympathy with Christ and into participation with His own life. By faith Christ unites them to himself. Faith working by love, draws them into living union with His own moral being. All this is done by the mind simply looking to Christ in faith.

When the serpent was up, no doubt many perished because they would not accept and act upon so simple a plan of remedy. Many perished because they did not and would not realize their danger. If they saw men cured, they would say, "We don't believe it was done by the brazen serpent on the pole. These people were not poisoned much and would not have died anyhow." They assume that those who ascribe their cure to the power of God are mistaken.

Many perished also from delay. They waited to see whether they were in danger of dying. And still they waited—till they were so bedizened and crazed, they could only lie down and die.

So now in regard to the gospel. Some are occupied with matters they believe are more important, and so they delay. Many are influenced by other's opinions. They hear many stories: "Such a man looked and yet lost his life. Another man did not look and yet was saved." So people have different opinions about their professedly Christian neighbors, and this stumbles many. They hear that some set out strong for Christianity, but seem to fail. They looked as they thought, but all in vain. Perhaps it was so, for they might have looked without real faith. Some will philosophize till they make themselves believe it is all a delusion to look. They think they see many pretend to look and appear to look, who yet find no healing. Who can believe where there are so many stumbling blocks?

We may suppose that discouraging appearances drove some into despair in the wilderness; and certainly we see that the same causes produce these effects here in the case of sinners. Some think they have committed the unpardonable sin. They class themselves among those who had once been enlightened, so now "there remaineth no more sacrifice for sins" (Heb. 10:26), but a certain looking for vengeance and fiery indignation. Some are sure it is too late for them now. Their heart is as hard as a stone. All is dark and desolate as the grave. See him? His very look is that of a lost soul! Ah, some of you are perhaps reasoning and disbelieving in this very way!

Many neglected to look, because they thought they were getting better. They saw some change of symptoms, as they supposed. So with sinners. They feel better for going to meeting, and indeed there is so much improvement, they take it they are undoubtedly doing well.

Many of the ancient Hebrews may have refused to look because they had no good hope, being full of doubts. If you had been there you would have found a great variety of conflicting views, often even between brothers and sisters, fathers and mothers, parents and children. Some ridicule; some are mad; some won't believe anyhow. And must I say it, some sinners who ought to be seeking Christ are deterred by reasons fully as frivolous and foolish as these.

It is easy for us all to see the analogy between the manner of looking and the reasons for not looking at the brazen serpent and to Christ the Savior. I need not push the analogy into its minute particulars any further. But the question for you all now is: "Do you really believe that as Moses lifted up the serpent in the wilderness, even so is the Son of man lifted up, that whosoever believeth in him shall not perish, but shall have eternal life?" Do you understand the simple remedy of faith? Perhaps you ask, "What were they to believe?" This, that if they really looked at the brazen serpent on the pole, they should certainly experience the needed healing. It was God's certified remedy, and they were so to regard it. And what are you now to believe? That Christ is the great antitype of that serpent lifted up in the wilderness, and that you are to receive from Him by simple faith all the blessings of a full and free salvation. Do you understand this? Do I hear you say to these things, "What? May I, a sinner, just fix my eye in simple faith on Jesus? Who? Who may do this? Is it I? How can it be that I should have this privilege?"

Are you wishing intensely that you could only feel so and so—according to some ideal you have in your mind? Do you understand that you are really to look by faith, and let this look of faith be to you as the touch of the poor woman with an issue of blood was to her dying body, believing that if you look in simple trust He surely will receive you, and give you His divine love and peace and life and light, and really make them pulsate through your whole moral being? Do you believe it? No, don't you see that you do not believe it? Oh, but you say, "It is a great mystery!" I am not going to explain it, nor shall I presume that I can do so, any more than I can explain how that woman was healed by touching the hem of the Savior's garment. The touch in this case and the looking in that, are only the means by which the power is to be received. The manner in which God operates is a thing of small consequence to us; let us be satisfied that we know what we must do to secure the operations of His divine Spirit in all things that pertain to life and godliness.

You have doubtless had confused notions of the way of salvation, perhaps contriving and speculating, and working upon your own feelings. Now you pray, and having prayed, you say, "Now let me watch and see if this prayer has given me salvation." This course is as much as if the Hebrew people when bitten by serpents and commanded to look to the serpent of brass, had gone about to apply here a plaster, there a blister, and then a probe, all the time losing sight of just that one thing which God told them would infallibly cure.

Oh! Why should you forget? Why not understand that all good needed by us comes from God to simple faith? When we see any need, there is Christ, to be received by faith alone, and His promises leave no need unprovided for.

Now, if this is the way of salvation, how extraordinary that sinners should look every other way but toward Christ, and should put forth all sorts of effort except the effort to look at once in simple faith to their Savior! How often do we see them discouraged and confounded, toiling so hard and so utterly in vain. No wonder they should be so greatly misled. Go around among the churches and ask, "Did you ever expect to be saved from sin in this world?" "No," they say, but they expect to be saved at death. Illogical! Inasmuch as He has been quite unsuccessful in His efforts to sanctify their souls during life, they think He will send death on in season to help the work through!

Can you believe this?

While Christians disown the glorious doctrine of present sanctification by faith in Christ, and according to each one's faith is so done to him, it cannot be expected that they will teach sinners with intelligible clearness how to look to Christ in simple faith for pardon. Knowing so little of the power of faith in their own experience, how can they teach others effectively, or even truthfully? Thus the blind leading the blind, it is no wonder that both are found together where the Bible proverb represents both the leaders and the led as terminating their mutual relations.

There seems to be no remedy for such a finality except for professing Christians to become the light of the world; and for this end, to learn the meaning and know the experience of simple faith. Faith once learned, they will experience its transforming power, and be able to teach others the way of life.

17

FAITH, THE WORK OF GOD*

"Then they said unto him, What shall we do that we might work the works of God? Jesus answered and said unto them, This is the work of God, that ye believe on him whom he hath sent" (John 6:28–29).

In the preceding context, Jesus rebukes the people for following Him, not because they saw His miracles, and in His miracles saw the proof that He came from God, but for the sake of the loaves and fishes; and then He takes occasion to exhort them to "labor not for the meat which perisheth, but for that meat which endureth unto everlasting life." Upon this they start up with the questions: "What is this *labor* of which you speak? What shall we do to secure this everlasting life?" To this Jesus answered: "This is the work of God, that ye believe on him whom he hath sent."

The letter of the commandment has to do with the outward act or doing, and is separate from the ultimate end or intention of the act. For example, in the act of going to meeting, the mere external act of going may be obedience to the simple letter of the precept. If all is right, the outward act may be to join in the singing, the prayer, or to participate in the instructions of the sanctuary. But the ultimate end of these actions will be to worship and glorify God. The letter of a precept says, "Do this. Abstain from this." And yet, everyone knows that all acts do in fact proceed from some ultimate end to which the spirit of the precept refers. In the case of going to church, the letter of the precept respects only the out-

---

*The Oberlin Evangelist, October 10, 1849.

ward going, and of course the outward going fulfills the letter of the precept. But the precept also has a spirit, and this refers to the ultimate intention of the act and requires that this shall be right before God.

This distinction is not only a very plain one, but in morals it is altogether fundamental. An act shall have a bad character, a good character, or none at all, according to its ultimate moral quality. For example, *giving to the poor* may result from a great variety of motives, and its real character can be determined only from its ultimate end.

God, therefore, not only requires the outward doing, but much more and above all the right *motives* so that a person would obey who had a right spirit until prevented from the outward act. For example, the precepts requiring attendance at public worship and giving to the poor would be obeyed in the mere intention if circumstances were such as absolutely to forbid the outward act. Yet, it should not be forgotten that if the outward act is possible, the sincere intention will always require and secure it. Still, it is true that if the intention exists, the deed, so far forth as its morality is concerned is actually done. If the intention is wrong, the command is disobeyed. If the intention is right, whether the person is able to carry it out or not in external action, the command is obeyed. If the intention is not right, there is no obedience no matter how the letter may be obeyed.

The Work God Does Not Require

What does not constitute that obedience acceptable to God? Certainly, it is not compliance with the mere letter of any precept whatever. So far as the executive acts of the will are concerned, none of these are the work God requires.

The work of God is not doing something in which the ultimate end is pleasing ourselves or promoting our own self-interest. In other words, it is not any action determined by hope of personal good or fear of personal evil. This can be no more doing God's work than a hired man would do his employer's work who should be purely selfish and aim to please himself only instead of pleasing his employer. If he feels no interest in his work for his employer's sake, and is interested only to serve himself, his hands may turn off a little business in a poor way for his master. But where no heart is, there is no valuable service.

So, and much more, in Christianity. Suppose a person prays, or preaches, or goes to meeting. If his ultimate object is to secure some good to himself, he is not doing the Lord's work but only his own. He is a really doing his own work as he who goes to California to dig for gold in its mines. The moral difference does not lie in the business done, but in the *spirit* of the act. One goes with a spade and mattock to dig for gold—all for himself alone. Another goes to his closet or to church to do his religious services and to work out his own salvation. If the latter is done as really for self as the other, and as truly without an ultimate regard to the will and glory of God, it is no more acceptable to God than the former. It matters not what the course of life is, if self and self only is the end.

Whatever is done simply in obedience to custom is not the work of God. It is astonishing to see how much is done for no other reason than that the church does so. The usages and customs of the church are held and deemed as law. But obedience to this law is not the work of God to which our text alludes.

Obedience to public sentiment is not true Christianity. It is amazing to see how much that passes for Christianity is done from regard to public sentiment. In places where the standard of piety as determined by public sentiment is very low, you will scarcely distinguish Christians from the most worldly people. But transfer them to other circumstances and relations where public sentiment requires much of them, and you will see their lives greatly modified. They will become very strict in their Christian duties, and very careful to meet all the claims that the current public sentiment makes upon them.

It is not strange that in some situations these people should seem to be very religious. Since I have been in Oberlin I have talked with hundreds who have told me how much their Christian life had improved since they have been here. But this change may have been simply the result of external circumstances—no principle at bottom controlling their conduct except a regard for public opinion. Such people are greatly in danger of misjudging their own character, and of becoming very self-complacent in the face of their making great progress in holiness, while really they ought only to condemn themselves for being under the control of public sentiment rather than faith working by love.

Nothing done in obedience to the commandments of human beings is doing the work of God. Human laws in civil governments, in the school, and in the family are good, but to suppose that obeying them is doing our whole duty to God is a great mistake. It is a part of our duty to God, no doubt, but it is not *the great thing* God requires. When regard to human authority is the ultimate motive, and we go no further than this, then plainly we render obedience simply to parents and not to God; that is, if in this very obedience they have no regard at all to God, they render Him no obedience at all. To do so is not "obeying parents in the Lord."

Nothing done from sheer superstition can be doing the work of God. This is most obvious. If I had time, I would point out various things done here that are real superstitions. Superstitions are not restricted to the Roman Catholics. They come down among Protestants in the form of traditions of the elders, with which people are exceedingly careful to comply, and thus think to work out great and important righteousness.

Nothing done from a mere sense of duty, without faith or love can be doing the work of God. Every mere legalist knows what it is to do things from a mere sense of duty. In fact, nothing is more common than for people to act on this principle. They meet a demand of conscience and conscience in some people seems to be developed only in certain directions and with reference to certain things. Usually people who say they act from conscience have reference only to external acts. They say it is right for me to do thus and thus toward my neighbor, but in this they think only of the external act, not of the internal motive.

But listen to that man who acts from a mere sense of duty: "I have been to meeting twice today. I went because I thought it to be my duty." You did, indeed! And is this the spirit of God's requirements? Where is the faith and love of the gospel in this act? It is not there. There is not a particle of evangelical obedience in such doings. No one ever assigns as a reason for true love to God: "I did it because I thought it was my duty!" To be sure, a person who does right from love to God is conscious of conforming to his conscience, but he does not act because he is lashed up to do his duty by a scourge he dare not resist and cannot endure.

Nothing done without regard to the ultimate end is obedience to God. Nothing done to obtain a hope of salvation or to support or revive an old hope is doing the work of God. Many toil earnestly for these ends, but toil to no good purpose.

Nothing done to obtain comfort is true Christianity. If people had hope of success, they might toil and labor for this event in hell. The rich man praying for a drop of water to cool his tongue might as well flatter himself that he is thereby doing the work of God. How vain for people to suppose that their labors to obtain rest of mind are really the work of God, unless those labors take the direction of faith and love. Intuitively the soul cries out, "O where shall rest be found, Rest for the weary soul."

Yet there is the utmost danger lest people seek success as an ultimate end, rather than the way of God. People need a monitor to follow them about, crying evermore in their care: "Brother, sister, that is not the work of God!" "What," you say, "perhaps—what! Does not God require me to pray?" Yes, but with faith, not without faith. "Does not God require me to give to the poor?" Yes; but not without faith and love. Oh, how some people need an angel at their elbow continually to keep them from falling into the pit. They are so prone to make mistakes. Many need to be warned most earnestly and made to see that their great efforts to obtain exemption from agonies of mind, conviction and distress, are not really the work of God.

Indeed, no matter what the effort may be, though made in ever so exact conformity to the letter, yet it is not acceptable obedience unless made in faith. Nothing whatever which is not faith and love, or the spontaneous results of these exercises, can be deemed real obedience to God. This is most manifest and needs to be thoroughly understood.

The Work God Requires

The Scripture text embraces all the work of God in one word: "Faith."

When Christ's hearers made this inquiry in our text, they had reference merely to executive or outward acts. They had fallen entirely from the spiritual apprehension of God's commands, and supposed their requirements to lie merely in the external act. They understood God as requiring a mere external course of life. Christ, therefore, understood them as inquiring: "Shall we sacrifice? Shall we give alms to the poor? Shall we make many offerings at the temple?"

Christ understood their inquiry and saw that they fell exceedingly short of the truth; therefore, He for the time being left out of view, utterly and purposely, all which they called *works*. No doubt they esteemed this a most marvelous answer. To them, His answer must have seemed equivalent to this: *Do not anything at all*. "You ask," says Christ, "what acts you shall do that you may work the works of God. I see that you have infinitely misapprehended the case. This is the work: *that you believe God—exercise faith*." "Faith? what is that?" they answer. "Do tell us what we shall DO!" "Do none of those things that you have in your minds."

Yet, we are not to suppose that Christ forbade the doing of any right external acts. He knew perfectly well, as we also do, that if the heart could be got into the right state all would be well. He, therefore, aimed at one blow to cut them square off from all their vain dependencies. "Do none of these things," He said, "as THE work of God; but *believe*." Suppose that they had replied, "We do believe already." Many thousands have said to me who yet were in a state similar to that of those Jews: "We certainly believe," and there is a sense in which they do; but it is not any sense that involves obedience and love. It is only a purely intellectual assent to the truth. But pure intellectual assent to the truth is not gospel faith.

The Conditions of Salvation

You will observe that we are not now inquiring into the *grounds* of salvation, but simply the *conditions* of salvation. Christ did not intend to teach that faith can be the *meritorious ground* of salvation, but simply *that without which* people cannot be saved.

It is remarkable that Christ speaks as if faith comprehended all God's requirements. Obviously Christ speaks of faith just as He speaks of love where He says love is the fulfillment of the law. In real love, we really fulfill the whole law, because love is connected with the whole circle of obedient activities and should be the moving spring of all our external actions. Faith sustains the same relation to all our activities that love does.

Faith is not a merely intellectual conviction. It is not opinion or any set of opinions. It is not a mere speculation nor a system of theology however firmly or intelligently held. Faith is no mere intellectual state of mind.

Faith is trust or confidence in the character of God. There can be no such thing as a rational belief of what God says unless we believe Him to be trustworthy. We never have confidence in the declarations of any being unless we presuppose confidence in his character. In faith, therefore, we voluntarily cast ourselves upon and confide in the truthfulness, wisdom, love and power of God. Confidence in God is the same sort of thing as confidence in any other person. In exercising confidence in another person, we really repose in the *character* of those in whom we trust.

Take for example the case of a student. He has no means of support. It is but natural, therefore, for him to be anxious, restless, and distressed lest he be obliged soon to abandon the pursuit of an education. To all human probability, he must soon turn away from his books and studies, and seek some means of livelihood in other pursuits. But tomorrow the mail brings him a letter from a friend—a man of great generosity, integrity, and wealth. His letter says, "I have heard of your case, of your anxieties, of your need, and of your strong desire to go on with your education. It gives me great pleasure to write to you and say that you may draw from me any amount you need." Now suppose the student does not believe this letter. Suppose he lacks confidence in the writer. "Oh," he says, "this looks very fair, but I am afraid he will fail in his business or at least that he will change his mind. I don't believe that I can rely on his promise." Now in this state of mind, he will not be at rest. Perhaps he will be as anxious as ever. But on the other hand, if he believes, he will be at rest. If he has confidence in the character of his friend, he will feel as calm as a summer evening. He can sleep as quietly as a baby. No longer will he let his heart burn up with intense, wasting anxieties.

This is so with regard to all confidence in God's wisdom and power. If any of you have ever been at sea in a fierce and dreadful storm, when every wave breaks over you, every plank creaks as though it will be wrenched apart, you know how anxiously you have looked to the captain—how you have watched his countenance and studied especially his confidence in his ship and its capacity to weather the storm. You noticed his composure as the masts twisted and bent up, yet breaking not; then you had an illustration of faith. You trusted in the captain's judgment and skill. He trusted in the seaworthiness of his ship and in his own experience.

So of faith in God. You need faith that God loves you and everybody else. If you believed that God loves you, and yet did not believe that He loves everybody else, you might have trouble. So if you admit that He loves others, but does not love you, you will find that more faith than this is needful before you can have universal peace.

You know how the little child feels toward his father. Even when the father is holding an axe or a knife the child is not afraid, because he knows his father. His father may play with the axe as if it were a feather, but his child cannot dream of danger or fear as long as the axe is in his father's hand. He believes his father loves him, and knows he will not hurt him, so that even an axe in his hand awakens no fear in the child's heart.

So with God. You are no more afraid when God plays with the

forked lightning than when he paints his rainbow on the vaulted sky in the stillness of an approaching sunset. This is faith. Faith trusts God amid the storm as in the calm, assured that God is forevermore the same and always infinitely good and wise.

Suppose you are sick. What then? Suppose your mother could save your life and restore you to health in a moment. You would feel very calm. And why? Because you have so much confidence in her love. "Ah," but you say, "I have confidence in God's love, but perhaps God does not see it best to save my life." So your mother might not see it best to save your life; and if she were as good as God, and as wise as God, she would do the very same thing as God. You may, therefore, be just as peaceful as if your destiny lay in the hands of the kindest and wisest earthly parent, for you may know that you shall live or die just as infinite Love and Wisdom shall appoint.[1]

Christ tasted death for everyone. Now, the faith God requires involves full belief in Christ's death on your behalf. Faith includes the confidence that Christ is ready, able and willing to save you. Suppose you are in deep waters, and you seem just ready to sink—when suddenly you see a person who is ready, willing and able to save you. The fact that you believe this fully will make you quiet under any circumstances of danger. This confidence will make you as calm as if your feet were already on a rock.

Faith implies that you trust in Christ as sustaining to yourself all His revealed relations—as being of God made unto you wisdom and righteousness, sanctification and redemption. You trust in the present sufficiency and fullness of His grace. You know He is adequate to meet and supply every need, and He is ready and at hand *now*. You see and believe that He can do for you all that you need.

You also see in Christ provision made for all the future, so that you have no more occasion to be anxious for the future than for the present. In fact, you believe in all His promises—taking every word of them as addressed to you and as good for your present use. You yield yourself up to His providence, assured that He pledges himself to make all things work together for good to His people. To His disposal, therefore, you yield up yourself entirely and most quietly for time and for eternity. You know you can trust His wisdom, and

---

[1]Finney himself was very near death in 1847, two years before this sermon was preached. The account of his near death experience was recorded by his wife and is published in *Answers to Prayer*. Finney's wife died shortly after Finney recovered from his illness.

you can cheerfully commit yourself to His safe conduct and preservation.

Some of you have seen the power of this faith illustrated in the dying saints of God. In talking with them, you found it impossible to name a thing that gave them any anxiety. "God," they said, "will keep all in His hand of love." You speak to that dying wife and mother: "Are you going to leave your husband? How can you bear to go?" And she replies, "God will take care of him." "But how can you leave your children, and your youngest one—that dear feeble child?" "God will take care of them." "Are you not afraid that you may die under a cloud, that you may dishonor God and may sin against His name in the last of your struggles?" "Aye, God knows how to take care of me and protect me." This is the universal answer. Everything is committed to God!

Press this dying mother yet further, say, "You will leave your children in a wicked world, a world full of temptations and snares. Your husband may marry badly and your children may suffer for lack of a mother's sympathy. You know not how many dangers and evils may befall them." What does she reply? "*God*," she says, "*will take care of that.*" This is the antidote for all cares and anxieties. God's immutable character and promises are a great sheet anchor to her soul. Stayed upon Christ, she is not afraid to leap over hell itself, making the entire sweep over its burning crater.

This faith is no visionary thing, no mere speculation. Nothing has ever been more abundantly attested by living and competent witnesses. But go up to that speculative believer. There he lies, on his dying bed. "Are you near your end?" He replies, "No doubt I am." "Have you any anxieties?" "Oh yes, anxieties enough. I am afraid about my children, my wife, my property—a thousand things." Now all this fear and anxiety is real unbelief.

To Do God's Work We Must Have God's Goal

Having the same goal or purpose as God is implied in doing the work of God. You must sympathize with God in the great end He pursues. This sympathy will be a natural result of really loving Him. When in the spirit of real love, you come to confide in His universal goodness, love and faithfulness, you cannot fail to have a universal sympathy with Him in respect to all His course in His government.

Spontaneous obedience to the letter of His commands is implied in doing the works of God. I have already said that faith and love are connected naturally with the corresponding outward acts; hence, the obedience of faith is perfectly spontaneous. How is it with the confiding wife? She has a perfect sympathy with her husband with respect to his goals and motives. Suppose that with a common object they set off upon a journey to realize this purpose. The wife knows perfectly that her husband understands best how to accomplish this end. Consequently, she needs no command. She needs only an expression of his will for the simple reason that she sympathizes with him in the common object and confides in his wisdom to achieve it.

So in regard to God. When you have perfect confidence in His character and sympathy with His ends, you will need only to know His will and obedience will not be forced, but entirely spontaneous—just like an angel, so far as you have real faith in God.

Absence of all fear that has torment is implied in doing the works of God. You see this beautifully exemplified in the case of many saints on their deathbeds when you cannot name a thing which they do not cheerfully and sweetly commit to God so as to have no anxieties remaining on their minds.

Doing the works of God implies dominion of the peace of God in your soul. This is the inevitable result of faith. God's faith in himself (if I may be allowed to speak in this way) is the ground of His own peace. His has perfect confidence in His own integrity and in all His attributes, both moral and natural. Having devoted these attributes to the great work of doing good with the assurance of success, He cannot fail to enjoy perfect peace of mind. Now, let a Christian believe about God what God believes, and he will have the very peace God has. God does not tremble through fear of the future, neither will the Christian.

Doing the works of God implies calmness and equanimity of soul. By this I do not mean that there will not be inequalities in the state of the sensibility. There were in Christ himself. Yet, the depths of the soul will be calm, for the elements of calmness and equanimity are naturally there.

Satisfaction with present allotments of providence is implied in doing the works of God. Whether sickness or health is your lot, all is well. You plainly see that everything comes from God and you trust Him to do all things in the best possible manner.

A quiet state of mind with respect to all the future is implied in doing the works of God. The believer may be totally ignorant of the future and be at rest about it. He does not wish to catechize the Omniscient One as if he could not wait for time to reveal coming events. He does not say, "Oh that God would let me turn over the leaves of the future that I might turn over the leaf of tomorrow today." It is enough to know that as the present is in the hands of God, so is the future and He does all things well.

Divine cheerfulness of attitude and temper is implied in doing the works of God. This is the natural and inevitable result of faith, even as sourness and moroseness of temper are the inevitable results of unbelief. Before my conversion, I could realize that if I had universal confidence in the present agency, wisdom and goodness of God, it could not fail to make me calm and cheerful under all circumstances. I saw that Christians were the only people who had any right to be cheerful.

Universal sympathy with goodness and universal opposition to all evil are implied in doing the works of God. What are called religious duties will be spontaneous, just as the affection and duties of a mother toward her children. She sits among her children in the midst of love—never so much in her element as when she is catching their smiles and responding with her own. Are not her maternal duties and affections the spontaneities of her heart? So are the Christian's when faith works by love and purifies the heart.

False Notions Concerning the Work of God

Many people look only to the letter of the law. They have, substantially, the Jewish notions of religion. All they think of is doing, doing, doing, without ever falling back upon faith as the mainspring of all they do.

The conscience of many people is only developed with respect to the letter of the law. They seem to have never developed their conscience with respect to anything beyond the outward moralities of religion. What a delusion! To have a conscience only with respect to the outward life and not to the heart, that which will not convict of wrong with respect to faith, how far apart this is from the doctrine of Christ! He said of the Holy Spirit that when He came, "He will reprove of sin, because they believe not on me." Did Christ say, "He will reprove the world for not fasting twice in a week, for not giving tithes of all one's mint, anise, and cummin, for lying, for licentiousness"? Nay, verily, but for not believing on Him! Christ seemed to have their state perfectly before His mind; therefore He said the Holy Spirit would come and teach them a better lesson than to fast and to make long prayers on the street corners to be seen by others. He would teach them the sin of unbelief.

How remarkable that people should have such a conscience! A conscience not developed at all toward the real things of God, but all their ideas of right and wrong relate to matters in which there is not a particle of right and wrong whatever! Shall I call this a *conscience*! It is not worthy of the name. Yet, it may answer my present purpose to use the name, for this thing of which I speak supplies to them the place and executes the functions that conscience ought to fill and execute. The delusion often remains unshaken even to death, that Christianity refers to nothing more or other than the outward life. For instance, a woman is absent from prayer meeting because her children are sick and her conscience is exceedingly troubled. What ails that woman? Oh, she has committed so great a sin! Does she not know that she may have committed more sin in her unbelief than she ever could commit under any circumstances in being absent from prayer meeting?

An occurrence in my life made an impression on me of the sin of unbelief, one I shall never forget. A friend of mine had manifested a great regard for my personal needs, and a strong determination to supply them. When I began to notice its effect upon my own feelings, it struck me forcibly that I did not have as much confidence in God as I had in that man. This thought came like a wave of death over my soul. Is it possible, I thought, that after all the revelations God has made of His love to me that I have not trusted Him as much as I trust one of my fellow mortals? And shall God never be able to gain my confidence? Shall my unbelief forever grieve His heart and bar me from His heart? This train of thought served to show me the greatness of my own sin of unbelief.

Many judge themselves more by their outward life than by their faith. They know very well that their faith does not correspond with the claims of God upon them, so they are averse to looking at that point. But their outward life comes nearer their own ideal. So with great pleasure they search their outward actions for some favorable testimony to support their hope.

Many compel themselves to obey the letter of the law, and then satisfy themselves with this as if they had now done all their duty. What a delusion and a mistake!

Becoming somewhat convicted, many begin to feel dissatisfied with themselves, and then set themselves about right doing and right feelings instead of believing in Christ. Someone says to them, "Go and visit, and labor and pray for souls. Then you will get joy and peace." So they rush upon outward doings for relief of their conscience and for rest of their minds. Christ would say to such people, "Would you know what to do that you may work the work of God? This is the work of God—that you believe." But you say, "I do believe." *What* do you believe? Do you believe *with all your heart*? Do you heartily embrace the *real* gospel and the *whole* gospel?

Others mistake conviction for faith. They think that views of truth are really the same thing as faith. Whereas, one may have strong convictions of truth, and yet be very far from yielding up the heart to the proper dominion of that truth.

Others make the mistake of resorting to works in order to get faith. Yes, they go into a perfect effervescence of feeling and agitation to try to get at faith. Now, all this results from misapprehension of what faith is. Many seem not to see that faith is the simplest thing in the world. Little children understand it and exercise it everyday. They have faith in their parents and friends, and it does not cost them a terrible struggle and a great fermentation of feeling to get it. It seems as natural to them as their very breath. Why should they not have confidence in their parents? Why not trust themselves implicitly to their parents' care!

Some rest in a perfectly spurious faith, and others stumble through a partial faith. They do not embrace *all* of the gospel. They seem to understand only a little of it. Hence, their faith does not embrace Christ as Savior from sin, present and future. They fail to embrace the fullness of the promises of gospel salvation, and go on ever more stumbling for the lack of a fuller and larger view of gospel truth.

Many begin at the wrong end in their Christian life. They expend their efforts upon works first and not upon faith. Hence, they are forever laboring and toiling uphill. They do not find the Spirit's aid to help them, for the good reason that they do not take hold of God's promises *by faith* for this blessing. Of course they drag along through life in this wretchedness, crying out as they groan along, "O wretched man that I am! who shall deliver me from the body of this death?" (Rom. 7:24). In fact, they live and die in the experience of Romans chapter 7. If they would at once believe and act as Paul did, how soon might they pass into the experience of Romans chapter 8.[2] Let them only thank God through Jesus Christ their Lord and then open their eyes to see that "there is therefore now no

---

[2]See *Principles of Victory* and *Principles of Liberty* for an analysis of what Finney means about these two experiences. These two books are a collection of his sermons on the Book of Romans.

condemnation to them which are in Christ Jesus" (Rom. 8:1), and also to see that "the law of the Spirit of life in Christ Jesus [may make them free] from the law of sin and death" (Rom. 8:2). How naturally and speedily might they enter upon a new stage of Christian experience! In Romans 7, Paul describes the case of one who begins at the wrong end, and labors hard uphill because he labors without faith.

Those who begin thus at the wrong end do not conceive rightly of a justified or gospel state of mind. Take the person of Romans 7: what conception has he of a justified state of mind as described in Romans 8? What does he know in his experience of that spontaneous faith and love, described so beautifully and so vividly in John 4 and 7? There Christ says of the real waters of life: "The water that I shall give him shall be in him a well of water springing up into everlasting life" (John 4:14); and "out of his belly shall flow rivers of living water" (John 7:38). The love and the faith of the gospel, having taken root *within*, develop themselves spontaneously and pour out their gushing influences over all the outward life.

Oh, when will Christians understand the difference between beginning outside as if they thought to work in their Christianity through the skin, instead of beginning with the heart and planting first of all its deep foundations there in faith and love!

One class of legalists have regard simply to the letter of the law, and of course their religion is made up of perpetual doing, doing, doing; while another class have caught a glimpse of the law and are, therefore, dissatisfied with themselves and groaning as in Romans 7, under a body of sin and death, but they do not come to Christ for relief and salvation. They have seen so much of the purity of the law and of the sin of their own hearts that they feel condemned; but not coming by faith to Jesus Christ, they remain under condemnation and uncleansed from sin. Occasionally, they have seasons of better feelings, occurring perhaps in the hours of Sunday worship or under some especially exciting circumstances; but before long these emotions subside and they are as much disgusted with their experience as ever.

Often it is the case that this class of people are not only dissatisfied with themselves but with everybody else. They look upon the religious state of their brethren through jaundiced eyes and see nothing as they think it should be. "How is it," they say, "that you can be satisfied with your present state or have any peace of mind at all? I am in as good a state as you are, but I am not by any means satisfied with myself. I live as near right as you do, but I am surely far from being right. You must be altogether deluded. You think yourself nearly or quite free from sin, but I know you are not, for if you are, I am too; but I know that I am not, and therefore know that you are not." Now, such people do not seem to consider that the outward life is not always an index of the inward life, and that of two people whose outward life is substantially the same, one may live by faith and walk humbly with God, while the other lives only by works and in the deepest guilt of unbelief.

Faith is Foundational

Christ speaks of faith as if it were the whole of Christianity. We have seen why He should. Faith is the natural root from which a religious life springs.

We may see why Paul says that faith establishes the law. Faith does so both because it embraces and honors God's system of atonement and because it works by love and thus begets a spirit of sincere obedience to law.

The exact difference between a legal and a gospel life is this: the gospel life is a spontaneity of faith and love; a legal life is a spontaneity of selfishness. Sincere and hearty obedience flows naturally from faith and love. It must be so and always will be. Just as naturally does selfishness, when it aims to be religious at all, puts on the type of legality.

Sinners look upon Christianity in a selfish light, and hence regard it as gloomy, cheerless, and full of painful self-denials. Judging of its duties by their own state of mind and principles of action, they see it only repulsive and profitless. Since it does not promise them earthly riches, or earthly honor, or sensual delight, they see no beauty in it that they should desire it. Since Christianity demands a reasonable subjection of those appetites which they delight to indulge, they think it a most burdensome system. If they would look at it, in a directly opposite point of view, they might see it as it is. Is it any self-denial or hardship for Love to seek to please? There is real affection between that mother and her child. Now why does she make up a little nosegay and bring it in so cheerfully and sweetly to her little one? Is this a grievous act of self-denial to the affectionate mother?

Or observe how the sea captain gathers up the choicest things he can find from the ends of the earth to bring home to the wife he loves. Is this a hardship? Does he drag out a miserable bondage in performing services of this sort for his beloved wife? If not, then you may know how to judge of the self-denials and hardships of the true Christian life. It is not the gospel Christian, but the legalist, who is dragging his snail's pace up the hard hill of his religious life. Ah, his whole religion is nothing better than *penance*—a penance of such sort as God neither asks nor accepts. Sinner, you misconceive of Christianity and your misconception results from your selfishness. If in the place of selfishness you had true love to God, you would see far more things in Christianity than what you see now. Go and ask that young convert how all these waters of life taste to him. He will tell you that they are sweeter than the honey or the honeycomb. If you would know this, *try it*. Oh, when will you understand what Christianity is and having understood it yield your heart at once in obedience to its claims? Then should your peace be like a river and your righteousness as the waves of the sea.

18

DIVINE MANIFESTATIONS*

"If ye love me, keep my commandments. And I will pray the Father, and he shall give you another Comforter, that he may abide with you for ever; Even the Spirit of truth; whom the world cannot receive, because it seeth him not, neither knoweth him: but ye know him; for he dwelleth with you, and shall be in you. He that hath my commandments, and keepeth them, he it is that loveth me: and he that loveth me shall be loved of my Father, and I will love him, and will manifest myself to him. Judas saith unto him, not Iscariot, Lord, how is it that thou wilt manifest thyself unto us, and not unto the world? Jesus answered and said unto him, If a man love me, he will keep my words: and my Father will love him, and we will come unto him, and make our abode with him" (John 14:15–17, 21–23).

"Wherefore come out from among them, and be ye separate, saith the Lord, and touch not the unclean thing; and I will receive you. And will be a Father unto you, and ye shall be my sons and daughters, saith the Lord Almighty. Having therefore these promises, dearly beloved, let us cleanse ourselves from all filthiness of the flesh and spirit, perfecting holiness in the fear of God" (2 Corinthians 6:17—7:1).

The one condition of acceptance with God is entire obedience to His law. You must fully set your heart to obey God in all things— at all times, under all circumstances—you must in fact obey the whole law of God in spirit; that is, to do all the will of God must

*The Oberlin Evangelist, March 18, 1846, Vol. VIII, No. 6.

be the supreme, fixed, strong purpose of your soul.

This is undoubtedly assumed in our texts, especially in the one from 2 Corinthians. In the context the apostle urges the church at Corinth not to connect themselves with unbelievers, urging as a reason that sin can have no fellowship with holiness; the temple of God no agreement with idols: "For ye," said he, "are the temple of the living God; as God hath said, I will dwell in them, and walk in them." The condition of this promise is that you come out from among them and be separate, and touch not the unclean thing; then God will receive you, and will be a father unto you and ye his sons and daughters. Dropping the borrowed language of the Old Testament, the apostle goes on to give in his own language the import of these promises and of their conditions. "Having therefore these promises, dearly beloved, let us cleanse ourselves from all filthiness of the flesh and of the spirit, perfecting holiness in the fear of God." These therefore are the conditions of God's dwelling in us: cleansing ourselves from all filthiness, and perfecting holiness in the fear of God. Becoming pure in heart and life—renouncing all filthiness of either the flesh or the spirit—this and nothing less than this can be the condition of acceptance with God.

The same truth is also plainly implied and taught in the passage from John's Gospel. "If ye love me, keep my commandments. And I will pray the Father, and he shall give you another Comforter." So again, "He that hath my commandments and keepeth them, he it is that loveth me: and he that loveth me, shall be loved of my Father, and I will love him and will manifest myself to him." Obedience and love, evermore inseparable, are here made the condition of the divine favor.

So everywhere throughout the Bible we are taught that God accepts only those who fully and most heartily obey Him. Indeed, it cannot possibly be otherwise. The nature of God forbids that it should be. What! God accept a rebellious spirit and own him as His child? God smile on a heart still sinning! This would subvert His throne and abolish all moral distinctions in His kingdom! This would treat sin and holiness the same, and show that He regards neither! This is just as impossible as for God to cease to be holy! Therefore, God must make sincere and full-hearted obedience the one condition of His favor. It would be infinitely dishonorable in Him to accept anything less. The same truth is implied in making repentance a condition of being accepted by God. For repentance is a hearty turning away from all sin to the full-hearted love and service of God.

Faith Produces Obedience

Full obedience is the condition of God's favor. But we still must look for the conditions of this obedience itself. How shall we obey? Under what influences and motives and efforts may we hope to yield this obedience?

We cannot hope to obey God apart from *faith*. It has often struck my mind forcibly in reading the seventh and eighth chapters of Paul's letter to the Romans that he is illustrating the impossibility of obeying the law of God without faith in Christ (not the impossibility of obeying it at all, but the obedience will be under *legal motives*). Hence, he shows that the law when it comes into contact with a depraved heart, the cross of Christ not being present, only provokes resistance and stirs up the depths of the heart's depravity. And the utmost that can be effected is to elicit ineffectual struggles between the reason and conscience on the one hand, and imperious lusts on the other. But faith coming in gives the victory. Such is manifestly the strain of his illustration in these chapters.

In Hebrews 11:6, we read that without faith it is impossible to please God. This is a most concise and explicit assertion to our point.

Galatians 5:6 teaches that "in Jesus Christ neither circumcision availeth any thing, nor uncircumcision; but faith (alone avails) which worketh by love." That faith which becomes efficient through love is the capital thing in the gospel scheme. This avails; nothing else does or can.

In Acts 15:9, we have a passage strikingly in point. Peter is there testifying before the great council at Jerusalem, as to the manner in which the Gentile converts were sanctified. He says, God gave them the Holy Spirit even as He did us, and "put no difference between us and them, *purifying their hearts by faith*." By faith, then, did they come into a state of purity of heart and thus sincerely and fully obey God.

To the same purpose is Acts 26:18, where the Lord appears to Paul and commissions him to go to the Gentiles and "open their eyes that they may receive forgiveness of sins and inheritance among them that are sanctified (how?) *by faith* that is in me." On this point we see that the testimony of Scripture is ample and explicit.

Specific Promises Require Specific Faith

That Christ will manifest himself to us is expressly stated in the passage taken from the Gospel of John. The entire scope of this passage is worthy of consideration. Christ was about to leave His disciples by His own death and ascension into heaven. Yet, He bid His disciples not to grieve and told them that He would come again. He would come himself with the Father and take up His abode with them. He said that the world would not see Him in these visitations and indwellings of His presence with them. Thomas asked how this could be that He would show himself to them yet the world would not see Him. And Jesus explained, "If a man love me, he will keep my words: and my Father will love him and we will come unto him, and make our abode with him." Love, therefore, leading the Christian to keep Christ's words; that is, love prompting and securing full obedience are the conditions revealed here.

So elsewhere throughout the Bible. So in our passage from Corinthians. "Come out from among them and be ye separate saith the Lord . . . and I will receive you." "Let us cleanse ourselves from all filthiness of the flesh and of spirit, perfecting holiness in the fear of God"; so shall we realize the fulfillment of those exceeding great and precious promises that pledge us the indwelling presence and manifestations of God.

According to the Bible, faith is the condition of real and full obedience, and any of God's work and manifestations to us. Now considering faith as one of the conditions of these divine manifestations, the question may be asked, "Must our faith fasten specifically on these promises of manifestations and plead with confidence for this particular blessing before it can be received?" This is an interesting and important question.

In answer to it I remark that this form of faith is not particularly alluded to among the conditions given in either of our texts. Obedience and love, purity of heart and life, are the things there specified.

Yet the general law in the spiritual world is clear and decisive on this point. When God gives a particular promise like this of manifesting himself to His people, He requires specific faith in that promise—a definite laying hold of those very words or at least of the idea of that promise and of pleading of the faithfulness of God for its fulfillment.

For example, famine rages in Israel. Drought has parched all the land. The Lord is about to send rain, and to send it in answer to prayer. Yet, he simply tells Elijah to go and meet Ahab. Elijah obeys. But he well understands that rain does not come without special prayer. In due season, he bows his soul with mighty energy for rain.

There are passages of Scripture that plainly show that specific blessings being promised, specific faith must take hold of those promises as a condition of their being given. In Ezekiel 36: 37, the Lord, having promised to cleanse His people and give them a new heart, declares explicitly, "I will yet for this be enquired of by the house of Israel, to do it for them." This is given here as a universal principle of the government of God. So far as we know, the Lord never departs from this principle in His spiritual administration toward His people. Whenever He has promised a blessing either to His Church or to individuals, the mere promise does not secure the bestowment. Faith must take hold of that promise. You must ask and ask believing that promised word of the Lord. Then He gives it and not before. Thus God elicits prayer, and makes us prize the blessing and love of the Giver.

Briefly, the conditions of receiving these manifestations are full-hearted obedience to all known duty, walking in faith, love, and obedience, and taking hold of God's promise for this blessing by faith. Take hold of this promise and wait earnestly and in confidence, honestly and earnestly meeting every revealed condition. Then shall the blessing be given.

The Meaning of "Manifest"

It would seem that it must mean something more than what we usually think for, the word *manifest* refers our minds more to *sight* than to faith. I will do more, Christ seems to say, I will make you *see*. Your apprehensions of God and of His Son shall be most vivid. It shall be as if you *saw* with open vision. This shall be more than mere faith.

It is also something more than love. At least more than such love as is implied in keeping God's commandments. For since love is a condition of these manifestations, and must precede them, it cannot be the blessing itself.

We have a clue to the real meaning of the paraphrase which our Lord himself gives: "My Father will love him, and we will come unto him, and make our abode with him." Oh there must be precious meaning in such words as these: "We will come unto him."

The Father and the Son will come to visit him and reveal themselves to his soul, and this for no transient hour but "we will take up our abode with him." This must be very like heaven! What more, we might almost ask, would be requisite to make one's bliss like heaven?

What then, I ask again, is implied in these promised manifestations? More of course than giving a person the Bible, and more than making a person understand the Bible. These gifts, great though they are, are never designated in such language as we find in the text.

Speaking positively, these manifestations imply *the baptism of the Holy Spirit*. The context plainly shows that Christ had this in His mind. After giving the promise as in our text, He proceeded to promise the Comforter, to show that He would teach all things and bring those things to their remembrance which Christ had said to them. "He shall glorify me, for he shall receive of mine, and shew it unto you" (John 16:14).

The text also shows that the blessing promised means the indwelling of the Father and of the Son by the Holy Spirit. And this, as I have said, is declared to be not a visit merely, but taking up an abode—not as a wayfaring man who tarries but for a night, but as a resident who makes your house His home.

Let it not be supposed from what I have said that the child of God to whom these manifestations are made, and who receives the special baptisms of the Holy Spirit, has of course never had the Holy Spirit before. Let no one imagine that the faith, love, and obedience which must precede these manifestations can ever exist without the Holy Spirit. By no means! But there is a higher kind and measure of the Spirit's influence and also a lower. The lower is essential to any sincere faith and love; the higher comes only in those glorious manifestations of which our Lord speaks here. This higher influence is said in our context to be *sent* by the ascended Savior on those who truly love Him and fully keep His commandments. The disciples plainly had received a lower measure of the Spirit's influence before. Now they receive a higher measure in the baptism of the Holy Spirit.

Another thing is implied in these manifestations. Christ will actually reveal himself to the mind so that it shall know Him in His official character and relations. And there is a deep and precious meaning in this. Often have I been struck with this in my own experience. Some new aspect of the Savior's character or some new point in His relations comes before my mind with great vividness. I wonder that I had not seen this before. I seem not to have been aware that Christ sustained this relation, and I now embrace Him in this new relation and rejoice that I find Him meeting and supplying one more need of my soul. Thus, for example, when Christ revealed a new feature of His relation to me through these words, "Thou shalt call his name *Jesus; for he shall save his people from their sins"* (Matt. 2:21). Then I saw Him not merely an atoning Redeemer, but a Sanctifier—one who came to save His people from sinning. Then my soul knew Christ in this other and more glorious relation.[1]

When Christ manifests himself to the soul, the Christian is rather a *knower* than a *believer.* He does indeed believe, but he also more than believes. He not merely believes that Christ died and made atonement, but he is made to know Christ. How natural is the language that a Christian enjoying these manifestations uses so spontaneously, "I believed before, but now I *know* it." I was often struck with the strong language of Elder Marks on his sick and dying bed. He did not say, "I believe," but "I *know.*" He would sit in his great chair, when he could not lie down, and laugh and then cry, overcome and convulsed often with deep, unutterable emotions because God was showing him his own blessed truth so that he *knew* it. Now in such cases, this strong perception we call seeing and knowing is not of the body but of the mind. It is not your external eye that sees, but your internal eye. Hence, your perceptions are so clear and so vivid.

Here we observe that when Christ manifests himself, there is something more than mere belief. There must be belief before this; a belief that begets love and obedience. But when Christ manifests himself by His Spirit, there is something more than this, Christ says, "The world seeth me no more, but ye see me" (John 14:19). Did He mean that He would come again during their lifetime in His body, and that they would see this? No, but that He would make such revelations of himself that they would know they had a personal interview with their Lord. He told them He was going away to heaven, but they need not grieve, for He would return again and show himself. Now, did all this mean only that they would have faith in Him? Much more than this: it meant that He would return and show himself and they would know assuredly

---

[1]After Finney preached this sermon, he published the material found in *Principles of Union with Christ*, a book which describes many of the relations we can have with Christ and is newly re-edited into a devotional format.

that Christ was with them.

Again, when Christ manifests himself to the soul, it must be that the mind in some way has an assurance that it is not deceived, and that the manifestation is actual. I have spoken of personal interviews with Christ. You are aware that in various ages there have been many saints who have asserted that they had interviews with Christ. There were many cases of this before Christ's incarnation. Christ manifested His glory to Moses, to Isaiah. After His resurrection and ascension, He manifested himself to John on Patmos and to Paul. In every age since, there have been those who have supposed themselves to have interviews with Christ. They are prone to say, "I have seen Him." I have heard a man in this place say that he had seen Christ. He could not rid himself of the impression that he had truly seen the Lord.

Now, on this point, I am not going to say that Christ manifests himself to the bodily eyes of the saints, but the revelation is such that they do not know but they see him with their eyes. Perhaps it seems to them altogether as if they did.

I have often alluded to the circumstances attending my own conversion. When Christ first revealed himself to me, I certainly seemed to see Him and to rush and fall at His feet. I felt a powerful drawing of soul toward Him, as if my very soul would be drawn out of me. I rushed into a private room and there seemed to meet Him. There—so it seemed—was Jesus, the very Savior.[2]

Now, I do not mention this because it is a peculiar case. It occurs or has occurred somewhat frequently in the experience of the people of God. Christians have often felt that they have seen Christ. They have no more question about this fact than about any other. They do not know that they see Him with the bodily eye, but their *mind* sees Christ, and it makes all the impression on the mind of seeing.

Christ does not *usually* manifest himself so that one sees a form and shape; but so that the soul is perfectly conscious of the presence of Christ. I know a minister who has told me that at one particular period of his life Christ was just as real to him as any man ever was. It seemed to him a matter of consciousness that Christ was present as much as any other man was present, as if Christ had actually come down from heaven and kept by his side daily. This is Christ's making himself manifest.

---

[2]For a detailed description of Finney's conversion see *Answers to Prayer* by Charles G. Finney.

It is intimated also that the Father comes and takes up His abode in the soul. This implies that the Holy Spirit reveals both Christ and the Father. Now it is certainly remarkable that in all Christian experience there is such a distinction between the Father and the Son. The Father is revealed as a father. Christ is revealed as Savior and Redeemer. The soul seems to know God distinctly in these two relations. It has no misgivings with respect to God's being indeed a father, more than any child has respecting his own earthly father. So also the soul regards Christ as really the Redeemer and comes to Him as such.

Another thing. These manifestations involve the establishment of the soul's love and confidence. This is no doubt one of the principal designed objects of those manifestations. In the case of the primitive disciples, Christ meant to give them such a hold of the gospel that they would be prepared for the coming trials and should make them *knowers* and not mere believers.

Another result. Whenever Christ is thus manifested the external evidences of Christianity no longer have any special force on the mind, comparatively. The mind's reliance is henceforth chiefly on the internal evidence. I have often thought that if Christ had not revealed himself to me so that my mind took hold powerfully of the internal evidence, and was impressed forcibly by the manifestations to which I have alluded, I would have been an infidel and would have apostatized utterly. It has often seemed that my natural incredulity is so great that nothing else but this could have kept me from being an infidel. My mind was in the habit of constant agitation under the questions: "How do I know this is true? How do I know but all this is a delusion?" Satan would often present these difficulties in the strongest light. I would set myself to reason upon them, and could see that according to all the rules of logic, all is clear and certain. Yet, at the same time, I was conscious of such a state of mind that I knew I would not have believed if Christ had not given me conscious and certain manifestations.

These manifestations greatly confirm the mind in its convictions. Christianity becomes such a matter of experience the soul has to believe. If Christ manifests himself to the soul at once, it can doubt no more. Yet, such manifestations may be frequent, and if the conditions are fulfilled, they will be.

Light from the Scriptures is another result. The promise as applied to us is that the Holy Spirit shall take of the Scriptures and show to us. People thus enlightened and privileged see more of the Bible than ever before. They have a new kind of confidence in it. They take up their Bibles and find there new things unseen before.

The Tragedy of a Truth Forgotten

Many people who profess to be Christians seem to have lost sight of this truth regarding the manifestations of God to the soul. It is remarkable to see to what an extent this is true. Perhaps they have lost sight of the strong faith that must precede them. Perhaps they conceive of nothing better in Christianity than a dim hope and enjoy nothing more. They seem to forget the conditions: "If a man love me, he will keep my words: and my Father will love him." In fact, some seem to have lost the whole subject.

There are few who understand this subject. They may have such manifestations, but have gotten the idea that it means more than it does or their notions of what it is are entirely vague. They call it, perhaps, assurance of faith, or assurance of hope. Others fail to attain these manifestations because they quite overlook the conditions, or seem to forget that there are any conditions at all. Or, as the case may be, they misapprehend the conditions and set themselves to get it in some antinomian or legal way, and hence fail of any good result.

Others have the idea that obedience itself depends upon divine manifestations, and hence suppose they cannot obey until they get these manifestations. But, this is not the Bible view of the subject. Our text says that if a man obey and love—then shall he have the manifestations—*then* and not before.

Some set themselves to seek for these manifestations selfishly, for the luxury they may afford. Of course, they fail of fulfilling the conditions and seek in vain. To seek these manifestations as some do that they may be distinguished and get honor to themselves, or if the motive be any other than the glory of God, the very seeking is an abomination to God, and will cause Him to manifest to such seekers His wrath rather than His glory.

When people set themselves to seek this blessing selfishly, they are commonly deluded by Satan, and suppose themselves to have obtained some great blessing when they have obtained no spiritual blessing at all. Satan transformed in appearance to an angel of light deceives such people and makes them believe that God has revealed himself to them, when it is only the devil. This is my opinion in such cases, and I will tell you why I think so. I have known several instances in which people have related a most remarkable experience of most astonishing manifestations of God to the mind as they supposed; but the results were a bitter, hard, acrimonious spirit, a spirit of fierce denunciation instead of gentleness and love, a spirit such as the Holy Spirit never begets, but which is the genuine offspring of Satan's manifestations. Forthwith, they plunge headlong into the most absurd errors, and the most anti-Christian practices. And yet, in all these things, they will most pertinaciously insist that God is leading them. I have known several who gave up family prayer, and closet prayer, and yet insisted that God led them in all this. By the fruits we may know that it was not God but Satan who induced them to abandon prayer.

This is the history of their case. They learn from the Bible that God promises manifestations. From merely selfish motives they seek this blessing, and God answers them according to their seeking and His promise. They set up the idol of their own selfishness in their hearts, and seeking God thus, He answers them according to their idols as He has said He would. The Lord allows Satan to deceive them. No wonder they are exceedingly positive and as bitter as they are positive. The hand of Satan is in all this. How else can you account for their state?

Yet, let it be well considered: such cases do not at all impair the integrity of these promises and ought not to shake our confidence in them. The false prophets revealed strange things; yet, we know that this was the work of Satan. There were true prophets nonetheless, and their messages were nonetheless worthy of confidence. Real prophecies did not fail of coming to pass, even though Satan deceived some false prophets.

It is doubted whether such people are for any considerable time very positive that God is leading them, and that the manifestations that they have are from Him. Usually God gives them so much light that they *might*, if they would, see that their leader is not God but Satan. Sometimes under these Satanic hallucinations the mind is thrown from its balance. Such cases are an exception to the remark last made.

Again I remark, it is of vast importance that this doctrine respecting divine manifestations should be fully developed throughout all the Church, and especially among all gospel ministers. Suppose that all ministers had these interviews with Christ and lived so near to him, and had Christ and the Father abiding continually in their hearts, would they not preach as if they had a Savior and *knew* Him? Would not all their preaching then be full of Christ, and would it not reveal Christ to their listeners? Verily they might then say with John, "That which we have seen and heard declare we unto you" (1 John 1:3).

It is one of the greatest difficulties with ministers that they have lost this experience. They do not know Christ by the living experience of their hearts through His presence abiding within them. All they can say about the gospel of Christ, they say upon their faith as opposed to the clearer vision of these promised manifestations. All is mere faith and often very dim. Oh, how much better to *see* Christ and be able to testify from the burning impressions made by such divine visions of Jesus!

It is indeed well to be able really and fully to believe that Christ is with us. But the mind needs greatly to *know* this and have it in the mind as a living, burning reality, kindling every energy of the soul by its presence and power. Every minister needs this in order to preach with energy and demonstration of the Spirit. The whole Church needs it and must have it before she will be clothed again with the glory and power of apostolic days.

Many people call these divine manifestations "sanctification." But this is not the Scriptural view. The Scriptures plainly represent obedience and love as the conditions, and these manifestations as consequent upon these conditions being fulfilled. Of course, sanctification precedes as a condition, and not merely an effect. At the same time, it is doubtless true that these abiding revelations of Christ to the soul exert a most hallowing agency, and may well be called a spiritual cleansing. They do indeed rectify the sensibility, mightily quickening it toward God and His truth, and thus serve to purify the soul. To the individual Christian, they are life, giving a glorious vitality to all his spiritual apprehensions. If all the Church were to come under this influence, if all missionaries went forth with this experience, if it were a universal fact among them that Christ manifested himself among them so that they should know Him as they know each other, and be as conscious of His presence and of His guidance too as they ever are of a Christian brother's presence and counsel, oh! what tremendous power would this give to the whole missionary enterprise!

This gave the early apostles their great power. Driven by fierce persecution, they assembled together. Christ came among them, and the whole place shook where they assembled. They prayed for a bold and fearless spirit that they might preach Christ in the face of scorn or scourging—and they received it. Nothing can daunt such men, and nothing can stand before them.

It would be richly instructive to read this portion of the apostles' history with the eye on this point, and see what the results were of having such manifestations as they had of Christ, and such baptisms of the Holy Spirit.

This great blessing should be sought by every Christian. No one should rest until he obtains it. Let his object in seeking it be the glory of God and this only. Let him know that it is for the glory of God that he should have it, and that he cannot eminently glorify God without it. Then, let him know that if he will fulfill the conditions, the blessing will surely be given.

Every Christian is authorized to take this ground and ought to take it at once: "If the conditions are within my power, then as the Lord liveth, I will have it." Let me say to those who doubt. This is the course you should pursue, for this will bring you the blessing you seek. You need not be afraid to come to Christ and tell Him all your difficulties. Come in the simplicity and fullness of your heart and say, "Lord, you know all things. You know that I love you. You know it is in my heart to know and do all your will. Now come and manifest yourself to me, and take up your abode in my heart."

You need, brethren, only to seek these blessings with all your heart and you will obtain. I have been greatly struck with the fact that within the circle of my own observation these blessings are obtained of the Lord usually in this manner. Led by the Spirit of the Lord, a person sets himself with great earnestness to mortify every lust and subdue every sin. He spares not his dearest idol. He loathes and abhors everything that can separate his soul from his Savior, and puts it utterly away. This being done, his Savior comes and makes His gracious presence manifest. This is just what we might expect from Christ's language. When a Christian puts down every appetite and lust of body and mind that leads his heart away from Christ, and does all this for Christ, then let him know that he may lay hold on this promise of the Savior and say: "Lord, I have humbly sought to fulfill all the conditions. Now, in thy mercy and faithfulness, bestow upon me the blessing." This is the remedy for doubting.

Then will the Savior come to your soul and reveal His glories. Then He will so attract your soul that you will cry after Him in the spirit of adoption, entreating Him to reveal himself yet more and more until you can say: "Surely the Lord hath done great things for me whereof I am glad and I will praise Him. Surely He hath done exceeding abundantly above all that I could ask or think: and to His name be all glory and praise forevermore."

19

THE ESSENTIAL ELEMENTS OF
CHRISTIAN EXPERIENCE*

"Blessed are they which do hunger and thirst after righteousness: for they shall be filled" (Matthew 5:6).

A great many things in the experience of Christians are exceedingly interesting when traced out in their natural history. Very commonly what is unique to Christian experience is forgotten; while that which is merely incidental is seen as the core of what Christianity is. The way some talk of their Christian experience leaves you in the dark as to its genuineness, even when they propose to give you the reasons of their hope. My design is to state some of the facts that belong to the life of God in the soul.

Thirsting after God is an important element all Christians must have. There are two kinds of hungering and thirsting, natural and spiritual. The objects on which the natural kind terminates are food and drink. By our very constitution these are necessary to our well-being in the present world. These appetites are natural and terminate on their appropriate objects. There is also spiritual hunger and spiritual thirst. These are as truly natural as the former. It is no more a figure of speech to use these terms in this case than in the other. The appetites that demand food and drink are facts and experiences. Everybody knows what it is to have them, and everybody knows in general what those things are that meet those needs. So also the spiritual appetites are things of fact and

---

Sermons on Gospel Themes, pp. 398–417.

experience. They stand in a similar manner related to the objects that meet the demand.

Sin: Part of the Race, but Not Part of the Body

That sin is a natural fact in the history of our race must be attributed to the fall of our first parents. Yet, whatever explanation be given of the introduction of sin into the human family, it now exists as an undeniable fact.

Some attention to the manner in which sin is first developed may serve to show its relation to what I have called the natural history of the race.

We all know it to be a fact that the natural appetites commence their development immediately after birth. The first awakening to a conscious existence in this world seems to be, if not occasioned by yet closely connected with, a constitutional demand for food. The alternations of demand and supply commence and go on while health continues—all the time developing the strength of this class of appetites. Commonly the natural appetites make their development far in advance of the spiritual appetites. Not much is said in the Bible as to the mode in which sin entered our world and acquired such relation to the human soul, but it is distinctly referred to Adam's first sin and is asserted to be in some way connected with that event. Facts show that sin has become natural to the race, so that all spontaneously, not of necessity yet spontaneously, if no special grace interpose, begin to sin as soon as they begin to act morally, or in other words, as soon as they become capable of moral action. Not that people are born sinners, not that they sin before they are born, not that sin is born in them, nor that they are beyond their control born into sin; but yet, the constitution of people—body and mind—is such, and the law of development is such, that we sin naturally (nonetheless voluntarily, responsibly, and guiltily). All sin is from free choice; the temptation to sin is developed in advance of those intellectual and moral powers that should counteract the excessive demands of the sensibility.

Mark the developments of the newborn child. Some pain or some appetite awakens its consciousness of existence, and thus is created a demand for the things it needs. Then the little infant begins to struggle for good—for that particular good that its newly developed sensibility demands. Want, the struggling demand for supply, and the gratification, form a process of development that gives such power to the sensibility that intense selfishness is generated; and before the conscience and the reason are perceptibly developed, the foundation for spiritual death has already been laid. If the Spirit of God does not excite spiritual wants and arouse the mind to efforts in obtaining them, the mind becomes so engrossed and its sensibilities acquire such habits of control over the will, that when the idea of right and wrong is first developed the mind remains dead to its demands. The appetites have already secured the throne. The mind seems to act as if scarcely aware that it has a soul or any spiritual wants. The spiritual consciousness is at first not developed at all. The mind seems not to know its spiritual relations. When this knowledge first forces itself upon the mind, it finds the ground preoccupied, the habits fixed, the soul too much engaged for earthly good to be called off. The tendency of this law of development is altogether downward; the appetites become more and more despotic and imperious; the mind has less and less regard for God. The mind comes into a state in which spiritual truth frets and chafes it, and of course it thoroughly inclines to spiritual apathy—choosing apathy, though not unaware of its danger before the perpetual annoyance of unwelcome truths. This tends toward a state of dead insensibility to spiritual want.

Spiritual needs, however, are always felt at some point. Sometimes they are weak at first, or sometimes the soul may be more strongly aroused to its spiritual relations, position, and wants. This brings on anxiety, desire, and a deep sense of what the soul truly needs. From this arises an influence that begins to counteract the power of appetite, operating as a balance and check to those long unrestrained demands. Here you may notice that just in proportion as the spiritual consciousness is developed, the mind becomes wretched, for in this proportion the struggle becomes intense and violent. Before this struggle, the man was dead. He was like an animal as to the unchecked indulgence of appetite—above the mere animal in some things, but below in others. He goes on without that counteracting influence that arises from the spiritual consciousness. You see some who live a giddy, aimless life. They seem not at all aware that they have a spiritual nature or any spiritual needs. When they awake to spiritual consciousness and reflection, conviction produces remorse and agony. This spiritual struggle, at whatever age it may occur, is in its general character the same as occurs in the infant when its spiritual consciousness is first awakened.

It is but natural that when the spiritual faculties are aroused, people will begin to pray and struggle under a deep sense of being wrong and guilty. At first this may be entirely selfish. But before conversion takes place, there will be a point in which the counter influences of the selfish against the spiritual will balance each other, and then the spiritual will gain the ascendancy. The animal and the selfish must relatively decline and the spiritual gain strength, till victory turns on the side of the spiritual powers. How commonly do you observe that when the mind becomes convicted of sin, the attractions of the world fade away; all it can give looks small; sinners can no longer take the pleasure in worldly things they once had. Indeed, this is a most curious and singular struggle. How rapid and great are the changes through which the sinner passes! Today, he quenches the light of God in his soul, and gropes on in darkness; tomorrow the light may return and reveal yet greater sin; one day he relapses back to worldliness, and gives up his soul to his own thoughts and pleasures; but before another has passed, there is bitterness in this cup and he loathes it, and from his soul cries out: This can never satisfy an immortal mind! Now he begins to practice upon external reformation; but soon he finds that this utterly fails to bring peace to his soul. He is full of trouble and anxiety for salvation, yet all his struggles thus far have been entirely selfish, and before he is converted he must see this to be the case.

He is in a horrible pit of miry clay. The more he struggles the deeper he sinks and the more desperate his case becomes. Selfish efforts for spiritual relief are just like a quagmire of thick clay. Each struggle plunges the sinking person deeper in the pit. The convicted person is ready to put himself to hard labor and mighty effort. At first he works with great hope of success, for he does not readily understand why selfish efforts will not be successful. He prays, but all in a selfish spirit. By this I mean that he thinks only of himself. He has no thought of honoring or pleasing God—no thought of any benefit to his fellow beings. He does not inquire whether his course of life and state of heart are such that God can bless him without detriment to the rest of His great family. In fact, he does not think of caring for the rest of that family nor for the honor of its great Father. Of course, such selfish praying brings no answer; and when he finds this to be the case, he frets and struggles more than ever. Now he goes on to add to his works and efforts. He attends more meetings, and reads his Bible more, and tries new forms of prayer. All is in vain. His heart is selfish still. What can I do? he cries out in agony; if I pray I am selfish, and if I desist from prayer, this too is selfish; if I read my Bible or neglect to read it, each alike is selfish, and what can I do? How can I help being selfish?

Alas, he has no idea of acting from any other or higher motive than his own interests. It is his darkness on this very point that makes the sinner's struggle so long and so unprofitable. This is the reason why he cannot be converted at once, and why he must sink and flounder so much longer in the quagmire of unavailing and despairing works. It is only when he comes at last to see that all this avails nothing that he begins to take some right views of his case and of his relations. When he learns that indeed he cannot work for his own salvation he begins to inquire whether his motives of heart are not radically corrupt.

Looking round and abroad, he begins to ask whether God may not have some interests and some rights as well as himself. Who is God and where is He? Who is Jesus Christ and what has He done? What did He die for? Is God a great King over all the earth, and should He not have due honor and homage? Was it this great God who so loved the world as to give His Son to die for it? "Oh, I see I have quite neglected to think of God's interests and honor! Now I see how infinitely mean and wicked I have been! Plainly enough, I cannot live so. No wonder God did not hear my selfish prayers. There was no hope in that sort of effort, for I had, as I plainly see, no regard to God in anything I was doing then. How reasonable it is that God should ask me to desist from all my selfish endeavors and to put away this selfishness itself, and yield myself entirely and forever to do or suffer all His blessed will!"

The Essence of Christianity

When you turn from your selfishness, and yield yourself entirely and forever to Jesus Christ, it is done! Now the long-troubled soul sinks into deep repose. It settles itself down at Jesus' feet, content if only Christ be honored and God's throne made glorious. The final result—whether saved or lost—seems to give him no longer that agonizing solicitude; the case is submitted to the Great Disposer in trustful humility. God will do all things well. If He takes due care of His own interests and glory, there will be no complaining—nothing but deep and peaceful satisfaction.

In the case of most young converts, this state of peaceful trust in God is subject to interruptions. The natural appetites have been denied—their dominion over the will disowned; but they are not dead. By and by they rise to assert their sway. They clamor for indulgence, and sometimes they get it. Alas, the young convert has fallen into sin! His soul is again in bondage and sorrow. Oh, how deeply is he mortified to think that he has again given away to temptation, and pierced the bosom on which he loved to recline! He had promised himself he should never sin, but he has sinned, and well for him if he finds no heart to evade or deny the fact. Better admit it all, and most freely, although it wounds his heart more than all his former sins. Mark his agony of spirit! His tears of repentance were never before so bitter! He feels disappointed, and it almost seems to him that this failure must blast all his plans and hopes of leading a Christian life. It does not work as he thought it would. He feels shy of God; for he says, "How can God ever trust me again after such developments of unfaithfulness." He can hardly get himself to say a word to God or to Christ. He is almost sure that he has been deceived. But finally he bethinks himself of the Cross of Calvary, and catches a faint ray of light—a beam of the light of love. He says, "There may be mercy for me yet! I will at least go to Jesus and see." Again he goes, and again he falls into those arms of love and is made consciously welcome. The light of God shines on his soul again, and he finds himself once more an accepted son in his Father's presence.

Here a new form of desire is awakened. He has learned something of his own weakness and has tasted the bitterness of sin. With an agony of interest never known before, he asks, "Can I ever be established in holiness? Can I have righteousness enough to make me stand in the evil day?" This is a new form of spiritual desire, such as our text expresses in the words "hunger and thirst after righteousness."

These extended remarks are only an introduction to my general subject, designed to get before your mind the true idea of hungering and thirsting after righteousness. This state of mind is not merely conviction; it is not remorse, nor sorrow, nor a struggle to obtain a hope or to get out of danger. All these feelings may have preceded, but the hungering after righteousness is none of these. It is a longing desire to realize the idea of spiritual and moral purity. He has in some measure appreciated the purity of heaven, and the necessity of being himself as pure as the holy there, in order to enjoy their bliss and breathe freely in their atmosphere. (This state of mind is not often developed by writers, and it seems rarely to have engaged the attention of the Church as its importance demands.)

When the mind gets a right view of the atmosphere of heaven, it sees plainly it can not breathe there, but must be suffocated, unless its own spirit is congenial to the purity of that world.

I remember the case of a man who, after living a Christian life for a season, relapsed into sin. At length God reclaimed him. When I next saw him, and heard him speak of his state of relapse, he turned suddenly away and burst into tears, saying, "I have been living in sin, almost choked to death in its atmosphere; it seemed as if I could not breathe in it. It almost choked the breath of spiritual life from my system." Have not some of you known what this means? You could not bear the infernal atmosphere of sin—so like the very smoke of the pit! After you get out of it, you say, "Let me never be there again!" Your soul agonizes and struggles to find some refuge against this awful relapsing into sin. Oh, you long for a pure atmosphere and a pure heart that will never hold fellowship with darkness or its works again.

The young convert, like the infant child, may not at first distinctly apprehend its own condition and wants; but such experience as I have been detailing develops the idea of perfect purity, and then the soul longs for it with longings irrepressible. "I must," says the now enlightened convert, "I must be drawn into living union with God as revealed in Jesus Christ. I cannot rest till I find God, and have Him revealed to me as my everlasting refuge and strength."

Some years ago, I preached a sermon for the purpose of developing the idea of the spiritual life. The minister for whom I preached said to me, "I want to show you a letter written many years ago by a lady now in advanced age, and detailing her remarkable experience on this subject. After her conversion she found herself exceedingly weak, and often wondered if this was all the stability and strength she could hope for from Christ and His gospel. 'Is this,' she said, 'all that God can do for me?' After a long time and with much prayer she examined her Bible. At last she found there lay a class of passages that revealed the real gospel— salvation from sinning. She saw the provisions of the gospel in full relief. Then she shut herself up, determined to seek this blessing. Her soul went forth to God, seeking communion with Him, and the great blessing she so deeply needed. She had found the promises in God's Word, and held on to them as if she could not let them go until they had all been fulfilled in her own joyful experience. She cried mightily to God. She said, 'If Thou dost not give me this blessing, I can never believe Thee again.' In the issue the Lord showed her that the provisions were already made, and were just as full and as glorious as they needed to be or could be, and that she might receive them by faith if she would. In fact, it was plain that the Spirit of the Lord was pressing upon her acceptance, so that she had only to believe—to open wide her mouth that it might be filled. She saw and obeyed; then she became firm and strong. Christ had made her free. She was no longer in bondage; her Lord had absolutely enlarged her soul in faith and love, and triumphantly she could exclaim: 'Glory be to God! Christ hath made me free.' "

The state of mind expressed by hungering and thirsting is a real hunger and thirst, with the object being the bread and water of life. These figures (if indeed they are to be regarded as figures at all) are kept up fully throughout the Bible, and all true Christians testify to the appropriateness of the language.

I have said that this state of mind implies conversion. Although the awakened sinner may have agonies and convictions, yet he has no clear conception of union with Christ, nor does he clearly apprehend the need to know the exceeding bitterness of sin as felt by one who has been near the Lord before he shall fully desire being made a partaker indeed of Christ's own perfect righteousness. By righteousness here, we are not to understand something imputed, but something real. It is imparted, not imputed. Christ draws the souls of His people into such union with himself that they become "partakers of the divine nature" (2 Pet. 1:4) or as elsewhere expressed, "partakers of his holiness" (Heb. 12:10). For this the tried Christian pants. Having had a little taste of it, and then having tasted the bitterness of a relapse into sin, his soul is roused to most intense struggles to realize this blessed union with Christ.

A few words should now be said on what is implied in being filled with this righteousness. Worldly men incessantly hunger and thirst after worldly good. But attainment never outstrips desire. Hence, they are never filled. There is always a conscious want that no acquisition of this sort of good can satisfy. It is most remarkable that worldly men can never be filled with the things they seek. This desire enlarges itself as hell, and is never satisfied. They really hunger and thirst the more by how much the more they obtain.

Let it be especially remarked that this being filled with righteousness is not perfection in the highest sense of this term. Men often use the term perfection, of that which is absolutely complete—a state that precludes improvement and beyond which there can be no progress. There can be no such perfection among

Christians in any world—earth or heaven. It can pertain to no being but God. He, and He alone, is perfect beyond possibility of progress. All else but God are making progress—the wicked from bad to worse, the righteous from good to better. Instead of making no more progress in heaven, as some suppose, probably the law of progress is in a geometrical ratio; the more they have, the farther they will advance. I have often queried whether this law that seems to prevail here will operate there, of what I may call impulsive progression. Here we notice that the mind from time to time gives itself to most intense exertion to make attainments in holiness. The attainment having been made, the mind for a season reposes, as if it had taken its meal and awaited the natural return of appetite before it should put forth its next great effort. Does the same law of progress operate even in heaven?

Here we see the operations of this law in the usual Christian progress. Intense longing and desire beget great struggling and earnest prayer; at length the special sought blessing is found, and for the time the soul seems to be filled to overflowing. It seems to be fully satisfied and to have received all it supposed possible and perhaps even more than was ever asked or thought. The soul cries out before the Lord, "I did not know there was such fullness in store for Thy people. How wonderful that God should grant it to such a one as myself!" The soul finds itself swallowed up and lost in the great depths and riches of such a blessing. Oh, how the heart pours itself out in the one most expressive petition: "Thy will be done on earth as in heaven!" All prayer is swallowed up in this." And then the praise, the FULLNESS OF PRAISE! All struggle and agony are suspended; the soul seems to demand a rest from prayer that it may pour itself out in one mighty tide of praise. Some suppose that persons in this state will never again experience those longings after a new baptism; but in this they mistake. The meal they have had may last them a considerable time—longer, perhaps, than Elijah's meal, on the strength of which he went forty days; but the time of comparative hunger will come round again, and they will gird themselves for a new struggle.

This is what is sometimes expressed as a baptism, an anointing, an unction, an ensealing of the Spirit, an earnest of the Spirit. All these terms are pertinent and beautiful to denote this special work of the Divine Spirit in the heart. They who experience it know how well and aptly it is described as eating the flesh and drinking the blood of the Lord Jesus, so really does the soul seem to live on Christ. It is also the bread and the water of life that are promised freely to him that is athirst. These terms may seem very mystical and unmeaning to those who have had no experience, but they are all plain to him who has known in his own soul what they mean. If you ask why figures of speech are used at all to denote spiritual things, you have the answer in the limits of the human mind in regard to apprehending spiritual things. Christ's language must have seemed very mystical to His hearers, yet it was the best He could employ for His purpose.

If any man will do His will, he shall know of His doctrine; but how can a selfish, debased, besotted, and disobedient mind expect to enter into the spiritual meaning of this language? How strangely must Christ's words have sounded on the ears of a Jewish priest: "God in us"; "The Holy Ghost dwelling in you"; "Ye shall abide in Me." How could they understand these things? "The bread that came down from heaven," what could this mean to them? They thought they understood about the manna from heaven, and they idolized Moses; but how to understand what this Nazarene said about giving them the true bread from heaven that would be for the life of the world, they could not see. No wonder they were confounded, having only legal ideas of religion, and having not even the most remote approximation to the idea of a living union with the Messiah for the purposes of spiritual life.

How to Receive Spiritual Fullness

In this passage, the only condition specified to receive spiritual fullness is that the soul hunger and thirst for it. But it is very common to have promises made in the Bible, and yet not have all the conditions to the promise stated in the same passage. If we find them elsewhere, we are to regard them as fixed conditions, and they are to be understood as implied where they are not expressed.

Elsewhere we are told that faith is a fundamental condition. Men must believe for it and receive it by faith. This is as necessary as receiving and eating bread is for the sustenance of the body. Ordinary food must be taken into the system by our own voluntary act. We take and eat; then the system appropriates. So faith receives and appropriates the bread of life.

In general, it is found true that before Christians will sufficiently apprehend the relation of this supply to their wants and to the means of supplying them, this hunger and thirst becomes very intense, so as to overpower and cast into insignificance all their other appetites and desires. As by a general law one master passion throws all minor ones into the shade, and may sometimes suspend them for a season entirely, so we find in this case a soul intensely hungering and thirsting after righteousness almost forgets to hunger and thirst even after common food and drinks. Place before him his study books, he cannot bring his mind to relish them now. Invite him to a singing concert, he has no desire for that now. Ask him into company, his mind is pressing in another direction. He longs to find God, and can take but little interest in any other friend at present. Offer him worldly society, and you will find he takes the least possible interest in it. He knows such companions will not understand what his soul so intensely craves, and of course it is vain to look for sympathy in that quarter.

It is an important condition that the mind should have somewhat clear apprehension of the thing needed and of the means of obtaining it. Effort cannot be well directed unless the subject be in some good measure understood. What is the ensealing of the Spirit? What is this baptism? Use all means to see what this is before you seek it and hope to gain it. True, no man can know before experience as he can and will know afterward; but he can learn something before and often much more after the light of experience shines in upon his soul. There is no more mystification than there is in hungering for a good dinner, and being refreshed by it after you have eaten it.

If we would have this fullness, we must be sure to believe this promise and all similar promises. We must regard them as truly promises of God—all yea and amen in Christ Jesus, and as good for our souls to rely upon as the promise of pardon to the penitent and believing.

We must ask and insist upon their fulfillment to our souls. We are authorized to expect it in answer to our faith. We should be first certain that we ask in sincerity, and then should expect the blessing just as we always expect God to be faithful to His Word. Why not? Has He said and shall He not do it? Has He promised and shall He not perform?

We must believe that the promise implies a full supply. Our faith must not limit the power or the grace of Christ. The Christian is not straitened in God. Let him take care, therefore, that he not straiten himself by his narrow conceptions of what God can do and loves to do for His hungering and thirsting children. Often there is need of great perseverance in the search for this blessing. Because of the darkness of the mind and the smallness of its faith the way may not for a long time be prepared for the full bestowment of this great blessing.

Getting to Know God Will Take an Eternity

The Antinomian Perfectionists mistook the meaning of this and of similar passages. They supposed that whoever believes gets so filled as never to thirst any more. But the fact is, the mind may rise higher and higher, making still richer attainments in holiness at each rising grade of progress. It may indeed find many resting places, as Bunyan gives to his pilgrim—here at the top of the hill Difficulty, there on the Delectable Mountains, where he passes through scenes of great triumph, great faith and great joy in God. Subsequently to these scenes will occur other periods of intense desire for new baptisms of the Spirit and for a new ascent upon the heights of the divine life. This is to be the course of things so long at least as we remain in the flesh, and perhaps forever.

Perhaps the blest spirits in heaven will never reach a point beyond which there shall not be the same experience—new developments of God made to the mind, and by this means new stages of progress and growth in holiness. With what amazement shall we then study these stages of progress and admire to look abroad over the new fields of knowledge successively opened, and the corresponding developments of mental power and of a holy character, all which stand related to these manifestations of God as effects to their cause! What new and glorious views have been bursting upon us, fast as we could bear them, for myriads of ages! Looking back over the past, we shall say— Oh, this everlasting progress—this is indeed the blessedness of heaven! How far does this transcend our highest thought when we looked forward to heaven from the dim distance of our earthly pilgrimage! Here there is no end to the disclosures to be made, nor to the truths to be learned.

If there was to be no more food, how could there be any more spiritual thirst and spiritual hunger? How, indeed, could there be more spiritual joy? Suppose that somewhere in the lapse of heaven's eternal ages, we should reach a point where nothing more remains to be learned—not another thing to be inquired after— not another fact to be investigated, or truth to be known. Alas, what a blow to the bliss of heaven!

We are told that the angels are desiring to look into the things of salvation. Oh yes, when they saw our Messiah born they were allowed to come so near us with their joyous outbursts of praise that even mortals could hear. Do you not suppose those angels too are growing in grace, and advancing in knowledge? No doubt they are, most wonderfully, and have been ever since they came into being.

How much more they must know of God now than they did before our world was created! And how much more they have yet to learn from God's government over our race! Do you think they have no more desire after the knowledge of God? And have they no more desire to rise to yet higher conformity of heart and character to the great Model of Heaven?

If so with angels, surely it is the same with their younger brethren—the holy who are redeemed from among men.

Imagine the error of thinking that by studying for a few years you would learn all human science. This would be a great mistake. After many years of study you might master many sciences and still have other heights to ascend—other vast fields of knowledge to explore. You might have the best of human teachers and the best possible opportunities for learning, yet still it would take many lives to master all there is in even human science. The mind is not made to be filled to satiety so that it craves no more—can receive no more. Like the trees planted on the rivers of the waters of life, which bring forth twelve manner of fruits and whose roots go deep and drink largely of those blessed waters—so is the mind that God has endowed with the functions of immortal progress.

As our ideal becomes elevated, and we see higher points to which we may arise, we shall have more enkindlings of desire, and more intense struggles to advance. What Christian does not find, as he reads the Bible over, new and deeper strata of meaning never seen before—new truths revealed and new beauties displayed. Old father O. used to say—"I am reading the Word of God. It is deep and rich, like the great heart of its Author. I have read now two hours and have only gone over but two verses. It will take me to all eternity to read through." So it was. He found more in the Bible than other men did. He went deeper, and the deeper he went, the richer did he find its precious ores of gold and silver.

So the Psalmist says—"Open Thou mine eyes that I may behold wondrous things out of Thy law" (Ps. 119:18). Have you not been so ravished with love to this blessed book that you wanted to clasp it to your bosom and become purified with its spirit? As you go down into its depths and find in each successive stratum of its deep thoughts new beauties and new fields of truth to explore, have you not been filled with intense desire to live long enough and have time and strength enough to see, to learn, and to enjoy it all? Like the successive landscapes as you ascend the lofty mountain's side, at each stage you see them spreading out in grander beauty and broader range—so, as you really study into the great and rich things of God's spiritual kingdom, there is no limit to this sweep of the knowledge of God, for the fields only become the broader and the more enchanting as you ascend. Do you not think that his soul must be truly blessed who eats and drinks and fills his soul with divine righteousness?

I am strongly impressed with the conviction that some of you need a new development of the spiritual life. You need to go deeper into the knowledge of God as revealed in the soul; you need to hunger and thirst more intensely, and be by this means filled as you have not often been as yet. Even though you may have tasted that the Lord is gracious, you yet need to eat and drink largely at His table. It will not avail you to live on those old dinners, long past and long since digested. You need a fresh meal. It is time for you to say—"I must know more about this being filled with righteousness. My soul languishes for this heavenly food. I must come again into this banqueting house to feast again on His love."

The full soul cannot be satisfied to enjoy its rich spiritual provisions alone. If well fed himself, he will be only more exercised to see others also fed and blessed. The Spirit of Christ in his heart is a spirit of love, and this can never rest except as it sees others reaching the same standard of attainment and enjoyment which is so delightful to itself.

Real Christians should be, and in the main they will be, growing better and holier as they come nearer heaven. On the other hand, how great and fearful is the contrast between an aged growing Christian and an aged sinner growing in depravity and guilt! The one is ripening for heaven, the other for hell. The one goes on praising and loving, laboring and suffering for God and for his generation according to the will of God; but the other goes on his downward course, scolding and cursing as he goes, abhorred of men and disowned of his Maker. You have seen the awful contrast. You could hardly believe that two men so unlike were both raised in the same township, taught in the same school, instructed in the same religious assembly, and presented with the same gospel; and yet see how manifestly the one is saved and the other damned. Each bears the sign beforehand—the palpable, unmistakable evidence of the destiny that awaits him.

Is it not full time that each one of you who has any spiritual life should stand out before the world and put on your beautiful garments? Let all the world see that there is a power and a glory in the gospel, such as human philosophy never has even approached. Show that the gospel begets purity and peace. Show that it enlarges the heart and opens the hand for good of all human kind. Show that it conquers selfishness and transforms the soul from hate to love.

Sinners, you who have earthly hunger and thirst enough, let your ears be opened to hear the glad tidings of real salvation. Ye whose hearts have never known solid peace—ye who are forever desiring, yet never satisfied—ye who cry in your inmost souls: Oh, for office! Oh, for honor! Oh, for wealth! See, here is that which is better far than all you seek. Here are durable riches and righteousness. Here are the first installments of pleasures that flow forever at God's right hand. Here is heaven proffered and even pressed upon your regard and your choice. Choose life before death, as you would be wise for your eternal well-being.

20

VICTORY OVER THE WORLD THROUGH FAITH*

"For whatsoever is born of God overcometh the world: and this is the victory that overcometh the world, even our faith" (1 John 5:4).

Overcoming the world means getting above the spirit of covetousness that possesses the men of the world. The spirit of the world is eminently the spirit of covetousness. It is a greediness after the things of the world. Some worldly people covet one thing and some another. But all classes of worldly people are living in the spirit of covetousness in some of its forms. This spirit has supreme possession of some minds.

Now the first thing in overcoming the world is that the spirit of covetousness in respect to worldly things and objects be overcome. The person who does not overcome this spirit of bustling and scrambling after the goods that this world proffers has by no means overcome it.

Overcoming the world implies rising above its engrossments. When a person has overcome the world, his thoughts are no longer engrossed and swallowed up with worldly things. A person certainly does not overcome the world unless he gets above being engrossed and absorbed with its concerns. Now we all know how exceedingly engrossed worldly people are with some form of worldly good. One is swallowed up with study, another with politics, a third with money-getting, and a fourth perhaps with fashion and with pleasure. But each in his chosen way makes earthly good the all-engrossing object.

Sermons on Gospel Themes, pp. 363–379.

The person who gains the victory over the world must overcome not one form only of its pursuits, but every form—must overcome the world itself and all that it has to present as an allurement to the human heart.

Overcoming the world implies overcoming the fear of the world. It is a mournful fact that most people, and indeed all people of a worldly character, have so much regard to public opinion that they dare not act according to the dictates of their consciences when acting thus would incur the popular frown. One is afraid lest his business should suffer if his course runs counter to public opinion; another fears lest if he stand up for the truth it will injure his reputation, believing that advocating an unpopular truth will diminish and perhaps destroy his good influence—as if a person could exert a good influence in any possible way besides advocating the *truth*.

Great multitudes, it must be admitted, are under this influence of fearing the world. Yet, some, perhaps many, of them are not aware of this fact. If you or if they could thoroughly sound the reasons for their backwardness in duty, fear of the world would be found among the chief. Their fear of the world's displeasure is so much stronger than their fear of God's displeasure that they are completely enslaved by it. Who does not know that some ministers dare not preach what they know is true, and even what they know is *important* truth, lest they should offend some whose good opinion they seek to retain? The society is weak perhaps, and the favor of some rich man in it seems indispensable to its very existence. Hence, the terror of these rich men is continually before their eyes when they write a sermon or preach or are called to take a stand in favor of any truth or cause that may be unpopular with people of more wealth than piety or conscience. Too many gospel ministers are so troubled by it that their time-serving policy is virtually renouncing Christ and serving the world. Overcoming the world is thoroughly subduing this servility to men.

Overcoming the world implies overcoming a state of *worldly anxiety*. You know there is a state of great carefulness and anxiety that is common and almost universal among worldly men. It is perfectly natural if the heart is set upon securing worldly good, and has not learned to receive all good from the hand of a great Father and trust Him to give or withhold with His own unerring wisdom. But he who loves the world is the enemy of God, and hence can never have this filial trust in a parental benefactor, nor the peace of soul that it imparts. Hence, worldly people are almost incessantly in a fever of anxiety lest their worldly schemes should fail. They sometimes get momentary relief when all things seem to go well; but some mishap is sure to befall them at some point soon, so that scarcely a day passes that does not bring some corroding anxiety. Their bosoms are like the troubled sea that cannot rest, whose waters cast up mire and dirt. But the person who gets above the world gets above this state of ceaseless and corroding anxiety.

The victory under consideration implies that we cease to be enslaved and in bondage to the world in any of its forms.

There is a worldly spirit and there is also a heavenly spirit. One or the other exists in the heart of everyone and controls his whole being. Those who are under the control of the world, of course have not overcome the world. No one overcomes the world till his heart is imbued with the spirit of heaven.

One form that the spirit of the world assumes is being enslaved to the customs and fashions of the day. It is amazing to see what a goddess fashion becomes. No heathen goddess was ever worshiped with costlier offerings or more devout homage or more implicit subjection. And surely no heathen deity since the world began has ever had more universal patronage. Where will you go to find the man of the world or the woman of the world who does not hasten to worship at her shrine? But overcoming the world implies that the spell of this goddess is broken.

Those who have overcome the world are no longer careful either to secure its favor or avert its frown. To them, the good or the ill opinion of the world is a small matter. "With me," said Paul, "it is a very small thing that I should be judged . . . of man's judgment" (1 Cor. 4:3). So of every real Christian. His care is to secure the approbation of God. This is his chief concern, to commend himself to God and to his own conscience. No one has overcome the world unless he has attained this state of mind. Almost no feature of Christian character is more striking or more decisive than this—*indifference to the opinions of the world.*

Since I have been in the ministry, I have been blessed with the acquaintance of some who were peculiarly distinguished by this quality of character, such as the Rev. James Patterson of Philadelphia. He was eminently distinguished in this respect. He seemed to have the least possible disposition to secure the applause of men or avoid their censure. It seemed to be of no consequence to him to commend himself to men. For him, it was enough if he might please God. Hence, he engaged in war against sin—all sin, however popular, however entrenched by custom or sustained by wealth or public opinion. Yet, he always opposed sin with a remarkable spirit—a spirit of inflexible decision and yet of great mellowness and tenderness. While he was saying the most severe things in the most decided language, you might see the big tears rolling down his cheeks.

It is amazing that most people never complained of his having a bad spirit. Much as they dreaded his rebuke and writhed under his strong and daring exposures of wickedness, they could never say that Reverend Patterson had any other than a good spirit. This was a most beautiful and striking exemplification of having overcome the world.

People who are not thus dead to the world have not escaped its bondage. The victorious Christian is in a state where he is no longer in bondage to others. He is *bound* only to serve God.

The Ones Who Will Overcome the World

Our scripture text gives the ready answer: "Whatsoever is born of God overcometh the world." You cannot fail to observe that this is a universal proposition—*all* who are born of God overcome the world—*all these*, and it is obviously implied that none others will. You may know who are born of God by this characteristic—they overcome the world.

This victory over the world results as naturally from the spiritual or heavenly birth as coming into bondage to the world results from the natural birth.

Let's take a closer look at the connection between natural birth and bondage to the world. This law obviously admits of a philosophical explanation, at once simple and palpable to everyone's observations. Natural birth reveals to the mind objects of sense and these only. It brings the mind into contact with worldly things. Of course, it is natural that the mind should become deeply interested in these objects thus presented through the external senses, especially as most of them sustain so intimate a relation to our sentient nature and become the first and chief sources of our happiness. Hence, our affections are gradually entwined around these objects and we become thoroughly lovers of this world before our eyes have been opened upon it many months.

Now, alongside this universal fact let another be placed of equal importance and not less universal, namely, that those intuitive powers of the mind that were created to take cognizance of our moral relations, and hence to counteract the too great influence of worldly objects, come into action very slowly, not developing as quickly as the external organs of sense. The very early and vigorous development of the latter brings the soul so entirely under the control of worldly objects that when the reason and the conscience come to speak, their voice is little heeded. As a matter of fact, we find it universally true that unless divine power interposes, the bondage to the world thus induced upon the soul is never broken. Thus, natural birth, with its attendant laws of physical and mental development, becomes the occasion of bondage to the world.

Right over against this lies the birth into the kingdom of God by the Holy Spirit. By this the soul is brought into new relation— we might rather say, into intimate contact with—spiritual things. The Spirit of God seems to usher the soul into the spiritual world in a manner strictly analogous to the result of the natural birth upon our physical being. The great truths of the spiritual world are opened to our view through the illumination of the Spirit of God. We seem to see with new eyes and have a new world of spiritual objects around us.

With regard to natural objects, people not only speculate about them, but *realize* them; so in the case of people born of God, spiritual things become not merely matters of speculation, but of full and practical *realization* also. When God reveals himself to the mind, spiritual things are seen in their real light and make the impression of realities.

Consequently, when spiritual objects are thus revealed to the mind, and thus apprehended, they will supremely interest that mind. Such is our mental constitution that the truth of God when thoroughly apprehended cannot fail to interest us. If these truths were clearly revealed to the most wicked person on earth, so that he should apprehend them as realities, it could not fail to rouse his soul to most intense action. He might hate the light, and might stubbornly resist the claims of God upon his heart, but he would feel a thrilling interest in truths that so take hold of the great and vital things of human well being.

Can there be a sinner on this wide earth, who does not see that if God's presence were made as manifest and as real to his mind as the presence of his fellow men, it would supremely engross his soul even though it might not subdue his heart? This revelation of God's presence and character might not convert him, but it would, at least for the time being, kill his attention to the world.

You often see this in the case of people deeply convicted. You have doubtless seen people so fearfully convicted of sin that they cared nothing at all for their food nor their dress. "Oh," they cried out in the agony of their souls, "what matter all these things to us, if we even get them all, and then must lie down in hell!" But these thrilling and all-absorbing convictions do not necessarily convert the soul, and I have alluded to them here only to show the controlling power of realizing views of divine truth.

When real conversion has taken place, and the soul is born of God, then realizing views of truth not only awaken interest, as they might do in an unrenewed soul, but they also tend to excite a deep and ardent love for these truths. They draw out the heart. Spiritual truth now takes possession of his mind, and draws him into its warm and life-giving embrace. Before, error, falsehood, death, had drawn him under their power; now the Spirit of God draws him into the very embrace of God. Now he is begotten of God, and breathes the spirit of sonship. Now, according to the Bible, the seed of God "remaineth in him." That very truth, and those movings of the Spirit that give him birth into the kingdom of God, continue still in power upon his mind and hence he continues a Christian. As the Bible states it, "he can not sin, because he is born of God" (1 John 3:9). The seed of God is in him, and the fruit of it brings his soul deeply into sympathy with his own Father in heaven.

The first birth makes us acquainted with earthly things, and the second birth with God. The first birth with the finite, the second with the infinite. The first with things correlated with our animal nature, the second with those great things that stand connected with our spiritual nature, things so lovely and so glorious as to overcome all the ensnarements of the world.

The first birth begets a worldly temper, and the second a heavenly temper. Under the first, the mind is brought into a snare; under the second, it is delivered from that snare. Under the first, the conversation is earthly; under the second, "our conversation is in heaven" (Phil. 3:20).

The Victory Comes Through Faith

The great agent is the Holy Spirit. Without Him, no good result is ever achieved in the Christian's heart or life.

The scripture text says, "This is the victory that overcometh the world, even our faith." Here the question might be raised, "Does this mean that faith of itself overcomes the world, or, is this the meaning, that we overcome by or through our faith?" Doubtless, the latter is the precise meaning. Believing in God, and having realizing impressions of His truth and character made upon our mind by the Holy Spirit, we gain the victory over the world.

Faith implies three things: 1. Perception of truth. 2. An interest in truth. 3. The committal or giving up of the mind to be interested and controlled by these objects of faith.

Perception of the truth must come first in order, for there can be no belief of unknown and unperceived truth. Next, there must be an interest in the truth that shall wake up the mind to fixed and active attention. Thirdly, there must be a voluntary committal of the mind to the control of truth. The mind must wholly yield itself up to God, to be governed entirely by His will, and to trust Him and Him alone as its own present and eternal portion.

Faith receives Christ. The mind first perceives Christ's character and His relation to us—sees what He does for us, and then deeply feeling its own need of such a Savior, and of such a work wrought in and for us as Jesus alone can do, goes forth to receive and embrace Jesus as its own Savior. This action of the soul in receiving and embracing Christ is not sluggish—it is not a state of dozing quietism. No; it involves the soul's most strenuous activity. And this committal of the soul must become a glorious, living, energizing principle—the mind not only perceiving, but yielding itself up with the most fervid intensity to be Christ's and to receive all the benefits of His salvation into our own souls.

Faith receives Christ into the soul as King, in all His relations, to rule over the whole being—to have our heart's supreme confidence and affection—to receive the entire homage of our obedience and adoration; to rule, in short, over us, and fulfill all the functions of supreme King over our whole moral being. Within our very souls, we receive Christ to live and energize them, to reign forever there as on His own rightful throne.

Now a great many seem to stop short of this entire and perfect committal of their whole soul to Christ. They stop short, perhaps, with merely *perceiving* the truth, satisfied and pleased that they have learned the theory of the gospel. Or perhaps some go one step further, and stop with being interested—with having their feelings excited by the things of the gospel, thus going only to the second stage; or perhaps they seem to take faith, but not Christ; they think to believe, but after all do not cordially and with all the heart welcome Christ himself into the soul.

All these various steps stop short of really taking hold of Christ. None of them result in gaining victory over the world.

The true Bible doctrine of faith represents Christ as coming into the very soul. "Behold I stand at the door, and knock: if any man hear my voice, and open the door, I will come in to him, and will sup with him, and he with me" (Rev. 3:20). What verse could more forcibly and beautifully teach the doctrine that by faith Christ is introduced into the very soul of the believer to dwell there by His gracious presence?

Since my mind has been drawn to the subject, I have been astonished to see how long I have been in a purblind state of perception in respect to this particular view of faith. For a long time, I had scarcely seen it; now I see it beaming forth in lines of glory on almost every page of the Bible. The Bible seems to blaze with the glorious truth, Christ *in the soul*, the hope of glory: God, Christ, dwelling in our body as in a temple. I am amazed that a truth so rich and so blessed should have been seen so dimly when the Bible reveals it so plainly. Christ received into the very soul by faith, and thus brought into the nearest possible relation to our heart and life; Christ himself becoming the all-sustaining Power within us, and thus securing the victory over the world. Christ, living and energizing in our hearts—this is the great central truth in the plan of sanctification, and this no Christian should fail to understand, as he values the victory over the world and the living communion of the soul with his Maker.

Christ Is Our Victory

It is in the very nature of the case impossible that if faith receives Christ into the soul, it should not overcome the world. If the new birth actually brings the mind into this new state, and brings Christ into the soul, then of course Christ will reign in that soul. The supreme affections will be yielded most delightfully to Him, and the power of the world over the mind will be broken. Christ cannot dwell in any soul without absorbing the supreme interest of that soul. And this is, of course, equivalent to gaining victory over the world.

He who does not habitually overcome the world is not born of God. In saying this, I recognize that a true Christian may sometimes be overcome by sin; but I do affirm that overcoming the world is the general rule, and falling into sin is only the exception. This is the least that can be meant by the language of our scripture text and by similar declarations that often occur in the Bible. Just as in the passage, "Whosoever is born of God doth not commit sin . . . and he cannot sin, because he is born of God" (1 John 3:9), nothing less can be meant than this—that he cannot sin uniformly; cannot make sinning his business and can sin, if at all, only occasionally and aside from the general current of his life. In the same manner, we should say of a man who is in general truthful, that he is not a liar.

I will not contend for more than this respecting either of these passages. But for so much as this I must contend, that the new-born souls spoken of here *do in general overcome* the world. The general fact respecting them is that they do not sin and are not in bondage to Satan. The affirmations of Scripture respecting them must at least embrace their general character.

What is a religion good for that does not overcome the world? What is the benefit of being born into such a religion if it leaves the world still swaying its dominion over our hearts? What good is a new birth that fails to bring us into a likeness of God, into the sympathies of His family and of His kingdom; that leaves us in bondage to the world and to Satan? What can there be of such a religion more than the name? With what reason can any man suppose that such a religion fits his heart for heaven, supposing it leaves him earthly-minded, sensual, and selfish?

Many unbelievers say the gospel of Christ is a failure, maintaining that it professes to bring people out from the world but it fails to do so; hence, the gospel is obviously a failure. Now, you must observe that the Bible does indeed affirm, that those who are truly born of God do overcome the world. This we cannot deny, and should not wish to deny it. Now, if the unbeliever can show that the new birth fails to produce this result, he has carried his point, and we must yield ours. This is perfectly obvious, and there can be no escape for us. But the unbeliever is in fault in his premises. He assumes the current Christianity of the age as a specimen of real Christianity, and builds his estimate upon this. He proves, as he thinks, and perhaps proves truly, that the current Christianity does not overcome the world.

We must demur to his assuming this current Christianity as real Christianity. Most are nominal professors who do not exhibit the true piety called for in the Word of God. And, moreover, if this current type of Christianity were all that the gospel and the divine Spirit can do for lost people, then we might as well agree with the skeptic, for such a religion could not give us much evidence of coming from God, would be of very little value to man, and scarcely worth contending for. Truly, if we must take the professedly Christian world as Bible Christians, who would not be ashamed and confounded in attempting to confront the unbeliever? We know but too well that the great mass of professing Christians do not overcome the world, and we would be confounded quickly if we were to maintain that they do. Those professing Christians themselves know they do not overcome the world, and would not be able to say that they exemplify the power of the gospel.

In view of facts such as these, I have often been astonished to see ministers setting themselves to persuade their people that they are really converted, trying to lull their fears and sustain their tottering hopes. Vain effort! Those same ministers, it would seem, must know that they themselves do not overcome the world; and equally well they must know that their people are in the same condition. How fatal, then, for them to gloss over such problems, saying, "Peace, peace, when there is no peace" (Jer. 8:11).

Let us sift this matter to the bottom, pushing the inquiry: "Do the great mass of professing Christians really overcome the world?" It is a fact beyond question that with them the things of this world are the realities, and the things of God are mere theories. Who does not know that this is the real state of great multitudes in the nominal Church?

Let the searching inquiry run through this congregation: "What are those things that set your soul on fire—that stir up your warmest emotions and deeply agitate your nervous system? Are these the things of earth, or the things of heaven; the things of time or the things of eternity; the things of self or the things of God? How is it when you go into your closets to pray? Do you go there to seek and find God? Do you in fact find there a present God, and do you hold communion there as friend with friend? How is this with you?"

Now you certainly should know that if your state is such that spiritual things are mere theories and speculations, you are altogether worldly and nothing more. It would be egregious folly and falsehood to call you spiritually-minded, and for you to think yourselves spiritual would be the most fatal and foolish self-deception. You give none of the appropriate proofs of being born of God. Your state is not that of one who is personally acquainted with God, and who loves Him personally with supreme affection.

Until we can put away from the minds of people the common error that the current Christianity of the Church is true Christianity, we can make but little progress in converting the world. For in the first place, we cannot save the Church itself from bondage to the world in this life, nor from the direst doom of the hypocrite in the next. We cannot unite and arm the Church in vigorous onset upon Satan's kingdom so that the world may be converted to God. We cannot even convince intelligent people of the world that our religion is from God, and that it brings to fallen humanity a remedy for their depravity. For if the common Christianity of the age is the best that can be, and this does not give people the victory over the world, what is it good for? And if it really is of little worth or none, how can we hope to make thinking people prize it as of great value?

There are but very few unbelievers who are as much in the dark as they profess to be on these points. There are very few of that class of people who are not acquainted with some humble Christians, whose lives commend Christianity and condemn their own ungodliness. Of course they know the truth, that there is a reality in the religion of the Bible, and they blind their own eyes selfishly and most foolishly when they try to believe that the religion of the Bible is a failure, and that the Bible is therefore a fabrication. Deep in their heart lies the conviction that here and there are people who are real Christians, who overcome the world and live by a faith unknown to themselves. In how many cases does God set some burning examples of Christian life before those wicked, skeptical people, to rebuke them for their sin and their skepticism—perhaps their own wife or their children, their neighbors or their servants. By such means the truth is lodged in their mind, and God has a witness for himself in their consciences.

I have perhaps before mentioned a fact that occurred in the South, and was stated to me by a minister of the gospel who was acquainted with the circumstances of the case. There resided in that region a very worldly and most ungodly man, who owned a great number of slaves, and was much given to horse racing. Heedless of all religion and avowedly skeptical, he gave full swing to every evil propensity. But wicked men must one day see trouble, and this man was taken sick and brought to the very gates of the grave. His weeping wife and friends gathered round his bed, and began to think of having some Christian called in to pray for the dying man's soul. "Husband," cried the anxious wife, "shall I not send for our minister to pray with you before you die?" "No," he said, "I know him of old. I have no confidence in him, I have seen him too many times at the horse races. There he was my friend, and I was his; but I don't want to see him now. Send for my slave, Tom. I have often overheard him praying, and I know he can pray. Besides, I have watched his life and his temper, and I never saw anything in him inconsistent with Christian character. Call him in. I would be glad to hear him pray."

Tom slowly and modestly came in, dropped his hat at the door, and looked at his sick and dying master. "Tom," said the dying skeptic, "do you ever pray? Do you know how to pray? Can you pray for your dying master and forgive him?" He said, "Oh yes, master, with all my heart," as he dropped on his knees and poured out a prayer for his soul.

Now the moral of this story is obvious. Place the skeptic on his dying bed, let that solemn hour arrive, and the inner convictions of his heart are revealed, and he knows of at least one man who is a Christian. He knows one man whose prayers he values more than all the friendship of all his former associates. He knows now that there is such a thing as Christianity. And yet, you cannot suppose that he has this moment learned a lesson he never knew before. No, he knew just as much before; an honest hour has brought the inner conviction of his soul to light. Unbelievers generally know more than they have honesty enough to admit.

The great error of those who profess Christianity, but are not born of God, is this: they are trying to be Christians without being born of God. They need to have that done to them which is said of Adam: God "breathed into his nostrils the breath of life; and man became a living soul" (Gen. 2:7). Their religion has in it none of the breath of God. It is a cold, lifeless theory. There is none of the living vitality of God in it. It is perhaps a heartless orthodoxy, and they may take a flattering unction to their hearts that their creed is sound; but do they *love* that truth they profess to believe? They think that they have zeal, and that their zeal is right and their heart right. But is their soul on fire for God and His cause? Where are they, and what are they doing? Are they spinning out some fond theory, or defending it at the point of the sword? Ah, do they care for souls? Does their heart tremble for the interests of the Church? Do their very nerves quiver under the mighty power of God's truth? Does their love for God and for souls set their orthodoxy and their creeds *on fire* so that every truth burns in their souls and glows forth from their very faces? If so, then you will not see them absent from the prayer meetings; but you will see that divine things take hold of them with overwhelming interest and power. You will see them living Christians, burning and shining lights in the world. Brethren, it cannot be too strongly impressed on every mind that the decisive character of true Christianity is energy, not apathy; that its vital essence is *life*, not *death*.

21

MEN INVITED TO REASON WITH GOD*

"Come now, and let us reason together, saith the Lord: though your sins be as scarlet, they shall be as white as snow; though they be red like crimson, they shall be as wool" (Isaiah 1:18).

God is a moral agent. If He were not, He could not have moral character. That He has moral character is sufficiently obvious from the revealed fact that man is made in His image. Everyone knows himself to have a moral constitution, and to be a moral being. Also, we necessarily conceive of God as a moral agent and cannot rationally think otherwise.

God is also a good being. He is not only moral, but holy and wise. He always acts upon good and sufficient reasons, and never irrationally and without reasons for His conduct. Hence, if we would appeal to God on any subject, we must address Him as a good being, and must make our appeal through His intelligence, expecting Him to be influenced more or less according as we present good and sufficient reasons.

God is always influenced by good reasons. Good reasons are more sure to have their due and full weight on His mind than on the mind of any other being in the universe. Nothing can be more certain than this, that if we present to Him good reasons and such as ought to influence Him, He will be influenced as much as He ought to be. Upon this we may rest with unlimited confidence.

Before entering upon the direct consideration of our text, we must first ask what this text invites us to do: "Come now, let us

---

Sermons on the Way of Salvation, pp. 93–111.

reason together." But what are we to "reason" about? The passage proceeds to say, "Though your sins be as scarlet, they shall be as white as snow; though they be red like crimson, they shall be as wool." In the previous context God brings tremendous charges against men. Their sins, hypocrisies, and apostasies have been provoking Him beyond measure. Now, therefore, He comes down to look into their case, to see if there is any hope of repentance, and proceeds to make a proposal. "Come now," He says, "let us reason together. Come near, if you will reason with me. Produce your strong reasons why your God should forgive your great sins."

The invitation, coupled with the promises annexed to it, implies that there are good and sufficient reasons why God should forgive the penitent. Hence the case is fair for practical results. The way is open for salvation. Sinners may so present their reasons before God as to insure success.

The nature of the case shows that we are to address our reasons and make our appeal, not to justice, but to mercy. We are to present reasons that will sanction the exercise of mercy. We have no hope from any appeal to justice. We must not come to demand the blessing we need; for it is assumed that our sins are as scarlet, hence, that there can be no such thing as our justification for them. We have to search for those considerations that may induce the Lord to exercise mercy in our case.

Why God Should Pardon Our Sin

You may plead that you entirely agree with God in all His course of actions. You must certainly take this position, for He cannot forgive you as long as you persist in self-justification. You know there is a breach of friendship between your soul and God. You have broken His laws. You either have good reason for your sin or you have not. If you have, God is wrong; if you have not, then you are wrong. You know how this case stands. You know beyond all question, with a force of reason that ought to silence all argument, that all the wrong is on your side and all the right on God's side. You might and should know also that you must confess this. You need not expect God to forgive you till you do. He *ought* not to publish to the universe that He is wrong and you are right, when there is no truth in such a proclamation. Hence you see that you must confess what your conscience affirms to be truth in the case. Now, therefore, will you honestly say, not as the decision of your conscience merely, but as the utterance of your *heart*, that you do accept the punishment of your iniquities as just? Do you honor and acquit your God in all the precepts of His law, and in all the course of His providence? Can you present this reason? So far as it goes, it is a good reason and will certainly have its weight.

You may come to God and acknowledge that you have no excuse whatever to make for your sin. You renounce the very idea of trying to come up with one. The case, you deeply feel, admits of none.

You must also be ready to renounce all sin, and be able in all honesty to say this before God. You must utterly cease from all rebellion against God, and be able to say so from your very heart, or else you cannot reasonably expect to be forgiven.

You must unconditionally submit to His discretion. Nothing less than this is the fitting moral position for a sinner toward God. You must unqualifiedly surrender yourself to His will and utterly renounce your own. This will be an important element in your plea before God for pardon whenever you can honestly make it.

You may plead the life and death of Jesus Christ as sufficient to honor the law and justify God in showing mercy. Plainly, our reasons must reach other points besides our own state of mind. They must also refer to the penalty of law, and show that such arrangements are made as will insure the honor and sustain the dignity of the law, though sin is forgiven. Hence we see how much it is worth to us that we are able to plead before God that Christ has fully honored the law, so that God can forgive sin without the danger of seeming to connive in it. The returning sinner may plead that forgiveness through Christ's death is safe to the government of God. Pardon must not put in peril the holiness or justice of Jehovah. The utmost expression He could make, or need to make, of His holiness and justice as touching the sins of man is already made in the death of Christ, "whom God hath set forth to be a propitiation through faith in his blood, to declare his righteousness for the remission of sins that are past . . . that he might be just and the justifier of him which believeth in Jesus" (Rom. 3:25–26).

Now, therefore, can you say that you are willing to accept the sacrifice He has made, and receive the gift of salvation through His blood as all boundless grace, and in no sense or measure of meritorious works? If you can truly say this, it will become a strong reason before God for Him to forgive you.

You may also urge His professed love for sinners. God has professed the greatest love for lost men and women. He has even spoken of loving them "with an everlasting love" (Jer. 31:3), and you are at liberty to urge this when you come to reason together with

God. You may plead that He has manifested this love in the gift of His dear Son, and hence you must be sure that you understand His language, and there cannot be any mistake in the matter. All your life long, too, He has been manifesting His love toward you in His kind providence; so that He has not ever left himself without witness to both the fact and the greatness of this love for the lost of our race.

He has also invited you to come and reason with Him. Therefore He has fully opened the way for the most free and fullest communion on this point. With amazing condescension, He allows you to come before Him and plead, filling your mouth with arguments. You may speak of all His promises, and of that solemn oath in which He swore by himself to the end that they all "might have a strong consolation who have fled for refuge to lay hold upon the hope set before us [in the gospel]" (Heb. 6:18).

You may also plead His honor, that, seeing He is under oath, and stands committed before the universe, you may ask Him what He will do for His great name if He refuses to forgive a repentant and believing sinner. You may plead all the relations and work of Christ. You may say to Him, "Lord, will it not induce other sinners to come to Thee? Will it not encourage thy Church to labor and pray more for salvation? Will not thy mercy shown to me prove a blessing to thousands?"

You may urge the influence of refusing to do so. You may suggest that His refusal is liable to be greatly misapprehended, that it may be a scandal to many, and that the wicked will be emboldened to say that God has made no such exceeding great and precious promises.

You may urge that there is joy in heaven, and on earth also, over every sinner pardoned and saved, that the saints everywhere will be delighted, and will exceedingly rejoice in the Lord their God. The Psalmist represents the young convert as saying, "The humble shall hear thereof and *be glad*" (Ps. 34:2). You may urge that since God loves to make saints happy in this world, He surely will not be averse to giving you His Spirit and putting away your sins. It will create such joy in the hearts of His dear people.

You may also plead the great abhorrence you have of living in sin, as you surely will unless He forgives you. You may also plead that God hates sin, and therefore must be more than willing to turn your heart away from sinning, and make it wholly pure before His eyes. You may urge on Him the worth of your soul, which He understands and appreciates far better than you do, inasmuch as

He gave up His only Son to die that souls might not perish. Ask Him if He does not know what it is for a soul to be saved, and what it is for a soul to be lost, and tell Him that the great question between these two momentous states is now pending in your case and must be soon decided for eternity! Ask Him, after all He has done and said about salvation, if He can refuse to save your perishing soul. Say, "O my God! Dost Thou not know how much my soul is worth, and how certainly it is lost forever unless thou interpose to save it?"

You may mention before Him your lost estate, that you are entirely dependent on His grace and mercy, that you are utterly lost to God, to happiness and to heaven, unless He has mercy on you. You may persuade Him by the love of His dear Son to take all these things into consideration.

You may also allude to His merciful disposition, and suggest how often His Word has affirmed that "he delighteth in mercy" (Mic. 7:18), and that while "judgment is his strange work, mercy is his delight." Ask Him if He will not gratify His own love of showing mercy, and give you the salvation you so much need. Remind Him that here is a great opportunity to magnify His mercy, and display the riches of His grace, and make an impression on the minds of both saints and sinners greatly to His own honor and to their good. Tell Him that to save one so lost and so vile as you cannot but glorify His great mercy far as the case is known in earth, or hell, or heaven. Tell Him how He has said, "It is more blessed to give than to receive" (Acts 20:35), and ask Him if He will not take advantage of this opportunity to show all men how He loves to act on this divine law of benevolence.

Tell Him, moreover, how wretched you are, and must be in your sins, if you cannot find salvation, and what mischief you will be likely to do everywhere on earth and in hell, if you are not forgiven and renewed in holiness. Tell Him that it is awful, and makes your soul shudder, to think of going on in sin and of becoming hardened past all repentance. Remind Him that He has invited you to come and reason with Him, and that He has virtually promised to hear and to consider your case. You do not come to justify yourself, but only to plead His great mercy and what Christ has done for you. With these very strong reasons you come before Him, on His own invitation, not to complain against His justice, but to intercede for His mercy; that you must beg of Him to consider the awful ruin of hell, and that you cannot escape without His help, and cannot endure its everlasting horrors. He has himself said, "Can thine heart endure, or can thine hands be strong, in the days that I shall deal with thee?" (Ezek. 22:14). Tell Him your heart *cannot* endure this, and that this should be a strong reason why He should have mercy on your soul.

Tell Him that you also commit yourself entirely to His hands, and resign everything to His discretion and to His supreme disposal. Tell Him you believe He will do the very best thing possible, and that you shall by no means shrink from confiding your whole case to His disposal. You are not disposed to dictate or control what God shall do, but are willing to submit all to His wisdom and love. In fact, you have such confidence in Him that you expect He will give you salvation, for you believe He has intended to encourage you to expect this great blessing, and on this ground you do expect to find mercy. You will therefore, at any rate, renounce all your sin henceforth and forever. Say, "O Lord, Thou knowest that I am purposed to renounce all sinning, and in this purpose I will persist, and die in it, if die I must, yea, go to hell, if so it must be, renouncing all my sin and trusting in Thy promised grace."

Let this be the manner of your reasoning together with God on this great question of the salvation of your soul.

Reasons We May Use to Plead for Entire Sanctification

You may plead your present justification. You have already found grace in His sight. This is a good reason to be used in your plea that He would fulfill all His promises to you, and not leave His great work already begun unfinished.

You may plead your relation to Him, to the Church, and to the world, that, having now been justified and adopted into His family, you are known as a Christian and a child of God, and it therefore becomes of the utmost consequence that you should have grace to live so as to adorn your profession and honor His name.

You may also plead your great responsibilities, and the weight of those interests that are depending upon your spiritual progress. Tell Him you have publicly committed yourself to His faithfulness, that you have trusted that He would keep you blameless and henceforth make His grace sufficient for you. You have professed to rely upon sanctifying grace, and how can you bear now to fail of finding all you need and all you have professed to expect?

You should notice, also, the matter of your example to others, especially the influence of your example. If it is known that you frequently fall into sin, how sad must be the influence! On the other hand, if God enables you to stand up and testify continually to His sustaining grace, what a testimony this is to His praise, and what a blessing to your Christian acquaintances!

Plead the desire you feel to be completely delivered from sin. Ask Him if He has not given you this very desire himself, and inquire if He intends to sharpen your thirst and yet withhold the waters of life. Ask Him if you must suppose that He means to enkindle the desire and yet leave it forever unsatisfied.

Plead also His expressed will. Revert to that explicit avowal, "This is the will of God, even your sanctification" (1 Thess. 4:3). Ask if He did not intend you should understand this as applicable to deliverance from *all* sin, and therefore as an unqualified expression of His desire and will that you should be altogether free from sin, even now. Ask if He has not so revealed His will on this point that you do not come to Him in any uncertainty as to His will. Has He not in many forms, and in forms most clear and decisive, signified His wish that you should be "perfecting holiness" (2 Cor. 7:1), and rise quite above all the power of temptation? Remind Him how He has pledged His Word of grace and held out before you most encouraging promises.

Tell Him also how the Church needs such witnesses to testify what grace has done, and what they have themselves experienced. Refer to what the world is saying because the Church is not sanctified, and show how great a scandal unsanctified professors of Christianity are to their brethren, because they testify falsely to the rich provisions of gospel grace. Show that the Church has many of them fallen almost out of sight of God's great grace, and so that they have become a sad stumbling block to the world. Consider how much scandal and unbelief exist everywhere, and ask how these great evils can be removed and evermore prevented.

Appeal to His great love for you, as manifested in what Christ has done, and in His present office as your Advocate on high, as evidenced also in the gift of the Holy Spirit. Tell Him you must and will confide in His love. Say, "I understand it; I must and will assume it. I cannot doubt. I must not disbelieve. I do not make my appeal to one who is an alien and a stranger, but to a kind and loving *Father*, and I come in simple confidence as His child." Say, "I dread to offend Thee, and I long to live worthy of my vocation, and cannot endure to misrepresent that great and blessed grace on which my hope reposes."

So you must come to reason with your Heavenly Father. By no means forget to urge the love He has professed, and to throw yourself upon His faithfulness, pleading that He will fulfill to you all that He has promised, and gloriously finish the work He has begun. Tell Him how you have stumbled many by your falls into sin and have given great occasion of reproach to the cause you love. Tell Him you cannot live so, that you are ready to die under this awful burden. Cry out before Him, "I have given your enemies occasion to doubt your sanctifying grace and to disbelieve your words of promise! O my Savior! Did you not give yourself to die for such a sinner as I am, to redeem me from all iniquity? And now, are you willing that your servants should be stumbled by me and fall over me into the depths of hell?"

Remind Him also of your dependence on Him and that you set out in the Christian life with the understanding that without His grace you could do nothing. Tell Him you have consecrated yourself to Him in distinct reliance upon His promised aid, and that you cannot endure to fall so far short of what you had been promised and expected. Tell Him of your willingness to make any sacrifice, that there is nothing you are unwilling to give up, that you are willing to forego your good name, and to lay your reputation wholly upon His altar; and you beg of Him, if He sees a single thing held so dear to your heart that you are not willing to sacrifice it for His sake, to show you what it is and press you to forsake it. Assure Him that if self-denial comes in His service you are willing to meet all the consequences. You are ready to confess His grace to you, and not conceal it from the great congregation. *Can you say this?* If so, do it! Tell Him you are ready to die to the world, ready to give it all up and renounce it utterly and forever. You are determined you will have no more fellowship with the works of darkness, to have the world become dead to you and you to the world. You are ready to meet all and bear all that the service of Christ may impose and involve. No matter if the world disowns you and casts you out from its regard and fellowship. You have counted the cost and are ready to meet it all. Urge as a further reason that you are willing to become dead to a worldly and unbelieving Church; that you are ready to die even to their good opinion, to be excommunicated if they will do it, to be cast out if they will cast you out. You shrink not from being reputed a heretic, if you may only have grace to overcome all sin and every temptation. You wish to please but one; and you are quite satisfied with pleasing God only. This shall be your object, and this, attained, shall fully satisfy your soul. You are willing to give up all idols and live to Him alone. No matter if your name is cast out as evil and trodden down as vile by the

Church, by her ministry, by all men, if you may only live to please God. Tell Him you are willing to renounce all creature help and all earthly reliances with only one great inquiry, *How can I most and best please God?*

Be sure to remind Him that you intend to be wholly disinterested and unselfish in this matter. You ask these things not for your own present selfish interest. You are aware that a really holy life may subject you to much persecution. You know that "all that will live godly in Christ Jesus shall suffer persecution" (2 Tim. 3:12); and you are well aware that if you receive this cleansing, it may bring on you much persecution. You come not therefore to ask for present personal good, for you expect only greater trials, but you will consent to endure anything that does not involve sin. You want to represent Him truly. You want to encourage all Christians, and all sinners too, to seek abounding grace by showing them how you have found mercy.

Then tell Him of your great weakness, and how you entirely distrust yourself; how, ofttimes, you are covered with confusion and filled with shame, so that you cannot lift up your head and you are constrained to cry, "O my God! Dost Thou not pity Thy child?" Tell Him you loathe yourself, that you would fain spew yourself out of your own mouth, because you so much dishonor Him. Tell Him you despair utterly of saving yourself, but that you still have unshaken confidence in Him. Remind Him, moreover, of His promises, and say that you are encouraged because you know that you are asking mercy of a most gracious God. Tell Him you shall go away greatly disappointed if you do not receive the grace you ask and need. As a dear sister said in a great struggle of her soul for spiritual blessings, "O my God, Thou has made me exceeding great and precious promises; now if Thou dost not give me these blessings, what can I say any more for Thee? How can I plead for Thee if Thou dost shut me up in my desolations? How can I ever again present Thy strong claims to be believed and trusted as to all Thy words of gracious promise?"

Thus making your strong issue, you come pleading not your goodness, but your badness; appealing not to God's justice but to His mercy; telling Him how poor you are and how rich He is, and that therefore you cannot bear to go away empty.

Whenever we have considered the reasons for God's actions till they have really moved and persuaded us, they will surely move Him. God is not slow, never slower than we, to see the reasons for showing mercy and for leading us to holiness.

Many fail in coming to God because they do not treat Him as a rational being. Instead of considering Him a rational being, they come without ever considering the reasons why He should and will forgive and sanctify. Of course, failing to have faith, and having views altogether dishonoring to God, they fail to get the blessing they seek.

Many do not present these reasons, because in honesty they cannot. Now God assumes that we ought to be in a state of mind to present all these reasons honestly. If we are not in such a state, we ought not to expect blessings. When we want anything of God, we should always consider whether we can present good reasons why it should be granted. If you were to apply to any other being—for example, the Governor, you would of course ask in the outset, "Can I give any good reasons?" If you are to appeal to justice, you must ask, "Have I any good reasons to offer?" So if you want favors on the score of mercy, what reasons have you to offer why they should be granted? If you have reasons, be sure to offer them, and by no means assume that you shall get your case without reasons.

All who are in need are invited to come and bring forward their strong reasons. If in sorrow, distress, affliction, come and present your plea. If you are a sinner, oppressed with a sense of sin, fear not to unburden your heart before God. All those who are under any affliction should come, like Job, and tell God how deeply you are afflicted. Why not? Did not saints of old say to God, "Doubtless thou art our Father, though Abraham be ignorant of us, and Israel acknowledge us not" (Isa. 63:16)?

Christian parents, you are invited to come and present your strong reasons why your children should be converted. Come and tell God how much you need this blessing. Tell Him you cannot endure that all your prayers in their behalf should come to naught, that the great labor of your life should fail, and worse than fail, as it must if your children of the covenant should disgrace Christianity and press their way through throngs of offered mercies down to hell.

Backsliders, come and tell God your case. Ask Him if He will not break your chains, bring you back, and put a new song into your mouth, even of praise for recovering grace.

Of all beings, God is most easily influenced to save. He is by nature disposed to save the lost. He loves to let His mercies flow. You have only to bring forth your strong reasons; indeed you have only to come in the spirit of a child, trustful and lowly, and your case is gained. You need not come with a bribe; you need not come and offer pay. No. You have only to come and say, "I want to serve God; for this end I need spiritual blessings." Tell Him how much He has loved you, and how often and richly He has manifested this love; and plead that He would still show forth this same love yet more abundantly, that you may still follow on in His service, and nevermore be confounded and put to shame and sorrow for your own grievous sins.

Oh, come and ask God if the growing people of this great nation, already outstripping the progress of the means of grace, must not become almost heathen, if His infinite mercy does not descend on all our schools and colleges and mold these young minds to himself! These young women, what shall their influence be when they become wives and mothers, and are scattered over the breadth of the land? And these young men, destined to stand on the high places of social and moral power, shall the Great West feel their influence? And the distant South, shall it and its peculiar institutions feel the touch of their power? And the East, shall it know the weight of their principle and of their educated and sanctified talent? Oh, have we not reason to plead mightily of God! Oh, how many young palpitating hearts are here which need to be drawn into God's work and into the spirit of full consecration to the Lord of Hosts! Christians, have you no plea, no *special*, peculiar plea, to urge in behalf of interests so great and so pressing? Sinners, have you not some plea to urge? Should not you be praying, "Oh my God, wash all my sins away! Fulfill Thy promise and make me white as snow! Let me not die, but live and declare the high praises of my God forevermore!"

BIBLIOGRAPHY

Sermons in this book are taken from *The Oberlin Evangelist*, a newspaper published by Oberlin College from 1839–1862, and from *The Penny Pulpit*, sermons published in England during his revival tour from 1849–51.

Additional sermons are from *Lectures To Professing Christians*, Oberlin, Ohio: E. J. Goodrich, 1880; *Sermons on Gospel Themes*, New York: Fleming H. Revell Company, 1876; and *Sermons on the Way of Salvation*, Oberlin, Ohio: E. J. Goodrich, 1891.

Additional sources for sermons on this theme are: *The Promise of the Spirit*, compiled and edited by Timothy L. Smith, Minneapolis: Bethany House Publishers, 1980; *Principles of Victory*, Minneapolis: Bethany House Publishers, 1981; and *Principles of Liberty*, Minneapolis: Bethany House Publishers, 1983.

Finney also discusses this theme in *The Heart of Truth*, Minneapolis: Bethany House Publishers, 1976; and in *Finney's Systematic Theology*, Minneapolis: Bethany House Publishers, 1976.

Other books published by Bethany House Publishers in the *Principles Series* are: *Principles of Prayer*, 1980; *Answers to Prayer*, 1983; *Principles of Devotion*, 1987; *Principles of Holiness*, 1984; *Principles of Union with Christ*, 1985; *Principles of Sanctification*, 1986; *Principles of Love*, 1986; *Principles of Revival*, 1987; *Principles of Discipleship*, 1988; *The Believer's Secret of Spiritual Power*, Minneapolis: Bethany House Publishers, 1987, a combination of devotional writings from Andrew Murray and Finney's *Power from on High*.